Values Concepts and Techniques
Revised Edition

Alfred S. Alschuler, Editor

nea PROFESSIONAL LIBRARY
National Education Association
Washington, D.C.

Acknowledgments

The editor gratefully acknowledges the first sources of his values, Alfred and Helene Alschuler.

He also acknowledges with thanks the assistance of Mario Fantini, Greg Laird, David C. McClelland, Sydney Simon, and Peter Wagschal in preparing the Revised Edition.

Copyright © 1976, 1982
National Education Association of the United States

NEA Stock No. 1487-1-00

"Strategies for Clarifying the Teaching Self"
Copyright © 1976, Stephen J. Taffee
"Values Clarification: Some Thoughts on How to Get Started"
Copyright © 1976, Joel Goodman
"Value Decisions and the Acceptability of Value Principles"
Copyright © 1976, W. Keith Evans and Terry P. Applegate

Library of Congress Cataloging in Publication Data
Main entry under title:

Values, concepts, and techniques.

   (NEA aspects of learning)
   Bibliography: p.
   1. Moral education—Addresses, essays, lectures.
I. Alschuler, Alfred S., 1939-
II. Series.
LC283.V33   1982   370.11'4   82-3569
ISBN 0-8106-1487-1   AACR2

NEA gratefully acknowledges the permissions given to use the following:

Part One

The Quest for Certainty by John Dewey. Copyright © 1960 by G.P. Putnam's Sons (Capricorn Books). Excerpted with permission.
"Toward a Common Scale of Measurement" by Robert S. Morison. *Daedalus*, The Journal of the American Academy of the Arts and Sciences, Vol. 94, No. 1; Winter 1965. Copyright © 1965 by *Daedalus*. Excerpted with permission.
The Function of Reason by Alfred North Whitehead. Copyright © 1957 by Princeton University Press. Excerpted with permission.

(Continued on page 310)

CONTENTS

Introduction to Revised Edition 5

Part One: Concepts

Editor's Note 7

- Freedom, Intelligence, and Valuing
  by Louis E. Raths 9
- The Cognitive-Developmental Approach to Moral Education by Lawrence Kohlberg 18
- Values Clarification: It Can Start Gently and Grow Deep by Sidney B. Simon and Polly deSherbinin 36
- Values Education in a Confluent Social Studies Curriculum by Kenneth K. Kickbusch 48
- Values Education Processes by William B. Hemmer 59
- School and Society: Barriers to Values Education
  by Michael Silver 64
- Confrontation, Insight, and Commitment: Moral Education and the Teacher
  by David Purpel and Kevin Ryan 72

Part Two: Techniques

Editor's Note 75

- Analyzing Value Conflict by Jack R. Fraenkel 77
- Strategies for Clarifying the Teaching Self
  by Stephen J. Taffee 87
- From Inculcation to Action: A Continuum for Values Education by Julia Bell, Sarah Bennett, and James Fallace 95
- Conducting Moral Discussions in the Classroom
  by Barry K. Beyer 103
- The Developmentalists' Approach to Alternative Schooling by Peter Scharf 121
- Humanizing Through Value Clarification
  by Mary M. Yanker 130
- Values Clarification vs. Indoctrination
  by Sidney B. Simon................................... 135

- Values Clarification: Some Thoughts on How to Get Started by Joel Goodman 144
- Value Decisions and the Acceptability of Value Principles by W. Keith Evans and Terry P. Applegate 148
- Exploring Social Issues: A Values Clarification Simulation Game by Judith Kirkhorn and Patrick Griffin 159
- Developing Values Awareness in Young Children by Alan J. Hoffman and Thomas F. Ryan 171
- The School Assembly as Creative Pace-Setter for Moral Development by Lisa Kuhmerker 177
- Nonsexist Teaching: Strategies and Practical Applications by David Sadker and Myra Sadker 189
- Multiculturalism in Moral and Values Education by Gwendolyn C. Baker 204
- Multiculturalism—Should We Clarify or Seek Values? by Claire B. Halverson 209
- Vocational Education and the Changing American Work Ethic by Charles W. Curry 225
- A Framework and Strategy for Examining Environmental Values by Elmer U. Clawson, Buckley R. Barnes, Marion J. Rice, James R. Richburg, and Roberta Rivner 235
- Pop Music and Values Clarification by Richard Simms 243
- Values and Health Education by Robert D. Russell 249
- Future Values for Today's Curriculum by Richard D. Van Scotter and Jon Cauley 257
- Interview: Alvin Toffler on the Role of the Future and Values in Education by Alvin Toffler, June Grant Shane, and Harold G. Shane 268
- The Challenge of Value Commitment by Lawrence Senesh 277

Selected Readings for the Revised Edition 288

Footnotes and References 291

Acknowledgments (continued from page 2) 309

INTRODUCTION TO REVISED EDITION

In the *Symposium* Alcibiades praised Socrates by saying, "He is exactly like the busts of Silenus which are set up in the statuaries' shops, holding pipes and flutes in their mouths; they open in the middle and have images of gods inside them.... [Socrates'] words are ridiculous when you first hear them, but he who opens [them] and sees what is within will find that they are the only words which have a meaning in them,...abounding in fair images of virtue and extending to the whole duty of good and honorable [human beings]." As values educators we face the same challenge described by Alicibiades—to open up our students and search beyond what may seem like ridiculous words at first, until we discover their images of virtue, goodness, duty, and honor.

The angry debate over values education today is not about whether schools can, do, and should influence students' images of virtue. Inevitably, the way the schools operate encourages certain values—respect for authority, compliance, punctuality. Whatever a teacher does constitutes a model of moral behavior—being helpful, kind, and showing respect for students, or by preferential treatment, distance, or disinterest. In fact, the public wants more than this indirect values education. According to several recent Gallup polls, about 80 percent of the general public supports deliberate efforts by schools to provide values education. However, vigorous differences exist among this group. At one end of the continuum, the "new religious Right" asserts that schools should teach students certain "correct" virtues and beliefs. At the opposite end of the continuum (and there are many groups in between), the "old liberal Left" advocates that schools should assist students in making their own informed choices, without prescribing "right" answers.

The ongoing debate about the best type of values education itself exemplifies a living national process of clarifying and developing values. The Right and Left argue for conflicting axioms to guide the education of our children. Disagreement exists about what is science, what is religion, what is acceptable evidence, what is investigation, what is indoctrination, what are the appropriate aims and methods of education. The battlegrounds have included the issues of prayer in the schools, the criteria for selecting and/or banning books, the content of family life and sex education, drug education, and the content of biology (should it include both the theory of evolution and "scientific creationism"?). Forums for debate range from the editorial columns of local newspapers to nationally televised religious programs and talk shows, from school committee meetings to state textbook adoption hearings, from pulpits to media campaigns.

All of the authors in this volume, the editor, and the National Education Association have chosen to help students discover their options, envision the likely consequences, then make their own choices about what is good and honorable, rather than to try to instill certain "correct" values. Consistent with this view, the articles in this book provide an array of alternatives for teachers. To prescribe a single best way for conducting values education would be a contradiction. Part One presents concepts of values, what values are, alternative processes for promoting value development, and the commitment needed from teachers to conduct values education. Part Two contains a set of useful techniques and another set of articles applying those techniques to divergent content areas from pop music to social issues such as racism and sexism. Given these resources, each teacher can decide what to do, when, and how.

Only a small number of events in a lifetime suddenly change the way a person lives—a deeply religious experience, getting married or divorced, the birth of a child, the death of a parent, involvement in a serious accident. These dramatic, singular events rapidly transform one's outlook, relation to others, and view of oneself. By comparison, daily learning in school is undramatic, regularized, and designed to promote steady, small changes. Obviously we do not want to create apocalyptic events that drastically alter students' personal lives. The concepts, techniques, and applications described in this volume enable teachers to conduct humane, gentle values education that can develop each student's unique virtues over time as profoundly as those rare life-changing events.

Alfred S. Alschuler
University of Massachusetts
in Amherst

Part One: Concepts

Editor's Note

Values are clear if a person acts to reach desired outcomes that are freely chosen from among carefully considered alternatives. Anything less—choice without action, action without forethought, or choice and action without caring—is a mere "value indicator," according to Raths in the first article. During the course of life, people pass through a predictable sequence of stages in the way they think about their alternatives and in the importance they attach to different types of outcomes. For Lawrence Kohlberg, the leading proponent of this "cognitive-developmental" theory, the purpose of values education is to help students engage in a higher stage of moral reasoning as they make their specific choices. As described in the second article, typically this method involves students at adjacent stages of development debating how they would resolve hypothetical moral dilemmas. Recently Kohlberg and his associates have created alternative "Just Community" schools where students and teachers resolve actual dilemmas through discussion and democratic decisionmaking. In contrast, "Values Clarification," as described by Simon and deSherbinin in their article, does not involve confrontation between individuals or decisions about problems in the immediate setting. Through questions, teachers help students move from value indicators to clear values, regardless of their stage of moral reasoning. Promoting the development of moral reasoning about clear values can be accomplished either by including these processes in traditional subject matter courses (according to Kickbusch in his article) or by setting aside separate times for exclusive attention to values education (according to Hemmer in his article).

A contradiction exists if teachers help students learn to make their own well-considered, free choices to create outcomes they cherish, and then send them back to classrooms where teachers make all significant decisions (subject matter content, style of teaching and learning, pace, objectives, outcome criteria, rewards and punishments). Similarly, it is contradictory to expect flexibility from teachers in a school administered through strictly hierarchical, authoritarian procedures. Values education implies educational practices in classrooms and schools that involve students with teachers and administrators in making democatic decisions. (Naturally, the form of responsible student participation should respect their developmental level.) Unfortunately, the educational context for values education is often less than ideal. As Silver points out in his article, teachers need to overcome these "barriers to values education." Such tasks "come with the territory," according to Purpel and Ryan, and require confrontation, insight, and commitment.

Although this summary is faithful to the authors' intentions, it may be misleading. Conducting values education does not require prior transformation of a school into a perfect model of democracy, any more than it requires a perfectly democractic society. Among the forces influencing student choices are parents and family life; religious training; messages from television, radio, newspapers, and advertising; mores of friends; and, obviously, each student's idiosyncratic history. Recognizing this combination of forces is reason for modest expectations about the total impact of our efforts, for empathy with students who must contend with so many conflicting pressures, and for determination to do our part as educators. These difficulties should not be cited as justifications for abandoning the effort.

Overemphasis on these external factors also is misleading. Such factors influence choices in the same way that the weather influences, but does not determine, our choices about going outside or staying inside. It is a uniquely human characteristic that ultimately we always choose our responses to events, whether or not we are conscious of choosing, whether or not we take responsibility for our choices. In this fact of human existence lies the potential power of values education. We can strengthen students' ability to exercise conscious choice on behalf of ends they value, in spite of inevitable counterpressures, obligations, claims on loyalties, inducements, and threats. Our educational assistance can make a pivotal difference in students' lives.

A.S.A.

FREEDOM, INTELLIGENCE, AND VALUING

Louis E. Raths, *Adjunct Professor, Department of Elementary and Early Childhood Education, State University College at Fredonia, New York.*

Anyone interested in values must believe that he or she has a conscious, is capable of awareness, and has sensitivity and perceptiveness. The person committed to values must have an aversion to the doctrine of determinism, because the realm of values is one that deals with choices. If there is no freedom of choice for individuals and groups in our world, then there is little or no need for the concept of values. Without freedom of choice there would be no freedom of speech. We would not have the choice whether to speak or not, whether to speak with passion and conviction or to speak with many qualifications and questions. Our lives would be determined, and choice would be unnecessary.

With this belief in one's own conscious, one's own awareness, and one's own perceptiveness, there is the concomitant acceptance of responsibility for the choices one makes. In a world of determinism it would not be possible to take personal responsibility for guiding one's own life or for sharing with others in the development of values, which hopefully shape a better life for all of us. Alfred North Whitehead indicated that in the beginning of human existence, the sole aim of people was to live. Tens of thousands of years later, with the development of agriculture and the taming of animals for domestic use and with the growth of small communities, the dominant aim became to live well. As this was achieved people began to see visions of living still better. For Whitehead, human evolution is ever upward with our goals continuing for a better and better way of life.[1] Sir Charles Scott Sherrington, also writing at about the same time, agreed with Whitehead that this latter period began about the era of the classical Greek civilization and other groups in West Asia.[2] Sherrington words the third alternative somewhat differently: he says in that latter time people came to see that they could live by values. Isn't it a little strange that this concept of shaping our world by values is so old, and yet in these 2500 years or more (4000 years since ancient India), we have made so little progress toward this goal? In reference to determinism, Harold Harris has said that evolution is a game that is played according to fixed rules—rules which limit life's possibilities but allow for a limitless number of variations. Harris has quoted Professor Christopher Lorguet-Higgins as saying, "Life is not merely programmed activity but self-programmed activity."[3] This indicates that any analogy between humankind and the computer is false: the computer cannot program itself.

These ideas of freedom and freedom of choice, of self-programming, and awareness and perceptiveness suggest that an extreme form of behaviorism in the social sciences is not an area of study that openly accepts the idea of values. The deterministic outlook practically excludes independent thinking of all kinds, regarding people as being totally molded or shaped by the milieu of those in authority. This outlook abrogates the concept of independent thinking for those subordinates who are being shaped.

Robert S. Morison says that:

> Science has progressively reduced the prestige and status of man in the scheme of things, first, by showing that he lives on a small planet in a rather out-of-the-way part of the universe, second by showing his close relationship with what are obviously lower animals, and finally, by showing that many, if not all, of his actions are determined by genetic and environmental variables over which he as conscious individual has little or no control.[4]

Morison goes on to say how odd it is that in the face of all this,

> Man has through his own unaided efforts developed instruments for looking further out and deeper into his universe than anyone could have imagined when he occupied his exhalted position as the center of

creation. Not only can he see and hear things no one ever thought of before, he has arranged them in ways to produce an extraordinary sense of order and predictability. Furthermore, the formulae which reflect the new found order can be used to heal the sick, feed the multitudes and destroy one's enemies on a scale which even the avenging Jehovah would have regarded as pretentious.[5]

Morison closes with the question of how we can bring peoples' destructive and constructive natures together in some coherent relationship and indicates that the resolution of their tension calls for an art of a high order.[6] In describing these two sides of human life, we can conjecture that the origin of human consciousness is as mysterious as the origin of life itself. In the words of Morison: "We seem to know more and more about how to live without finding out any more about why it is worthwhile to live."[7]

The great majority of professional educators, including the present writer, believe that our values come from our experiences. Genetically we may inherit nervous systems that are unique to ourselves, and we may inherit bodily structures that tend to facilitate different kinds of awareness and perceptiveness. Nevertheless, we tend to accept the idea that, concerning values, we are what we experience. The word itself is often used loosely. Whitehead indicates that the conventional view of experience is simplistic. He indicates that it is not a neat and tidy finite experience which is uniformly illuminated, and he says with conviction that no notion could be further from the truth. Whitehead goes on:

> The equating of experience with clarity of knowledge is against evidence. In our own lives, and at any one moment, there is a focus of attention, a few items in clarity of awareness, but interconnected vaguely and yet insistently with other items in dim apprehension, and this dimness shading off imperceptively into undiscriminated feelings.[8]

John Dewey described character as the interpenetration of habits.[9] In other words, the idea of character is no more clear than the idea of experience. Character too is made up of many things in which there are perhaps a few items in clarity of awareness, but all of them are interconnected vaguely in terms of present knowledge. Even so, most of us continue to believe that our values come from our experiences. Very often we associate them with our hearth and home and the immediate family or the extended family. We associate them with the kind of life we are living. We associate them with our participation in social institutions: the school; the church; the government; the world of art, books, drama, music, and dance; and just about everything that has touched our lives in one way or another. In our adult life we are apt also to indicate that our work has had an influence upon our values and that our near and close relationships with other people have indeed had their influence. We include feelings of love and sadness and of joy. All of this and more is the stuff from which we have squeezed values and all of this constitutes for us that realm we call experience.

Both Whitehead and Dewey have said that the quality of an experience is to be judged by the thinking that has been involved in it, the connections that have been made between the immediate experience and our existence past, present, and future. If one thinks about this, it necessarily follows that although several of us may have shared the same outward situation, each of us may have had a distinctly different experience. Perhaps at this time we need to turn to definitions or concepts of value.

Dewey clearly indicates that his concept of values includes:

1. The idea of prizing, cherishing, and holding dear
2. The idea of reflection and making connections between the factors of the situation in one's existence to the end that intelligence is employed and that improved judgment is concluded
3. The idea that action in support of an approved value will be taken. [10]

This would suggest that in a situation of choice—

●One would most certainly consider all of the available alternatives that seem to be significant.

●One would reflect upon the grounds which would sustain each of them and the further consequences toward which each one would lead.

●After having applied intelligent reflection on these matters, one would make a choice leading to a course of action which would tend to preserve the values that were prized.

It seems evident enough that these three operations could not be carried on in a totalitarian society where individual choice is not permitted. Commitment to the idea of choosing freely involves the same principles for the society as for the individual member. Free choice places upon each of us a responsibility to organize our behavior so that the means we use will be consistent with the ends we seek.

As we have experiences and from them generate concepts of value, the resultant values become rules which will govern future conduct, or (according to Dewey's general position) they become principles and generalizations drawn from past experiences that are not absolute but serve as guides to a situation in which we find ourselves. A rather simple example might be that we carry upon our backs a bag that is full of principles and values and rules that have come to us by way of experiences. When we meet a new experience we may indeed thrust our hand into the bag and look for an appropriate solution to the problem at hand, but we find almost always that the situation is different from any that we have experienced before and because of our cumulative experiences we too are different. Hence, it follows that what we extract from the bag is not an answer to the present situation, but something to examine and look at carefully in order to grasp its relevance to what we are about to decide and then either to modify and adapt it or create something entirely new that will meet the value we desire to support.

Dewey compares the methods of science with the so-called ordinary common sense methods.[11] His writings clearly indicate that when a scientist is moved to test a new hypothesis, the methods used to test other hypotheses in the past may not be appropriate. So, the scientist changes his or her behavior in order that an adequate test can be made of the hypothesis which is being subjected to inquiry. On beginning an experimental work, the scientist does not contrast what he or she is doing with some generalization about absolute truth or absolute perfection. Rather the scientist, confronted by a problematic situation, has an hypothesis which he or she has chosen as appropriate for the occasion. The procedure for carrying through the requirement may involve instruments and behaviors never before utilized. If, however, they are necessary for the valid and reliable testing of the hypothesis and presumably the solution of the problem, the scientist sees to it that the necessary arrangements take place. Dewey suggests that in the so-called humanities, the problems are more difficult, contain many more factors usually, and are less likely to be capable of reduction to the simplicity of one factor at a time. But over and over again he insists that if we are to use the methods of intelligence in the field of values and the means consistent with those ends, we can achieve a great deal more than we are now doing by appealing to custom, prejudice, nationalism, or mysticism. To sum up, Dewey's concept of value puts a great emphasis upon prizing and cherishing and upon choosing in terms of consequence and carefully calculated action that supports what is prized.

Dewey says, "A moral law, like a law in physics, is not something to swear by and stick to at all hazards; it is a formula of the way to respond when specified conditions present themselves. Its soundness and pertinence are tested by what happens when it is acted upon."[12] Whitehead says pretty much the same thing: "In scientific investigations the question, True or False?, is usually irrelevant. The important question is, In what circumstances is this formula true, and in what circumstances is it false? If the circumstance of truth be infrequent or trivial or unknown, we can say, with sufficient accuracy for daily use, that the formula is false."[13] Both quotations emphasize process and are a definite rejection of static absolutes.

Neither is suggesting that the experiences of the past, personal and social, are unimportant. Quite obviously we would be without any ideas whatever if the past were an entire blank. The past may give us suggestions and guides, but in decision-making situations of a complex nature the past does not give us answers. We can say that all of our lives we do carry with us at least fragments of the experiences we have endured and reflected upon. Our past experiences constitute a resource for us in the situations which we are destined to meet in the future. They are not absolutes dictating what we shall do in any one situation; nevertheless, our past experiences help enlighten the current situation and its possibilities as we begin value inquiry.

Concepts of what constitutes value are themselves values or value indicators. To be for freedom of choice, and at the same time free to add other choices as one perceives them, is in itself a very important value. To esteem being free to exercise the operations of intelligence in examining a situation is also a value. To esteem being free to suggest hypotheses and to recommend action based upon the preservation of the values in the definition is also a value. To want a world for children in school where they can express (1) purposes of their own, (2) interests of their own, (3) attitudes of their own, (4) aspirations of their own, (5) beliefs of their own, (6) feelings of their own, (7) thinking that is theirs, and (8) activities that they enjoy, is indeed to champion a life for these children. To seek and promote a life that contains these eight is indeed to reveal a value orientation. In *Values and Teaching*, I have referred to these eight categories as possible habits of behavior that connect to Dewey's definition of character.[14] The teaching profession should place great emphasis upon changing the college preparation of teachers and upon changing the behavior of our administrators and teachers so that classrooms could constitute lives for children in which these eight habits of behavior could be expressed and, on numerous occasions, be made the beginning point of value inquiry. In this way educators would be treating the area of values as scientists treat the area of material things.

In thinking about each one of these eight categories every teacher could begin by asking children questions when statements of purposes are made, when statements of attitudes are spoken, when feelings are expressed or beliefs shared, or when thinking is stated. The questions should help young people see more clearly what they believe, what their purposes are, and what their thinking implies. The questions are oriented to Dewey's conception of values: they represent an effort to find out what is prized or cherished, what alternatives have been considered, what processes of intelligence have been employed, what ends are sought in the practical situation, what means have been chosen to meet those ends, and whether or not they are consistent with each other. All of this may suggest an intensely individualistic concern with values. However, this method of inquiry does not necessarily restrict questions to the personal domain, but concerns the consequences of one's own actions for self, for peers, for family, for social institutions, and for society at large as well.

In *Values and Teaching*, some 35 different questions were suggested for the exploration of the eight categories of habits. Their underlying assumption is that if teachers created situations in which children could adopt these habits, teachers would then be in a situation to observe, listen, and react to the value indicators that are implied by the habits themselves. Teachers would also be in a situation to carry on a very limited interaction with the student, involving perhaps not more than a few minutes. It was not intended that any student be asked 35 questions in sequence nor was it implied that these questions exhausted all possibilities. The idea was to have a curriculum in which purposes and interests would generate related activities. It was further hoped that as students were repeatedly asked to consider alternatives and consequences and to see the significance of acting in terms of what was deemed desirable, these students would learn that achieving certain values would require a change in behavior.

There have been a number of trials involving this kind of interaction between teachers and students and, in a large number of instances, children have changed their behavior without being told to do so. For example, some children had been thought of as apathetic and listless, and, yet, over a period of a semester or longer a change took place. They began to participate more, seeming to generate purpose within themselves. Some children who were characterized as extremely flighty tended to become more organized in their approach to experience and more selective in choosing their activities. Similarly, some children who were conformists seemed to develop some independence of mind. The effort was made in every such trial to stay away from telling children what they ought to do or be or believe. This did not mean that their teachers were tolerant of everything that was said or done—just as in the adult world, accepting dissent or difference does not always mean approval or toleration for the sake of tolerance. Most frequently we use it as a point of inquiry with the idea that, from interaction with the dissenter, we may learn more about ourselves and the dissenter. If we believe in freedom of speech and the right to dissent, we acknowledge that in our role as teachers we can accept much that is different without necessarily approving it.

The major aim in this whole area of values is freedom and freedom controlled by intelligence. It invites the current generations of men, women, and children to look at values in the same way that scientists look at experimentation in their own fields. Specifically, it suggests to teachers that—

●When students are put in a position of comparing one alternative to another, they are using a method of intelligence.

●When students are seeking to classify factors in a situation in order to understand it more fully, they are using the operations of intelligence.

●When students are delving into some of the assumptions which underlie one hypothesis or another, or one alternative or another, they are using the methods of intelligence.

●When students are being critical of all the alternatives and thinking that might be employed at the moment, they are also using the methods of intelligence.

●When students are imagining alternatives other than those presented, they are also using the methods of intelligence to extricate themselves from a problematic situation.

●When students are assembling and organizing data, they are also using the methods of science in anticipation of a course of action.

These show what is meant by taking the time to become familiar with the situation itself, to look at it in terms of what is prized, and to use the methods of intelligence for making a choice and arranging for a course of action. Of course, such purposeful and arranged behavior will not always produce what is anticipated. However, of the many ways for arriving at a decision, this method of valuing seems to be about the best available.

Originally in developing values-clarifying operations that grow out of an activity-oriented curriculum, my intention was to place a premium on children's purposes, interests, and needs. I did not envision entire books devoted to hundreds of examples of "choice" situations which had little or nothing to do with the ongoing curriculum. As history has revealed, it is very possible to trivialize the values-clarification approach. For example, a teacher may use many problematic situations within one classroom hour: from dropping the hydrogen bomb, to kissing on the first date, to drinking too much cola, to showing up late when you have an engagement with your best friend. Although multiplicity of examples is not a bad thing, when examples are offered in profusion, there is the temptation for teachers to use them in almost any sequence. Merely using them is thought of as dedicating one's self to the clarification of values. However, examples should focus upon those issues, problems, or concerns which the teacher believes to represent serious and significant matters in the lives of children and in the existence of our society. The use of trivial problem situations does a disservice to the serious task of clarifying values; they may titillate students but the question may be asked whether they make any kind of lasting contribution to character development.

By using authentic values-clarifying ideas daily in the classroom and by creating situations in which children will live and express their living, we are respecting the dignity of the individual as well as the right of every individual to seek a better life. For in the process we will be emphasizing the value of the freedoms of speech, thought, assembly, and religion, in addition to the revolutionary principle of the Declaration of Independence that "All governments derive their just powers from the consent of the governed." D.W. Brogan says of this value statement: "There is the revolutionary slogan, coming from the pen of a young, erudite, Virginia slave-holder. The Revolution was on the march from that moment; it still is."[15] As with the potential in us for continuing moral development, we can expect that if we apply ourselves to the task, the revolution will continue, on and on and on.

THE COGNITIVE-DEVELOPMENTAL APPROACH TO MORAL EDUCATION

Lawrence Kohlberg, *Director of the Center for Moral Education, Graduate School of Education, Harvard University.*

The cognitive-developmental approach was fully stated for the first time by John Dewey. The approach is called *cognitive* because it recognizes that moral education, like intellectual education, has its basis in stimulating the *active thinking* of the child about moral issues and decisions. It is called developmental because it sees the aims of moral education as movement through moral stages. According to Dewey:

> The aim of education is growth or *development,* both intellectual and moral. Ethical and psychological principles can aid the school in the *greatest of all constructions—the building of a free and powerful character.* Only knowledge of the *order and connection of the stages in psychological development can insure this.* Education is the work of *supplying the conditions* which will enable the psychological functions to mature in the freest and fullest manner.[1]

Dewey postulated three levels of moral development: 1) the *pre-moral* or *preconventional* level "of behavior motivated by biological and social impulses with results for morals," 2) the *conventional* level of behavior "in which the individual accepts with little critical reflection the standards of his group," and 3) the *autonomous* level of behavior in which "conduct is guided by the individual thinking and judging for himself whether a purpose is good, and does not accept the standard of his group without reflection."[2]

Dewey's thinking about moral stages was theoretical. Building upon his prior studies of cognitive stages, Jean Piaget made the first effort to define stages of moral reasoning in children through actual interviews and through observations of children (in games with rules).[3] Using this interview material, Piaget defined the pre-moral, the conventional, and the autonomous levels as follows: 1) the *pre-moral stage,* where there was no sense of obligation to rules; 2) the *heteronomous stage,* where the right was literal obedience to rules and an equation of obligation with submission to power and punishment (roughly ages 4-8); and 3) the *autonomous stage,* where the purpose and consequences of following rules are considered and obligation is based on reciprocity and exchange (roughly ages 8-12).[4]

In 1955 I started to redefine and validate (through longitudinal and cross-cultural study) the Dewey-Piaget levels and stages. The resulting stages are presented in Table 1 on the next page.

We claim to have validated the stages defined in Table 1. The notion that stages can be *validated* by longitudinal study implies that stages have definite empirical characteristics.[5] The concept of stages (as used by Piaget and myself) implies the following characteristics:

1. Stages are "structured wholes," or organized systems of thought. Individuals are *consistent* in level of moral judgment.

2. Stages form an *invariant sequence.* Under all conditions except extreme trauma, movement is always forward, never backward. Individuals never skip stages; movement is always to the next stage up.

3. Stages are "hierarchical integrations." Thinking at a higher stage includes or comprehends within it lower-stage thinking. There is a tendency to function at or prefer the highest stage available.

Each of these characteristics has been demonstrated for moral stages. Stages are defined by responses to a set of verbal moral dilemmas classified according to an elaborate scoring scheme. Validating studies include:

1. A 20-year study of 50 Chicago-area boys, middle- and working-class. Initially interviewed at ages 10-16, they have been reinterviewed at three-year intervals thereafter.

2. A small, six-year longitudinal study of Turkish village and city boys of the same age.

Table 1. Definition of Moral Stages

I. Preconventional level

At this level, the child is responsive to cultural rules and labels of good and bad, right or wrong, but interprets these labels either in terms of the physical or the hedonistic consequences of action (punishment, reward, exchange of favors) or in terms of the physical power of those who enunciate the rules and labels. The level is divided into the following two stages:

Stage 1: *The punishment-and-obedience orientation.* The physical consequences of action determine its goodness or badness, regardless of the human meaning or value of these consequences. Avoidance of punishment and unquestioning deference to power are valued in their own right, not in terms of respect for an underlying moral order supported by punishment and authority (the latter being Stage 4).

Stage 2: *The instrumental-relativist orientation.* Right action consists of that which instrumentally satisfies one's own needs and occasionally the needs of others. Human relations are viewed in terms like those of the marketplace. Elements of fairness, of reciprocity, and of equal sharing are present, but they are always interpreted in a physical, pragmatic way. Reciprocity is a matter of "you scratch my back and I'll scratch yours," not of loyalty, gratitude, or justice.

II. Conventional level

At this level, maintaining the expectations of the individual's family, group, or nation is perceived as valuable in its own right, regardless of immediate and obvious consequences. The attitude is not only one of *conformity* to personal expectations and social order, but of loyalty to it, of actively *maintaining*, supporting, and justifying the order, and of identifying with the persons or group involved in it. At this level, there are the following two stages:

Stage 3: *The interpersonal concordance or "good boy—nice girl" orientation.* Good behavior is that which pleases or helps others and is approved by them. There is much conformity to stereotypical images of what is majority or "natural" behavior. Behavior is frequently judged by intention—"he means well" becomes important for the first time. One earns approval by being "nice."

Stage 4: *The "law and order" orientation.* There is orientation toward authority, fixed rules, and the maintenance of the social order. Right behavior consists of doing one's duty, showing respect for authority, and maintaining the given social order for its own sake.

III. Postconventional, autonomous, or principled level

At this level, there is a clear effort to define moral values and principles that have validity and application apart from the authority of the groups or persons holding these principles and apart from the individual's own identification with these groups. This level also has two stages:

Stage 5: *The social-contract, legalistic orientation,* generally with utilitarian overtones. Right action tends to be defined in terms of general individual rights and standards which have been critically examined and agreed upon by the whole society. There is a clear awareness of the relativism of personal values and opinions and a corresponding emphasis upon procedural rules for reaching consensus. Aside from what is constitutionally and democratically agreed upon, the right is a matter of personal "values" and "opinion." The result is an emphasis upon the "legal point of view," but with an emphasis upon the possibility of changing law in terms of rational considerations of social utility (rather than freezing it in terms of Stage 4 "law and order"). Outside the legal realm, free agreement and contract is the binding element of obligation. This is the "official" morality of the American government and constitution.

Stage 6: *The universal-ethical-principle orientation.* Right is defined by the decision of conscience in accordance with self-chosen *ethical principles* appealing to logical comprehensiveness, universality, and consistency. These principles are abstract and ethical (the Golden Rule, the categorical imperative); they are not concrete moral rules like the Ten Commandments. At heart, these are universal principles of *justice,* of the *reciprocity* and *equality* of human *rights,* and of respect for the dignity of human beings as *individual* persons ("From Is to Ought," pp. 164, 165).

—Reprinted with permission from *The Journal of Philosophy,* October 25, 1973.

3. A variety of other cross-sectional studies in Canada, Britain, Israel, Taiwan, Yucatan, Honduras, and India.

With regard to the structured whole or consistency criterion, we have found that more than 50% of an individual's thinking is always at one stage, with the remainder at the next adjacent stage (which he is leaving or which he is moving into).

With regard to invariant sequence, our longitudinal results have been presented in the *American Journal of Orthopsychiatry* (see footnote 12), and indicate that on every retest individuals were either at the same stage as three years earlier or had moved up. This was true in Turkey as well as in the United States.

With regard to the hierarchical integration criterion, it has been demonstrated that adolescents exposed to written statements at each of the six stages comprehend or correctly put in their own words all statements at or below their own stage but fail to comprehend any statements more than one stage above their own.[6] Some individuals comprehend the next stage above their own; some do not. Adolescents prefer (or rank as best) the highest stage they can comprehend.

To understand moral stages, it is important to clarify their relations to stage of logic or intelligence, on the one hand, and to moral behavior on the other. Maturity of moral judgment is not highly correlated with IQ or verbal intelligence (correlations are only in the 30s, accounting for 10% of the variance). Cognitive development, in the stage sense, however, is more important for moral development than such correlations suggest. Piaget has found that after the child learns to speak there are three major stages of reasoning: the intuitive, the concrete operational, and the formal operational. At around age 7, the child enters the stage of concrete logical thought: He can make logical inferences, classify, and handle quantitative relations about concrete things. In adolescence individuals usually enter the stage of formal operations. At this stage they can reason abstractly, i.e., consider all possibilities, form hypotheses, deduce implications from hypotheses, and test them against reality.[7]

Since moral reasoning clearly is reasoning, advanced moral reasoning depends upon advanced logical reasoning; a person's logical stage puts a certain ceiling on the moral stage he can attain. A person whose logical stage is only concrete operational is limited to the preconventional moral stages (Stages 1 and 2). A person whose logical stage is only partially formal operational is limited to the conventional moral stages (Stages 3 and 4). While logical development is necessary for moral development and sets limits to it, most individuals are higher in logical stage than they are in moral stage. As an example, over 50% of late adolescents and adults are capable of full formal reasoning, but only 10% of these adults (all formal operational) display principled (Stages 5 and 6) moral reasoning.

The moral stages are *structures of moral judgment* or *moral reasoning. Structures* of moral judgment must be distinguished from the *content* of moral judgment. As an example, we cite responses to a dilemma used in our various studies to identify moral stage. The dilemma raises the issue of stealing a drug to save a dying woman. The inventor of the drug is selling it for 10 times what it costs him to make it. The woman's husband cannot raise the money, and the seller refuses to lower the price or wait for payment. What should the husband do?

The choice endorsed by a subject (steal, don't steal) is called the *content* of his moral judgment in the situation. His reasoning about the choice defines the structure of his moral judgment. This reasoning centers on the following 10 universal moral values or issues of concern to persons in these moral dilemmas:

1. Punishment
2. Property
3. Roles and concerns of affection
4. Roles and concerns of authority
5. Law
6. Life
7. Liberty
8. Distributive justice
9. Truth
10. Sex

A moral choice involves choosing between two (or more) of these values as they *conflict* in concrete situations of choice.

The stage or structure of a person's moral judgment defines: 1) *what* he finds valuable in each of these moral issues (life, law), i.e., how he defines the value, and 2) *why* he finds it valuable, i.e., the reasons he gives for valuing it. As an example, at Stage 1 life is valued in terms of the power or possessions of the person involved; at Stage 2, for its usefulness in satisfying the needs of the individual in question or others; at Stage 3, in terms of the individual's relations with others and their valuation of him; at Stage 4, in terms of social or religious law. Only at Stages 5 and 6 is each life seen as inherently worthwhile, aside from other considerations.

Having clarified the nature of stages of moral *judgment,* we must consider the relation of moral judgment to moral *action.* If logical reasoning is a necessary but not sufficient condition for mature moral judgment, mature moral judgment is a necessary but not sufficient condition for mature moral action. One cannot follow moral principles if one does not understand (or believe in) moral principles. However, one can reason in terms of principles and not live up to these principles. As an example, Richard Krebs and I found that only 15% of students showing some principled thinking cheated as compared to 55% of conventional subjects and 70% of preconventional subjects.[8] Nevertheless, 15% of the principled subjects did cheat, suggesting that factors additional to moral judgment are necessary for principled moral reasoning to be translated into "moral action." Partly, these factors include the situation and its pressures. Partly, what happens depends upon the individual's motives and emotions. Partly, what the individual does depends upon a general sense of will, purpose, or "ego strength." Krebs' study is an example of the role of will or ego strength in moral behavior: Slightly more than half of his conventional subjects cheated. These subjects were also divided by a measure of attention/will. Only 26% of the "strong-willed" conventional subjects cheated; however, 74% of the "weak-willed" subjects cheated.

If maturity of moral reasoning is only one factor in moral behavior, why does the cognitive-developmental approach to moral education focus so heavily upon moral reasoning? For the following reasons:

1. Moral judgment, while only one factor in moral behavior, is the single most important or influential factor yet discovered in moral behavior.

2. While other factors influence moral behavior, moral judgment is the only distinctively *moral* factor in moral behavior. To illustrate, we noted that the Krebs study indicated that "strong-willed" conventional stage subjects resisted cheating more than "weak-willed" subjects. For those at a preconventional level of moral reasoning, however, "will" had an opposite effect. "Strong-willed" Stages 1 and 2 subjects cheated more, not less, than "weak-willed" subjects, i.e., they had the "courage of their (amoral) convictions" that it was worthwhile to cheat. "Will," then, is an important factor in moral behavior, but it is not distinctively moral; it becomes moral only when informed by mature moral judgment.

3. Moral judgment change is long-range or irreversible; a higher stage is never lost. Moral behavior as such is largely situational and reversible or "loseable" in new situations.

Moral psychology describes what moral development is, as studied empirically. Moral education must also consider moral philosophy, which strives to tell us what moral development ideally *ought to be*. Psychology finds an invariant sequence of moral stages; moral philosophy must be invoked to answer whether a later stage is a better stage. The "stage" of senescence and death follows the "stage" of adulthood, but that does not mean that senescence and death are better. Our claim that the latest or principled stages of moral reasoning are morally better stages, then, must rest on considerations of moral philosophy.

The tradition of moral philosophy to which we appeal is the liberal or rational tradition, in particular the "formalistic" or "deontological" tradition running from Immanuel Kant to John Rawls.[9] Central to this tradition is the claim that an adequate morality is *principled*, i.e., that it makes judgments in terms of *universal* principles applicable to all mankind. *Principles* are to be distinguished from *rules*. Conventional morality is grounded on rules, primarily "thou shalt nots" such as are represented by the Ten Commandments, prescriptions of kinds of actions. Principles are, rather, universal guides to making a moral decision. An example is Kant's "categorical imperative," formulated in two ways. The first is the maxim of respect for human personality, "Act always toward the other as an end, not as a means." The second is the maxim of universalization, "Choose only as you would be willing to have everyone choose in your situation." Principles like that of Kant's state the formal conditions of a moral choice or action. In the dilemma in which a woman is dying because a druggist refuses to release his drug for less than the stated price, the druggist is not acting morally, though he is not violating the ordinary moral rules (he is not actually stealing or murdering). But he is violating principles: He is treating the woman simply as a means to his ends of profit, and he is not choosing as he would wish anyone to choose. (If the druggist were in the dying woman's place, he would not want a druggist to choose as he is choosing.) Under most circumstances, choice in terms of conventional moral rules and choice in terms of principles coincide. Ordinarily, principles dictate not stealing (avoiding stealing is implied by acting in terms of a regard for others as ends and in terms of what one would want everyone to do). In a situation where stealing is the only means to save a life, however, principles contradict the ordinary rules and would dictate stealing. Unlike rules which are supported by social authority, principles are freely chosen by the individual because of their intrinsic moral validity.[10]

The conception that a moral choice is a choice made in terms of moral principles is related to the claim of liberal moral philosophy that moral principles are ultimately principles of justice. In essence, moral conflicts are conflicts between the claims of persons, and principles for resolving these claims are principles for justice, "for giving each his due." Central to justice are the demands of *liberty, equality,* and *reciprocity.* At every moral stage, there is a concern for justice. The most damning statement a school child can make about a teacher is that "he's not fair." At each higher stage, however, the conception of justice is reorganized. At Stage 1, justice is punishing the bad in terms of "an eye for an eye and a tooth for a tooth." At Stage 2, it is exchanging favors and goods in an equal manner. At Stages 3 and 4, it is treating people as they desire in terms of the conventional rules. At Stage 5, it is recognized that all rules and laws flow from justice, from a social contract between the governors and the governed designed to protect the equal rights of all. At Stage 6, personally chosen moral principles are also principles of justice, the principles any member of a society would choose for that society if he did not know what his position was to be in the society and in which he might be the least advantaged.[11] Principles chosen from this point of view are, first, the maximum liberty compatible with the like liberty of others and, second, no inequalities of goods and respect which are not to the benefit of all, including the least advantaged.

As an example of stage progression in the orientation to justice, we may take judgments about capital punishment.[12] Capital punishment is only firmly rejected at the two principled stages, when the notion of justice as vengeance or retribution is abandoned. At the sixth stage, capital punishment is not condoned even if it may have some useful deterrent effect in promoting law and order. This is because it is not a punishment we would choose for a society if we assumed we had as much chance of being born into the position of a criminal or murderer as being born into the position of a law abider.

Why are decisions based on universal principles of justice better decisions? Because they are decisions on which all moral men could agree. When decisions are based on conventional moral rules, men will disagree, since they adhere to conflicting systems of rules dependent on culture and social position. Throughout history men have killed one another in the name of conflicting moral rules and values, most recently in Vietnam and the Middle East. Truly moral or just resolutions of conflicts require principles which are, or can be, universalizable.

We have given a philosophic rationale for stage advance as the aim of moral education. Given this rationale, the developmental approach to moral education can avoid the problems inherent in the other two major approaches to moral education. The first alternative approach is that of indoctrinative moral education, the preaching and imposition of the rules and values of the teacher and his culture on the child. In America, when this indoctrinative approach has been developed in a systematic manner, it has usually been termed "character education."

Moral values, in the character education approach, are preached or taught in terms of what may be called the "bag of virtues." In the classic studies of character by Hugh Hartshorne and Mark May, the virtues chosen were honesty, service, and self-control.[13] It is easy to get superficial consensus on such a bag of virtues—until one examines in detail the list of virtues involved and the details of their definition. Is the Hartshorne and May bag more adequate than the Boy Scout bag (a Scout should be honest, loyal, reverent, clean, brave, etc.)? When one turns to the details of defining each virtue, one finds equal uncertainty or difficulty in reaching consensus. Does honesty mean one should not steal to save a life? Does it mean that a student should not help another student with his homework?

Character education and other forms of indoctrinative moral education have aimed at teaching universal values (it is assumed that honesty or service are desirable traits for all men in all societies), but the detailed definitions used are relative; they are defined by the opinions of the teacher and the conventional culture and rest on the authority of the teacher for their justification. In this sense character education is close to the unreflective valuings by teachers which constitute the hidden curriculum of the school board.[14] Because of the current unpopularity of indoctrinative approaches to moral education, a family of approaches called "values clarification" has become appealing to teachers. Values clarification takes the first step implied by a rational approach to moral education: the eliciting of the child's own judgment or opinion about issues or situations in which values conflict, rather than imposing the teacher's opinion on him. Values clarification, however, does not attempt to go further than eliciting awareness of values; it is assumed that becoming more self-aware about one's values is an end in itself. Fundamentally, the definition of the end of values education as self-awareness derives from a belief in ethical relativity held by many value-clarifiers. As stated by Peter Engel, "One must contrast value clarification and value inculcation. Value clarification implies the principle that in the consideration of values there is no single correct answer." Within these premises of "no correct answer," children are to discuss moral dilemmas in such a way as to reveal different values and discuss their value differences with each other. The teacher is to stress that "our values are different," not that one value is more adequate than others. If this program is systematically followed, students will themselves become relativists, believing there is no "right" moral answer. For instance, a student caught cheating might argue that he did nothing wrong, since his own hierarchy of values, which may be different from that of the teacher, made it right for him to cheat.

Like values clarification, the cognitive-developmental approach to moral education stresses open or Socratic peer discussion of value dilemmas. Such discussion, however, has an aim: stimulation of movement to the next stage of moral reasoning. Like values clarification, the developmental approach opposes indoctrination. Stimulation of movement to the next stage of reasoning is not indoctrinative, for the following reasons:

1. Change is in the way of reasoning rather than in the particular beliefs involved.

2. Students in a class are at different stages; the aim is to aid movement of each to the next stage, not convergence on a common pattern.

3. The teacher's own opinion is neither stressed nor invoked as authoritative. It enters in only as one of many opinions, hopefully one of those at a next higher stage.

4. The notion that some judgments are more adequate than others is communicated. Fundamentally, however, this means that the student is encouraged to articulate a position which seems most adequate to him and to judge the adequacy of the reasoning of others.

In addition to having more definite aims than values clarification, the moral development approach restricts value education to that which is moral or, more specifically, to justice. This is for two reasons. First, it is not clear that the whole realm of personal, political, and religious values is a realm which is nonrelative, i.e., in which there are universals and a direction of development. Second, it is not clear that the public school has a right or mandate to develop values in general.[15] In our view, value education in the public schools should be restricted to that which the school has the right and mandate to develop: an awareness of justice, or of the rights of others in our Constitutional system. While the Bill of

Rights prohibits the teaching of religious beliefs, or of specific value systems, it does not prohibit the teaching of the awareness of rights and principles of justice fundamental to the Constitution itself.

When moral education is recognized as centered in justice and differentiated from value education or affective education, it becomes apparent that moral and civic education are much the same thing. This equation, taken for granted by the classic philosophers of education from Plato and Aristotle to Dewey, is basic to our claim that a concern for moral education is central to the educational objectives of social studies.

The term *civic education* is used to refer to social studies as more than the study of the facts and concepts of social science, history, and civics. It is education for the analytic understanding, value principles, and motivation necessary for a citizen in a democracy if democracy is to be an effective process. It is political education. Civic or political education means the stimulation of development of more advanced patterns of reasoning about political and social decisions and their implementation in action. These patterns are patterns of moral reasoning. Our studies show that reasoning and decision making about political decisions are directly derivative of broader patterns of moral reasoning and decision making. We have interviewed high school and college students about concrete political situations involving laws to govern open housing, civil disobedience for peace in Vietnam, free press rights to publish what might disturb national order, and distribution of income through taxation. We find that reasoning on these political decisions can be classified according to moral stage and that an individual's stage on political dilemmas is at the same level as on nonpolitical moral dilemmas (euthanasia, violating authority to maintain trust in a family, stealing a drug to save one's dying wife). Turning from reasoning to action, similar findings are obtained. In 1963 a study was made of those who sat in at the University of California, Berkeley, administration building and those who did not in the Free Speech Movement crisis. Of those at Stage 6, 80% sat in, believing that principles of free speech were being compromised, and that all efforts to compromise and negotiate with the administration had failed. In contrast, only 15% of the conventional (Stage 3 or Stage 4) subjects sat in. (Stage 5 subjects were in between.)[16]

From a psychological side, then, political development is part of moral development. The same is true from the philosophic side. In the *Republic,* Plato sees political education as part of a broader education for moral justice and finds a rationale for such education in terms of universal philosophic principles rather than the demands of a particular society. More recently, Dewey claims the same.

In historical perspective, America was the first nation whose government was publicly founded on postconventional principles of justice, rather than upon the authority central to conventional moral reasoning. At the time of our founding, postconventional or principled moral and political reasoning was the possession of the minority, as it still is. Today, as in the time of our founding, the majority of our adults are at the conventional level, particularly the "law and order" (fourth) moral stage. (Every few years the Gallup Poll circulates the Bill of Rights unidentified, and every year it is turned down.) The Founding Fathers intuitively understood this without benefit of our elaborate social science research; they constructed a document designing a government which would maintain principles of justice and the rights of man even though principled men were not the men in power. The machinery included checks and balances, the independent judiciary, and freedom of the press. Most recently, this machinery found its use at Watergate. The tragedy of Richard Nixon, as Harry Truman said long ago, was that he never understood the Constitution (a Stage 5 document), but the Constitution understood Richard Nixon.[17]

Watergate, then, is not some sign of moral decay of the nation, but rather of the fact that understanding and action in support of justice principles are still the possession of a minority of our society. Insofar as there is moral decay, it represents the weakening of conventional morality in the face of social and value conflict today. This can lead the less fortunate adolescent to fixation at the preconventional level, the more fortunate to movement to principles. We find a larger proportion of youths at the principled level today than was the case in their fathers' day, but also a larger proportion at the preconventional level.

Given this state, moral and civic education in the schools becomes a more urgent task. In the high school today, one often hears both preconventional adolescents and those beginning to move beyond convention sounding the same note of disaffection for the school. While our political institutions are in principle Stage 5 (i.e., vehicles for maintaining universal rights through the democratic process), our schools have traditionally been Stage 4 institutions of convention and authority. Today more than ever, democratic schools systematically engaged in civic education are required.

Our approach to moral and civic education relates the study of law and government to the actual creation of a democratic school in which moral dilemmas are discussed and resolved in a manner which will stimulate moral development.

For many years, moral development was held by psychologists to be primarily a result of family upbringing and family conditions. In particular, conditions of affection and authority in the home were believed to be critical, some balance of warmth and firmness being optimal for moral development. This view arises if morality is conceived as an internalization of the arbitrary rules of parents and culture, since such acceptance must be based on affection and respect for parents as authorities rather than on the rational nature of the rules involved.

Studies of family correlates of moral stage development do not support this internalization view of the conditions for moral development. Instead, they suggest that the conditions for moral development in homes and schools are similar and that the conditions are consistent with cognitive-developmental theory. In the cognitive-developmental view, morality is a natural product of a universal human tendency toward empathy or role taking, toward putting oneself in the shoes of other conscious beings. It is also a product of a universal human concern for justice, for reciprocity or equality in the relation of one person to another. As an example, when my son was four, he became a morally principled vegetarian and refused to eat meat, resisting all parental persuasion to increase his protein intake. His reason was, "It's bad to kill animals." His moral commitment to vegetariansim was not taught or acquired from parental authority; it was the result of the universal tendency of the young self to project its consciousness and values into other living things, other selves. My son's vegetarianism also involved a sense of justice, revealed when I read him a book about Eskimos in which a real hunting expedition was described. His response was to say, "Daddy, there is one kind of meat I would eat—Eskimo meat. It's all right to eat Eskimos because they eat animals." This natural sense of justice or reciprocity was Stage 1—an eye for an eye, a tooth for a tooth. My son's sense of the value of life was also Stage 1 and involved no differentiation between human personality and physical life. His morality, though Stage 1, was, however, natural and internal. Moral development past Stage 1, then, is not an internalization but the reconstruction of role taking and conceptions of justice toward greater adequacy. These reconstructions occur in order to achieve a better match between the child's own moral structures and the structures of the social and moral situations he confronts. We divide these conditions of match into two kinds: those dealing with moral discussions and communication and those dealing with the total moral environment or atmosphere in which the child lives.

In terms of moral discussion, the important conditions appear to be:

1. Exposure to the next higher stage of reasoning.

2. Exposure to situations posing problems and contradictions for the child's current moral structure, leading to dissatisfaction with his current level.

3. An atmosphere of interchange and dialogue combining the first two conditions, in which conflicting moral views are compared in an open manner.

Studies of families in India and America suggest that morally advanced children have parents at higher stages. Parents expose children to the next higher stage, raising moral issues and engaging in open dialogue or interchange about such issues.[18]

Drawing on this notion of the discussion conditions stimulating advance, Moshe Blatt conducted classroom discussions of conflict-laden hypothetical moral dilemmas with four classes of junior high and high school students for a semester.[19] In each of these classes, students were to be found at three stages. Since the children were not all responding at the same stage, the arguments they used with each other were at different levels. In the course of these discussions among the students, the teacher first supported and clarified those arguments that were one stage above the lowest stage among the children; for example, the teacher supported Stage 3 rather than Stage 2. When it seemed that these arguments were understood by the students, the teacher then challenged that stage, using new situations, and clarified the arguments one stage above the previous one: Stage 4 rather than Stage 3. At the end of the semester, all the students were retested; they showed significant upward change when compared to the controls, and they maintained the change one year later. In the experimental classrooms, from one-fourth to one-half of the students moved up a stage, while there was essentially no change during the course of the experiment in the control group.

Given the Blatt studies showing that moral discussion could raise moral stage, we undertook the next step: to see if teachers could conduct moral discussions in the course of teaching high school social studies with the same results. This step we took in cooperation with Edwin Fenton, who introduced moral dilemmas in his ninth- and eleventh-grade social studies texts. Twenty-four teachers in the Boston and Pittsburgh areas were given some instruction in conducting moral discussions around the dilemmas in the text. About half of the teachers stimulated significant developmental change in their classrooms—upward stage movement of one-quarter to one-half a stage. In control classes using the text but no moral dilemma discussions, the same teachers failed to stimulate any moral change in the students. Moral discussion, then, can be a usable and effective part of the curriculum at any grade level. Working with filmstrip dilemmas produced in cooperation with Guidance Associates, second-grade teachers conducted moral discussions yielding a similar amount of moral stage movement.

Moral discussion and curriculum, however, constitute only one portion of the conditions stimulating moral growth. When we turn to analyzing the broader life environment, we turn to a consideration of the *moral atmosphere* of the home, the school, and the broader society. The first basic dimension of social atmosphere is the role-taking opportunities it provides, the extent to which it encourages the child to take the point of view of others. Role taking is related to the amount of social interaction and social communication in which the child engages, as well as to his sense of efficacy in influencing attitudes of others. The second dimension of social atmosphere, more strictly moral, is the level of justice of the environment or institution. The justice structure of an institution refers to the perceived rules or principles for distributing rewards, punishments, responsibilities, and privileges among institutional members. This structure may exist or be perceived at any of our moral stages. As an example, a study of a traditional prison revealed that inmates perceived it as Stage 1, regardless of their own level.[20] Obedience to arbitrary command by power figures and punishment for disobedience were seen as the governing justice norms of the prison. A behavior-modification prison using point rewards for conformity was perceived as a Stage 2 system of instrumental exchange. Inmates at Stage 3 or 4 perceived this institution as more fair than the traditional prison, but not as fair in their own terms.

These and other studies suggest that a higher level of institutional justice is a condition for individual development of a higher sense of justice. Working on these premises, Joseph Hickey, Peter Scharf, and I worked with guards and inmates in a women's prison to create a more just community.[21] A social contract was set up in which guards and inmates each had a vote of one and in which rules were made and conflicts resolved through discussions of fairness and a democratic vote in a community meeting. The program has been operating four years and has stimulated moral stage advance in inmates, though it is still too early to draw conclusions as to its overall long-range effectiveness for rehabilitation.

One year ago, Fenton, Ralph Mosher, and I received a grant from the Danforth Foundation (with additional support from the Kennedy Foundation) to make moral education a living matter in two high schools in the Boston area (Cambridge and Brookline) and two in Pittsburgh. The plan had two components. The first was training counselors and social studies and English teachers in conducting moral discussions and making moral discussion an integral part of the curriculum. The second was establishing a just community school within a public high school.*

We have stated the theory of the just community high school, postulating that discussing real-life moral situations and actions as issues of fairness and as matters for democratic decision would stimulate advance in both moral reasoning and moral action. A participatory democracy provides more extensive opportunities for role taking and a higher level of perceived institutional justice than does any other social arrangement. Most alternative schools strive to establish a democratic governance, but none we have observed has achieved a vital or viable participatory democracy. Our theory suggested reasons why we might succeed where others failed. First, we felt that democracy had to be the central commitment of a school, rather than a humanitarian frill. Democracy as moral education provides that commitment. Second, democracy in alternative schools often fails because it bores the students. Students prefer to let teachers make decisions about staff, courses, and schedules, rather than to attend lengthy, complicated meetings. Our theory said that the issues a democracy should focus on are issues of morality and fairness. Real issues concerning drugs, stealing, disruptions, and grading are never boring if handled as issues of fairness. Third, our theory told us that if large democratic community meetings were preceded by small-group moral discussion, higher-stage thinking by students would win out in later decisions, avoiding the disasters of mob rule.[22]

Currently, we can report that the school based on our theory makes democracy work or function where other schools have failed. It is too early to make any claims for its effectiveness in causing moral development, however.

---

*A description of these schools is found on pp. 121-129.

Our Cambridge just community school within the public high school was started after a small summer planning session of volunteer teachers, students, and parents. At the time the school opened in the fall, only a commitment to democracy and a skeleton program of English and social studies had been decided on. The school started with six teachers from the regular school and 60 students, 20 from academic professional homes and 20 from working-class homes. The other 20 were dropouts and troublemakers or petty delinquents in terms of previous record. The usual mistakes and usual chaos of a beginning alternative school ensued. Within a few weeks, however, a successful democratic community process had been established. Rules were made around pressing issues: disturbances, drugs, hooking. A student discipline committee or jury was formed. The resulting rules and enforcement have been relatively effective and reasonable. We do not see reasonable rules as ends in themselves, however, but as vehicles for moral discussion and an emerging sense of community. This sense of community and a resulting morale are perhaps the most immediate signs of success. This sense of community seems to lead to behavior change of a positive sort. An example is a 15-year-old student who started as one of the greatest combinations of humor, aggression, light-fingeredness, and hyperactivity I have ever known. From being the principal disturber of all community meetings, he has become an excellent community meeting participant and occasional chairman. He is still more ready to enforce rules for others than to observe them himself, yet his commitment to the school has led to a steady decrease in exotic behavior. In addition, he has become more involved in classes and projects and has begun to listen and ask questions in order to pursue a line of interest.

We attribute such behavior change not only to peer pressure and moral discussion but to the sense of community which has emerged from the democratic process in which angry conflicts are resolved through fairness and community decision. This sense of community is reflected in statements of the students to us that there are no cliques—that the Blacks and the whites, the professors' sons and the project students, are friends. These statements are supported by observation. Such a sense of community is needed where students in a given classroom range in reading level from fifth-grade to college.

Fenton, Mosher, the Cambridge and Brookline teachers, and I are now planning a four-year curriculum in English and social studies centering on moral discussion, on role taking and communication, and on relating the government, laws, and justice system of the school to that of the American society and other world societies. This will integrate an intellectual curriculum for a higher level of understanding of society with the experiential components of school democracy and moral decision.

There is very little new in this—or in anything else we are doing. Dewey wanted democratic experimental schools for moral and intellectual development 70 years ago. Perhaps Dewey's time has come.

VALUES CLARIFICATION: IT CAN START GENTLY AND GROW DEEP

Sidney B. Simon, *Professor of Humanistic Education, University of Massachusetts, Amherst*

Polly deSherbinin, *Educational Writer and Visiting Lecturer in Journalism, University of Massachusetts, Amherst.*

There's no place to hide from your values. Everything you do reflects them. Even denying that your values show in your every act is a value indicator.

For example, when you sell something—like a used car—how important is what you choose to tell the potential buyer? Deciding what to say about what you know of all the defects in that heap may not lead to a very deep dilemma, but the way you make up your mind is part of a lifelong search for the meaning and significance of living. Through the process of working on their values through values clarification, many people have found their daily lives taking on new order and direction.

The process of values clarification involves knowing what one prizes, choosing those things which one cares for most, and weaving those things into the fabric of daily living. It is sometimes taught by working on real-life situations, at other times by dealing with made-up stories, but always by grappling with issues that are of real concern in people's lives.

Let us return to the example of the used car. You and the potential buyer of your car are just stepping up to the corpus delicti. Some fascinating issues are about to unfold.

Are you going to tell the person at your side everything you know is wrong with the car? Think about that. For each thing you tell, the threat increases that you will eventually sell for less money than you'd hoped. Further, if your prospective customer hears a long list of defects, a quick change of heart might very well ensue.

It's a fairly simple issue. If you reveal all the defects, the price will go down; if you scare the potential buyer enough, you may not be able to sell at all. What to do? Withhold some of the information? Where do you draw the line? Will you tell the interested party anything he or she asks, but hold back information not asked for? (A lot of people, by the way, respect that stance.)

You may decide upon a more complex solution to this moral issue—adopting a double standard. You may want to spill the beans if the prospective buyer is a friend or neighbor, but play it cozy if he's a stranger responding to a newspaper ad.

You may refine your position in a still different situation. What if the person looking at your car is a dealer? You may now consider a third standard, feeling that if this dealer isn't shrewd enough to spot the defects, then let the buyer truly beware.

Consider other variations on the theme as you twist and turn in the grip of this value issue. Say you know that the brake fluid is leaking slowly. In an emergency, the brakes may fail.

The problem can get increasingly complex. Things like a small leak in the muffler may not make much difference now, but if the buyer doesn't check, he or she might be poisoned by carbon monoxide gas.

We've just talked about life and death issues. Many people, even though it would cost them money, would mention the defective brakes or muffler or have them repaired before selling the car. But where do you stand?

The values clarification process is at work when you consider what may be a minor decision like your approach to selling a car. It comes into play with heavy issues, too; e.g., will you use drugs? Drug educators across the country increasingly use values clarification techniques.

Originally, drug programs specialized in scare techniques. Students were generally shown the horrendous problems created by using drugs. Ironically, research tells us this approach had the unforeseen effect of interesting more people in drugs. To many young people, danger did not seem to be a deterrent. Those were the days when an ex-drug user might be brought into the high school auditorium to show the scars on his arms and to tell lurid tales of his life as a junkie. Students who were into drugs would try to unveil him as a fraud. The pharmaceutical approach—telling students everything they never wanted to know about drugs—seemed to be equally ineffective.

In contrast, drug educators report reaching students by examining their values. Instead of focusing exclusively on drugs, they involve young people in looking at their total lives. The young discover what they prize and cherish. They begin to think about the consequences of their actions. Eventually they learn techniques for examining the harder issues in their lives, such as whether or not to use drugs.

A time-tested values clarification strategy which educators find particularly effective is to ask people to list 20 things in their lives they really love to do. Of course, drug users will put "getting stoned" on their list, but as they begin to think of the 19 other things they cherish doing, many of them come to see that getting stoned stands in the way of a variety of delights in living.

Another strategy that helps teachers show young people what unique and precious human beings they are is called "the coat of arms."[1] They divide a diagram of a coat of arms into six large spaces and ask each person to make drawings as follows in all but the last space:

First space—something you are very, very good at and something you are struggling to get better at

Second space—a value about which you would never budge

Third space—your most significant material prossession

Fourth space—your greatest achievement of the last year and your greatest setback or failure

Fifth space—what you would do if you were guaranteed success for a year in any undertaking

Sixth space—three words you'd like people to say about you if your life ended today

Young people often gather in small groups to share their coats of arms with each other, thoughtfully and respectfully, or they enjoy taping them to the wall and taking each other on "gallery walks." It can also be played in a number of variations.

In Simi Valley, California, Jane Stenger asked the young people she was working with to list both "what brings sunshine into my life" and "what brings pain into my life." One student wrote of his sunshine, "Talking with_____while sitting in the dark watching the wind blow and the rain fall brings sunshine and warmth to my heart." In the other column, the student wrote, "Watching and hearing_____want his real family's love and concern he deserves, but knows he won't get the love he longs for with his deep, hurt heart."

As young people get in touch with themselves, life begins to look different to them, and they gather courage to make new decisions. A recent study of 851 students, grades 5 through 10, was made by a delinquency-prevention organization in Visalia, California. It was found that, following values clarification training, the young people cut back significantly in their use of drugs.[2]

The term *values clarification* was first used by Louis Raths while he taught at New York University during the late fifties. Working from John Dewey's book, *Theory of Valuation,* Raths refined Dewey's ideas and created values clarification strategies based on the recorded thoughts of the great philosopher.

Doctoral candidates flocked to the classes Raths taught, often consisting of more than 100 students. He had the gift of personally touching his students and inspiring them to set their own lives in order. His relationship with his wife, his family, and his colleagues reflected his deep commitment to living his own radiant values.

Raths was also interested in the emotional needs of human beings. In some respects his work in this area went even further than that of Abraham Maslow. He also accomplished important work both in power theory and critical thinking theory. In short, Raths is a major figure in education, one who may have an important place in history.

What can be accomplished by values clarification? It is the hope of those involved in this new work that all students will learn the process during their years in school. It seems ultimately important that every human being be given the opportunity to become clearer about what he or she wants, is living for, and may perhaps die for.

Every man, woman, and child needs help in trying to make sense out of the confusion and conflict of today's world. For example, how does one know how to use a Saturday? How can one raise his children better than he himself was raised? Where does one get insight into how each unique human being needs to live? What are the immutable bases for personal relationships? These are among the vital questions values clarification strategies deal with.

Now, clearly, values clarification is not a panacea. It is not meant to "cure" people. But it does provide them with insight into how they look at choices and how they work at making decisions.

It is useful to enumerate the specific aims of values clarification:

1. *It helps people to be more purposeful.* When you know what you want, you don't fritter away your time on pursuits that seem less than beneficial to you. (A new values clarification strategy, by the way, asks people to list ways they fritter away their time.)

An excellent strategy for helping people become more purposeful is the "priority ladder" which helps them find out what is most important to them.[3] People are asked to place 10 or so items, such as the following, on their own personal ladders, with the highest priority at the top:

I want to have a clarified set of values to live by.
I want more intimacy with more people different from me.
I want to learn how to change.
I want to live more fully.
I want to help make the world a better place in which to live.
I want more ritual and celebration in my daily living.
I want feedback from people so I know how to act.
I want to be more authentic, open, and trusting.
I want to handle my anger more constructively.
I want to live more justly.

Afterwards, people range themselves on rungs of a ladder drawn on the floor. When, for example, the leader reads, "I want to live more fully," each person stands on the rung on which he or she placed that item, and looks around to see where he or she is standing in relation to others. Often people exchange with others on the ladder their reasons for placing themselves where they did.

Let us turn to another example. In Rochester, New York, a newspaper reports a high school administrator speaking of the importance of being purposeful.[4] He is telling members of the Parent/Teacher Association that people with clear values have "considerable purpose and pride in what they do." But, he continues, many people "at the other end of the continuum have a great deal of confusion." They're unsure about their lives and their surroundings. "Some people," the article continues, "are apathetic, flighty, make inconsistent choices or self-destructive decisions. Others are drifters. Some try too hard to conform to the crowd, while others are chronic dissenters." Still others, the administrator concludes, like the class clown or the class bully, are role players "whose counterfeit existence conceals their lack of a real one."

Research has been completed which backs up this principal's

contention that when children have clear values they work more purposefully. According to a recent study, a group of fifth-grade children who participated in values clarification sessions developed a more favorable attitude toward learning and felt more positive about themselves than their classmates did.[5]

In another study, conducted in South Burlington, Vermont, with a small but carefully selected group of 10 fifth-graders who habitually acted up in the classroom, it was found that, when values clarification activities were introduced during the school day, these youngsters took part in them to a notably greater extent than they had in normal classroom activities. They also became far less noisy and recalcitrant.[6]

2. *It helps people become more productive.* Perhaps this seems too commercial or mechanistic as a way of looking at life, but to be productive is very gratifying—to have a sense of accomplishment, to feel at the end of a day that you've used it well.

Here again the upper New York State school administrator sheds light for the benefit of local newspaper readers on one way in which values clarification can help students become more productive. He argues that in the face of the twentieth-century knowledge explosion, teaching only facts no longer suffices. "Time was when a teacher could point to a body of knowledge to learn," he says. "But today it's inconceivable that any individual student can internalize all available knowledge. Students have to have some process by which they can identify the knowledge that will be useful to them." He is speaking of values clarification.

Turning to another strategy, "New Year's Eve"[7] suggests a series of steps that will help people become more productive during the year to come. Participants ring in the New Year with the reminder, "Each New Year's Day is like being born again.

The first strategy is to list "the very best things that happened to you in each of the months last year." Participants are then encouraged to record a high point at the end of each month of the coming year. By comparing the two years, they can watch the direction in which their lives are going.

The second strategy is to list "20 things I love to do." In a column adjacent to the list, participants are asked to check those which cost them absolutely nothing each time they do them; to check those which they did five years back; and those which mean physical, emotional, or intellectual risk. These columns are infinitely expandable at the invention of the participants.

The third strategy is to look closely at the just-completed chart for "what leaps out at you about the life that you lead?"

Then complete each of five sentences: (1) I learned that I . . . . (2) I was disappointed that I . . . . (3) I was happy to see that I . . . . (4) I discovered that my life would be better if I . . . . (5) I see that by next Saturday I should . . . .

The fourth strategy is to list the resolutions a participant "has made, plans to make, or needs to make." After considering which ones mean a genuine gain and which can actually be achieved, he or she is asked to sift out the five most valuable resolutions.

The fifth strategy is to sign a contract to live by each resolution until a date the participant decides upon in advance and to give a copy of the contract to a person who also signs it and promises to help celebrate on the appointed date if contract terms have been observed. Ceremonies include burning the contract.

3. *It helps people sharpen their critical thinking.* You can find people who have been in values clarification for some time who can see through other people's foolishness. They're not taken in by smooth talkers. They seem to get a large picture of what's good and beautiful and right, and to know what's wrong. They're less vulnerable to fads and to hopping on the latest bandwagon of new things to own, to do, and to believe in.

4. *It helps people have better relations with each other.* When people know what they want, believe strongly, and follow up on commitments, they are nicer people to have around. You can count on them. And, indeed, when conflict arises, they know how to work it through.

Because they are purposeful and creative, they're better able to share and give warmly and consistently of themselves. If everyone in a high school is taking values clarification, you might expect more than the average number of thoughtful and considerate students, ones who know how to work on decent relationships with each other.

In the same newspaper article mentioned above, a guidance counselor speaks of the problems of students in his school who live in the isolation of a tract home. They have no sidewalks and no street lights; streets are too dangerous for bicycling. He says kids come to school in need of a place to be together and to learn to get along with each other. One of the hardest things for people to learn, he believes, is how to get along with others. "A great deal of your ability to do that stems from being able to understand why you are the way you are," the guidance counselor says. Getting along also requires young people to understand that "what's important to me is fine for me, but that doesn't make it right for you," the administrator adds in support of values clarification.

Above all, perhaps, people who work on their values tend to be more zestful. They have more than physical energy; they seem to know how to bank energy to spend on things which bring particular gratification and well-being. They rarely flip-flop around like Marty the butcher and his friend Ange in the Paddy Chayefsky movie *Marty*. Every time they have a night off, they rerun the same old dialogue: "What do you want to do tonight?" Marty asks. "I dunno, Marty, what do you want to do?" is always the answer. It is, in fact, a poetic and poignant commentary on people who don't know what they want and therefore have no idea how to ask for it.

How does values clarification work in schools? The following methods are ways frequently used:

1. *Time set aside during a course.* English, history, or social studies teachers may set aside one day a week to work on values clarification. Some report extending the time to two or even three days a week by popular request.

2. *Is an elective.* Some students work on values clarification techniques and issues every school day, five days a week, in a credit course called *values clarification or clarifying your values.*

3. *Backing up subject matter.* Traditionally, subjects are taught in terms of facts. Take, for example, the story of the Pilgrims. The facts include their departure for Holland from England, sailing on the *Mayflower,* landing at Plymouth Rock, and celebrating the first Thanksgiving.

Many teachers then delve into concepts. They may ask students to discuss cultural assimilation: Is America really a melting pot? Or they may discuss the relative advantages of the wilderness and of civilization, or what is necessary to survival. Or they may inquire into reasons for which men everywhere invent ceremonies like Thanksgiving.

Out of the Pilgrim story can also come teaching of values. The scary question is raised, "What does this have to do with me?" Teachers may ask students to think about the pride they feel in their own ethnic group, as well as what they are not proud of. Or when pondering the concept of wilderness, they may be asked to think about how self-sufficient they are, which electrical appliances they could do without for a month, what in themselves remains savage and untamed.

Or they may think about things in their own lives they'd like to celebrate and try to create a new ritual to do it justice.

4. *Career and drug education programs.* In addition to exploring careers or drugs as such, values clarification allows students to look at their lives and the choices they make.

5. *And other ways.* Actually, values clarification is being used in a broad spectrum of ways. For example, it can be used in very small doses (e.g., a teacher hands out a sheet once a month to help kids define their values), or in large doses (e.g., a full-scale credit course is set up).

It's interesting to see that some schools start with values clarification groups which evolve after a semester's course into human relations T-groups. The students at Staples High School in Westport, Connecticut, are particularly involved in both kinds of work.[8]

It may help to understand the use of values clarification in schools by placing it against a backdrop of the traditional way of teaching values, which is by moralizing. Moralizing teachers tell children what they should think and believe and what they should value.

Moralizing offers the illusion of looking like the right way to go, but its whole focus—trying to shape and manipulate people into accepting a given set of values—is doomed to failure. The problem is that if a student has not been taught to examine and weigh his own values, he is prey to the next fast-talking moralizer who comes down the road. The next one might, in fact, be hustling drugs.

It's confusing, because each of us obviously carries around certain beliefs and attitudes which *have* been preached to us. However, there is much evidence to indicate that when those morals, beliefs, and attitudes have been developed through a values clarification process, they have more significance for the people who hold them. True values are so much a part of us that we won't give them up even if bamboo splints are driven under our fingernails; but ideas we get as a result of preaching often vanish with the next wind and the next moralizer.

Many observers feel that young people learn the most from watching older people. In what is known as "modeling," teachers are encouraged always to say "Thank you," to hold doors for others, etc.—in short, to live by what they believe, in the hope that students will emulate them.

Young people who are surrounded by good models—good parents, good teachers, good ministers, good rabbis, good neighbors—tend to reflect their good behavior. Values clarifiers believe, however, that people who go through the process of deciding what they value will in the end reflect the ways one would hope, in any event, that all good teachers would behave.

Where is values clarification headed? The use of values clarification is constantly expanding in a number of areas, some of which are listed here:

1. *Among teachers.* Large numbers of teachers every year attend values clarification workshops. That should mean that there will be a marked increase in the number of teachers offering the technique and inventing new strategies tailored to the needs of their students.

2. *Curriculum packages.* More and more people are beginning to produce curriculum packages of which values clarification is the whole or a significant part. Merrill Harmin at Southern Illinois University created "Making Sense of Our Lives" for young people.[9] Using posters and other materials, he offers strategies to encourage young people to go well beyond the fine-thanks-how-are-you level of relationship.

Another such package was developed and sponsored by the Center for Learning, Inc., in Villa Maria, Pennsylvania,[10] and has found equal success in both public and Catholic schools. A favorable review in a Catholic journal praises the approach and suggests that it is a "vital first step in religious and psychological development."[11]

A third is Wayne Paulsen's "Deciding for Myself," a values clarification series for high school students.[12]

3. *Colleges and junior colleges.* Recently, increasing numbers of guidance and personnel people have been requesting values clarification workshops. Indications are that counseling centers will be offering students small groups in which to clarify values; more electives listed in course catalogues also seem to be in the offing.

Young people at junior colleges are frequently marginal students, in the sense that they don't meet the usual four-year college entrance requirements, and thus have a particular need to make sense of their lives. Although junior colleges haven't yet developed values clarification as one of the tools by which students can grow and develop, it works well as a vital component of the work in personal growth which many of them need. We will see more of it in junior colleges.

4. *Parents.* Values start at home. Family work with values is becoming one of the major directions in values clarification and should continue into the future. In fact, Sally Olds and Sidney

Simon are completing a book for Simon and Schuster on values clarification in the family. It is designed to help parents help their children choose from among the staggering array of choices they must make in their lives today.

5. *Sexuality education.* Many sexuality educators see great potential in making values clarification available to young people as they sort through the large numbers of options that are open to them. For example, each person's answer to the omnipresent question of whether to have premarital sex is ultimately based on values.

Students are frequently gripped by the ability of the values clarification process to fill an important need in their lives. Although values clarification is basically moral, it tries not to push any single set of answers. Instead, it encourages people to search out their own answers to life's baffling variety of choices.

6. *Religious education.* Another area in which values clarification is used to examine moral dilemmas is in religious education. Values clarification already has a solid place in Sunday and church schools, where thousands of teachers are using it. These teachers are face to face with the question of whether moralizing is a suitable way to deal with religious education. They are out on the risky frontier of letting go of some absolute answers.

How does values clarification fit into the human potential movement? People in values clarification work feel the need to extend it in two directions. One is the outer focus, toward social psychology, economics, social planning, and even toward the educational implications of Charles Darwin, Karl Marx, and other more contemporary social thinkers.

On the other hand, values clarification skills are a natural companion of other skills which help people to live their lives more fully. For example, it can go hand in hand with Carl Roger's work which emphasizes warmth and genuineness among people.

Values clarification can borrow something from Harvey Jackins's re-evaluation counseling model, in which people make commitments to help each other grow. Generally, people divide the time they have for each other into two equal segments during which each works as both client and counselor. This reciprocity generates power that penetrates deeply into people's lives; values clarification techniques can be used in exactly the same way to accomplish this.

More and more, people working in T-groups are also coming to see that values clarification exercises rapidly advance their aims of getting people close to others' thoughts and feelings.

It has also found its way into the training of Gestalt therapists. Gestalt teachers have sensed that its various strategies are useful in clarifying the way people respond to each other's problems.

Other counselors simply fit a values clarification exercise into a transactional analysis technique. One way that transactional analysis workers have used values clarification is to ask a client to respond to a values question as if the child inside of him or her is speaking; then the parent inside, and then the adult.

People generally respond warmly to values clarification work and speak of its power in their lives.[13] It is a nonthreatening way for people to start thinking productively about themselves. They feel in control of what they are doing. Further, they are frequently gratified by almost immediate success in seeing their lives with greater clarity.

It can start gently and can grow deep.

VALUES EDUCATION IN A CONFLUENT SOCIAL STUDIES CURRICULUM

Kenneth K. Kickbusch, *Project Director, Nicolet Confluent Project, Nicolet High School, Glendale, Wisconsin.*

Watching values education materials proliferate is like watching Topsy grow: there is no end in sight and the accumulated mass is becoming unmanageable. This does not mean that the quality of recent publications on values education is suspect or that they have nothing new to offer the classroom teacher. Exciting new models and new strategies appear in a number of recent publications.[1] However, while new models and strategies abound, the formidable task of curriculum integration remains.

If values education is to survive the current challenge posed by the back-to-basics movement, teachers must make the leap from classroom experience to learning theory, performance objectives, and integrated curriculum. Making that leap is a demanding and rigorous experience. Not making that leap leaves values education and the classroom teacher vulnerable. Since 1960 there have been numerous trends or tendencies in social studies education. Social studies teachers were beleaguered in the early sixties by the techniques of inquiry, discovery, conceptual frameworks, and social science disciplines; in the late sixties by the reforms known as alternative or humanistic education; and in the early seventies by a new movement which featured a combination of the new social studies, humanistic education, and the problems/issues approach. While these developments are a compliment to the creative dynamism of social studies educators, the rapidity of change has confused some classroom teachers. This confusion stems from the failure of the innovators in our profession to provide an integrative model which is easily understood by both the teacher and the community.

Confluent education offers one model for integrating values education within the social studies curriculum. Since 1973 the Nicolet Confluent Social Studies Project has sought to develop a working model for the integration of disparate cognitive and affective goals. The Project has worked to incorporate values education, cognitive knowledge, self-concept, personal and political efficacy, and interpersonal effectiveness in a sequential four-year high school curriculum. Its model neither permits the teacher to ignore the values issue nor allows the values issue to dominate the educational process. Central to confluent education is a balance that approximates reality, i.e., a recognition that values questions permeate every human decision but are not the only element in each decision.

Confluent educational philosophy is characterized by a deliberate effort to integrate goals which are sometimes viewed as incompatible. It is defined as the integration or flowing together of the cognitive and affective domains of learning. While it is subsumed under a general humanistic philosophy which encompasses affective education, confluent education is distinct from affective education. The distinction ensues from the degree to which both the cognitive and affective domains of learning are merged. The degree of their confluence can be portrayed as a smooth and flowing river of two elements, in each of which there are elements of the other.[2] The two are so intertwined that one does not take precedence over the other, for each one serves to enhance the other. Because of its affective and cognitive elements, the confluent framework is particularly useful in values education.

The basic premise of confluent theory is that the affective and cognitive domains of learning are inseparable and of equal importance. The confluent philosophy attends to students' emotional and intellectual experiences and growth. It helps them make the connections between the two and to integrate their thoughts and feelings in their lives. Combining the affective and the cognitive in one's teaching style is an attempt to make the process and the product more humane. By integrating the two domains, the teacher may help students reduce and overcome some of their basic psychological conflicts, particularly during adolescence. These conflicts have been variously named: identity crisis, value relativism, social isolation, apathy, and alienation. Because most formal schooling has not fostered a confluent outlook, many students have left school, since it is not vital in their lives, or have stayed on in boredom without knowing why (alienation).

Proponents of confluent education argue that accepting and working with emotions in the classroom not only produces healthier persons but also increases intellectual achievement. Involved and excited students will learn more and retain it longer than those who are not. Proponents of confluent education regard emotions as central to the motivation necessary for learning. Emotions are not to be denied, viewed as subjective or illegitimate, and left outside the classroom door. Negative motivation or emotions are not to be buried under a new values clarification technique because concerns, wants, interests, fears, anxieties, and joys contain the seeds of motivation. By recognizing the existence and validity of the learner's inner concerns, teachers will show that they believe the learner's personal experiences are real and have a dignity of their own. In such a learning environment, teachers need competencies beyond the cognitive level.

The role of values education within the confluent model can best be explained by first examining that model (see Figure 1). The model begins with students' "concerns" and "blockages." Concerns and blockages exist in every learning situation and represent what educators call motivation. "Jack is not motivated" is another way of saying that Jack, at the moment, has concerns of greater consequence to him than the curriculum. They can be the explicit concerns of adolescents, who are aware of them and can verbalize them. Questions such as: Do I have friends? Do my friends really like me? Am I really dumb? Why won't my father allow me to set my own standards? and What should I do about this drug thing? are questions which adolescents bring to school and into the classroom. Some of them are identity questions, some are value questions, and some are fears; but all of them are real and significant for the adolescent.

If not worked through, these concerns may become blockages and will inhibit learning. Teachers often call this condition a lack of motivation and many assume personal responsibility for it. The most common response of teachers is either to jazz up their teaching style or to use new motivational materials. Occasionally, their response will, by accident, meet the needs that Jack feels. In confluent education these concerns and blockages are legitimate avenues for exploration. To do this the staff must be trained to recognize how the student is responding at a given moment and to

Figure 1

CONFLUENT MODEL

Student Component
Cognitive/Affective

Concerns/Blockages

Personal Loadings

Content Loadings ⟶

G — Self-Concept
O — Values Clarification
A — Moral Reasoning
L — Efficacy
S — Interpersonal Effectiveness
— Cognitive Knowledge

Knowledge Component
Cognitive/Affective

Social Education
  Cognitive Structures
  Social Awareness
  Citizenship Participation

Social Science

History

Staff Component
Cognitive/Affective

Knowledge
Skills
Awareness

Cognitive Competency
Affective Awareness

Affective Competency
Cognitive Knowledge

Confluent Curriculum

Confluent Instructional Style

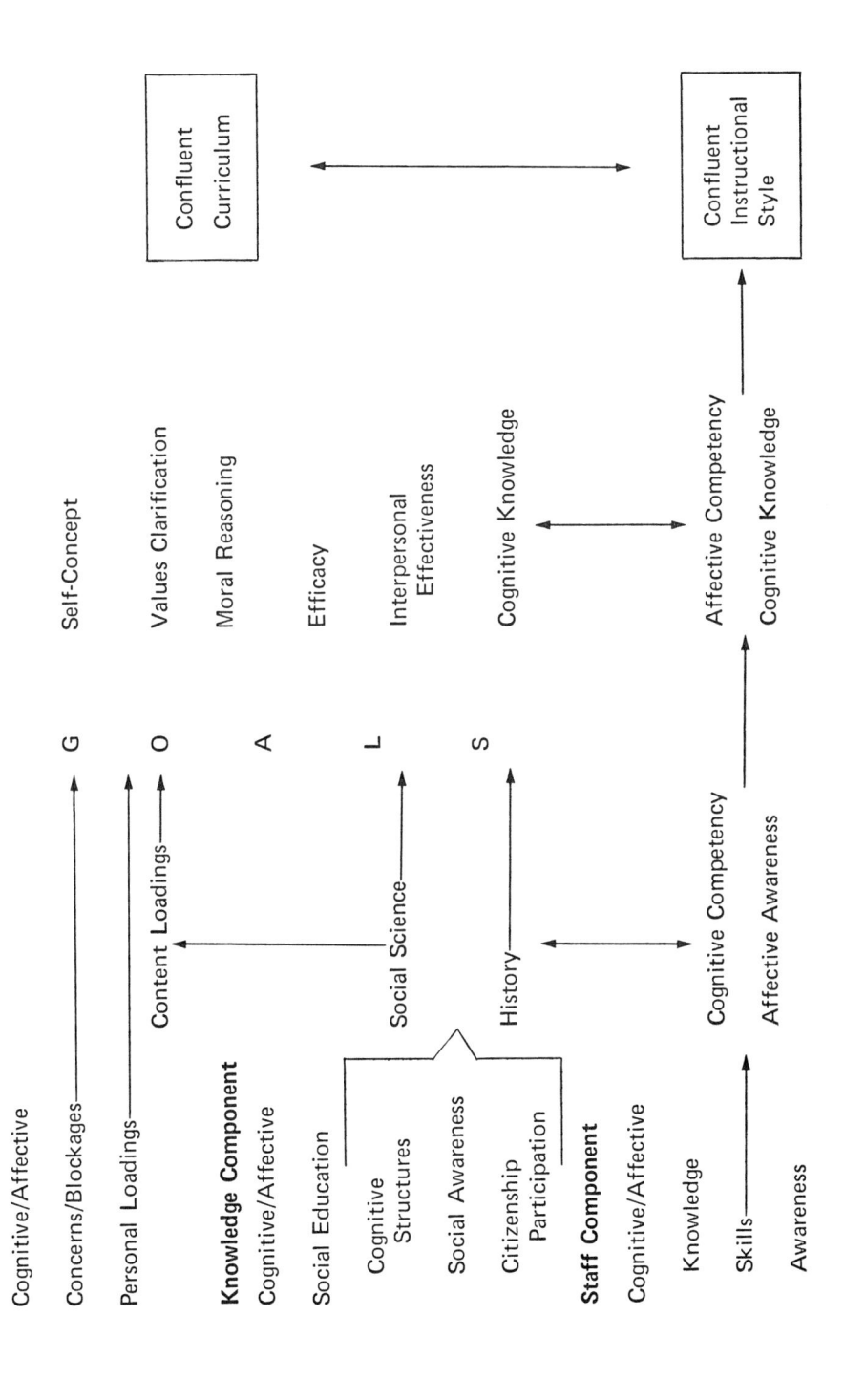

learn how to work with that response. If a value conflict is the apparent concern, an appropriate values clarification or moral reasoning activity can be used. The intention here is not therapeutic; it is developmental. Confluent theory recognizes that each of us has concerns, but having concerns does not mean we are sick. As teachers we are not trained to do therapy nor do we pretend that confluent education is a substitution for therapy where it is needed. Our goal, rather, is to provide the support needed for healthy personal growth and development. In this way we seek to help students recognize and work through those personal concerns which stand in the way of learning (blockages).

Personality ("personal loadings") and the emotional responses generated by the subject matter ("content loadings") exist in every learning situation.[3] Subject matter carries with it an inherent affective aspect that is dependent on the personality of the individual student. Issues such as drug use and abuse, abortion, capital punishment, and the feminist movement may provoke highly emotional responses from students. Value conflicts are in these responses; teachers should try to make them more evident to the student. Once value positions have been clarified, it is possible to present a dilemma that encourages students not only to state their positions but to verbalize their reasoning processes as well. The opportunity this presents for role-taking and public expression of value positions can provide the setting for strengthening self-concepts, developing empathic response styles, and stimulating the development of a more adequate reasoning process. Other content will probably be deemed dull or boring by students, suggesting that they see the connection between the subject matter and their personal lives as remote.

Personality ("personal loadings") influences how a student learns a particular subject matter. The student may have an initial desire to learn or a lack of desire ("orientation loading"), the student may be excited or bored while in the learning process ("engagement loading"), and the student will determine either to complete the learning task or not to complete it ("accomplishment loading").[4] Again, these are motivational factors which either can be obscured (or obliterated) by artificial techniques in an attempt to elicit the socially acceptable response from the student or can become the basis for learning and growth.

The knowledge component of the confluent model establishes a working definition of social education which includes a cognitive structure and the goals of social awareness and citizenship participation. An incredible variety of vehicles exist to present this content. Their selection and choice remain with the community and the classroom teacher. However, if the previously mentioned goals of social education are to be achieved, deliberate and explicit experiences must be created. That set of experiences is summarized within the goal segment of the model (Figure 1).

The interrelationships among the respective confluent goals are difficult to delineate, but several suggestions can be made. An inadequate self-concept may prevent students from verbalizing their value preferences; on the other hand, a supportive classroom environment fostering interpersonal relationships may encourage students with poor self-concepts to share value choices and further stimulate the moral reasoning process. Feelings of personal powerlessness (lack of "efficacy") may prevent a student from completing a research project ("cognitive knowledge") in a neighborhood library. And, finally, cognitive knowledge without social awareness or feelings of efficacy may not significantly alter voter turnout in the coming years. Once goals have been integrated, separating them, even for the purposes of an intellectual discussion, is difficult.

Confluent education also demands new knowledge and a new commitment from social studies teachers. Cognitive competency is not to be neglected in lieu of new and additional affective goals. Teaching confluently demands much more of the teacher than does a traditional methodology. Its complexity is not often recognized by the critics of affective education, who tend to believe that education should concern only those things that appear to be pleasurable. This represents an interesting commentary on what education should be, inasmuch as for others learning is legitimate education only if it is painful. Either view may be a product of one's own experience.

To merge the two domains of learning requires a redirection in thinking and exposure to new experiences. Nine parameters of confluent education have been identified.[5] If their elements are to be included implicitly or explicitly in any lesson or human interaction, then teachers must be cognitively aware of their significance. It is imperative that teachers seriously consider them within the context of their own lives, for if these elements are important to the life experiences of each student, teachers must examine their own lives within that framework as well. This means formal values clarification work and training, experiences in the use of and creation of moral dilemmas, participation in Gestalt and sensory awareness training, work with communication skills, an understanding of small group processes, and the capacity to carry their integration into curriculum writing and ultimately the classroom.

Until educators can grow, they will tend to be stuck with cookbook approaches. They will not be able to improvise and create learning experiences that are appropriate for their students. It's not possible for the teacher to relate the values, emotions, and interests of each student to the content of each course of study. Even if it were possible, the resulting dependency relationship of student to teacher would be unhealthy. Rather, the teacher's task should be to develop processess which will assist students in making these connections on their own.

The preceding discussion has placed values education into the specific context of confluent education. Integrating values education into confluent curriculum may occur at several levels. There may be an opportunity to consider values issues while working with student concerns and blockages. In fact, a values conflict will often emerge in the examination of a blockage. This becomes an opportunity for the individual student, as well as for the entire class, to examine and identify the conflicting value positions. It creates a sense of contact and connectedness between the blocked student and peers with the realization that such conflicts are not unique to the individual but are present (though not often verbally shared) in the lives of others as well.

Content loadings are frequently emotional responses based on strong value positions. An opportunity to clarify and state those positions would permit a more adequate cognitive examination of the issue. A new value dilemma can be raised following the consideration of additional factual information. With a focus on reasons rather than on decisions, students will be more open to share their value positions.

The opportunities for teaching values in confluent education lie in spontaneous responses to unpredictable circumstances. Teachers must be competent to work with these situations as they occur. Deliberate integration of values education with a cognitive structure is not difficult. Because a value-free social studies content cannot exist, curriculum writers must make choices and selections in structuring a confluent experience. For example, while interpersonal affectiveness is a legitimate continuous goal, it might best receive special emphasis during the first few weeks of the semester. There will be personal growth and the class will learn how to function as a social unit. Some affective goals are integrated more naturally with specific cognitive content. The appropriateness of the context will determine which goals are implemented at what point in the curriculum.

Each course in the Nicolet Confluent Project utilizes two values approaches: values clarification and cognitive moral development. In two-semester courses, the first semester tends to emphasize personal values clarification and the second semester uses moral dilemmas to provide role-taking opportunities for the student. In one-semester courses both activities occur as the time is appropriate.

The Project uses a valuing model that is based on the process outlined by Louis Raths.[6] Students are taught the seven subprocesses identified by Raths so that they can draw distinctions between personal values and value indicators. The seven value criteria may, to students at the outset, appear to be rather forthright, but the aura of simplicity is quickly dissipated when the implications of those criteria are examined. Choosing freely has little significance until the question of genuine choice is raised. If all options are pre-packaged by parents, schools, or peers, is it possible to choose freely? Or, must we be content with choosing from among censured alternatives? Do we choose freely or is it merely an illusion? What are the social limitations imposed on the universe of choices? Having considered the value criteria, students are prepared to engage in the clarification process as they confront value issues within the context of the curriculum. The intent is forthright: Students will be expected to clarify for themselves what they value. Consequences of value choices are examined within the present social framework.

The second phase of the values education goal in the Nicolet Confluent Project involves cognitive moral development. Values clarification is used as an entry to raise the students' level of cognitive moral reasoning.

Lawrence Kohlberg has established a positive relationship between Piaget's logical stages and the development of moral judgment or reasoning (Figure 2). In his research Kohlberg identified six universal stages in moral thought.* The six stages have been divided into three major levels of moral reasoning: preconventional. conventional, and postconventional.[7] As with Piaget's logical stages, moral stages follow an invariant universal sequence of development. Logical development is viewed as a necessary but not sufficient condition for movement from one moral stage to another. With the ability to operate at the formal operational thinking level, the adolescent gains the awareness that any given

---

*See "Definition of Moral Stages" on p. 20.

society's definition of right and wrong is only one among many. It opens the door to value relativism, which may be a crucial factor in some of the adolescent's own conflicts.

Why should the school concern itself with the level of moral reasoning? The claim for increasing the stage level of moral decision-making rests on the claim for the greater adequacy of one stage of reasoning over another. As a moral concept is defined at each succeeding stage, the definition becomes more adequate in that it becomes more differentiated (value of life differentiated from value of property), more integrated (value of life enters a hierarchy where it is higher than property), and more universal (any life is valuable regardless of status or value of property).[8] Each successive moral stage handles more moral problems, conflicts, or points of view in a more stable self-consistent way. It is important to note one other aspect of Kohlberg's theory. As a general rule, persons at the same stage of moral reasoning can come to different conclusions about appropriate action in the same situation. The stages do not generate a moral guidebook containing right answers for all situations. Justice, and the value and equality of all human beings, is the central principle in the Kohlberg model. Justice or equality is not a set of prescriptions but a principle for resolving competing claims. Morality is the notion of reciprocity between the individual and others in a single social environment.

The classroom approach to cognitive moral development is a product of cognitive-developmental learning theory. Learning is a change in one's pattern of thinking or organizing information. This sort of change occurs as a result of the interaction between the student and his or her environment. Learning is neither just maturation nor only the accumulation of information. So the classroom process, which is designed to move the student to a higher stage of moral reasoning, involves creating opportunities for interaction. Thought and growth are stimulated through genuine conflict or dilemmas growing out of the subject matter under consideration. Role-taking opportunities for the student must be structured so as to provide stimuli that will produce conflict—but not conflict to the degree that would prevent the student's identification with the problem. In most classrooms a range of two or three levels of moral reasoning will exist among students. If the cross-stimulation and provocation that result as reasons for decisions are shared, they will produce growth in the student's level of moral reasoning. Changing someone's mind on a particular issue is not the goal. Rather the dilemmas offer the students the opportunity to engage in the stimulating exchange and re-evaluation of reasons for their

Figure II.

Relations between Piaget logical stages and Kohlberg moral stages.
(all relations are that attainment of the logical stages is necessary, but not sufficient, for attainment of the moral stage)

Logical Stage	Moral Stage	
Symbolic, intuitive thought	Stage 0: The good is what I want and like.	
Concrete operations, Substage 1 Categorical classification	Stage 1: Punishment-obedience orientation.	Pre-conventional
Concrete operations, Substage 2 Reversible concrete thought	Stage 2: Instrumental hedonism and concrete reciprocity.	
Formal operations, Substage 1 Relations involving the inverse of the reciprocal	Stage 3: Orientation to inter-personal relations of mutuality.	
Formal operations, Substage 2	Stage 4: Maintenance of social order, fixed rules, and authority.	Conventional
Formal operations, Substage 3	Stage 5A: Social Contract, utilitarian law-making perspective.	
	Stage 5B: Higher law and conscience orientation.	Post-conventional
	Stage 6: Universal ethical principle orientation.	

Source: Lawrence Kohlberg and Carol Gilligan, "The Adolescent as Philosopher," *Daedalus* (Fall, 1971); p. 1072.

actions.[9] Values education within this confluent model will aid students in clarifying their own values and stimulate them to move beyond moral relativism.

The values education process and the confluent model which provides the context for this process are based on an amalgam of two learning theories: cognitive developmental learning theory and Gestalt learning theory. Cognitive developmental learning theory makes the following four assumptions: (1) that learning involves a change in mental structure or in the way students think rather than repetition or the accumulation of information, (2) that learning is the result of interaction between students and their environment, (3) that cognitive development leads to a greater balance or more reciprocity between students and their environment, and (4) that affective and cognitive development are parallel.[10] Curriculum developed within the confluent model reflects these propositions as learning experiences for students are created. Although cognitive developmental learning theory recognizes the parallel development of cognitive and affective learning, little real consideration is given to the affective component.

Gestalt learning theory focuses on the affective domain and can help clarify questions about the confluent experience. Gestalt psychology views the personality as a flow of life energy which, when blocked, can be freed through the use of awareness and present experiencing techniques.[11] Its intent is to enable the student to live a rich emotional life without trying to stifle or avoid those emotions. By accepting, exaggerating, and exploring here-and-now behavior, a student can work through emotional blocks or conflicts which are preventing growth and learning.

Confluent education is a process of "leading out" an individual's abilities, talents, and uniqueness. Its aim is the balanced development of the student toward intellectual and emotional maturity. Significant questions for the student (e.g., Who am I? What are my values? What is important?) have a central place in the confluent experience. Values education presents educators, and confluent educators in particular, with a great challenge. The confluent process is desperately needed, yet it is easily misunderstood and vulnerable to critics if improperly implemented and remains subject to a great deal of debate by educators themselves. Confluent education provides a theoretical framework, an integrative model, and a classroom instructional process which will provide values education the legitimacy it needs in order to survive in the social studies.

VALUES EDUCATION PROCESSES

William B. Hemmer, *Associate Professor of Curriculum and Instruction, State University of New York, Brockport.*

What is values education? Teachers have long heard insistent voices in the community asking or demanding that the schools teach values.

Usually, when a group demands that values be taught, they mean inculcated. For most teachers in the past, teaching values has meant inculcation, moralizing, persuading, inspiring, or outright indoctrination. All teachers use inculcation to some extent. The process involves limiting the students' choices to those that are acceptable. For example, students are taught to respect the right of others to express their ideas freely in class. Teachers may try to model the desired behavior and set a good example for their students. Sometimes teachers use models from the present or the past, such as President Ford, George Washington, or Nathan Hale. Through rules and regulations, and every school and classroom has many of these, the right to make free choices is limited. Behavior that deviates too far from the norm is punished while exemplary behavior is praised.

Other characteristics of the inculcation approach include presenting certain values as cultural dogma, unquestioned wisdom, or principle because everyone always does it that way. Pledging allegiance to the flag and respecting teachers, principals, and parents are often presented in this manner.

Sometimes teachers attempt to develop the conscience of the child by arousing feelings of guilt, if the child's conscience doesn't indicate the proper decision or action. We may tell our students, "You should know better than to do that!" or "Aren't you sorry you did that?" At other times, educators use the old propagandist trick of card-stacking. This involves telling all the good things about the "good guys" while telling all the bad things about the "bad guys." For example, during the mid-1960's, the FBI was often portrayed as the good guys fighting for peace and justice while the "left wing radicals" protesting the war in Viet Nam were portrayed as subversives and communists who abused drugs, who were cowardly, and who were undermining the moral fabric of the country.

Teachers, and parents, who use inculcation note that the older the child gets, the less successful the inculcation process is. With secondary students it is sometimes as productive as banging one's head against the proverbial stone wall.

Another problem has been whose values should be taught— the teacher's, the school's, the church's, the Democrats', the Republicans', the atheist's? Since the community is nearly always made up of divergent and diverse groups, there is usually no agreement on what values should be taught.

The new wave of interest in values education, however, does not involve the inculcation process, holding that values can't really be taught, and centers its interest around the process of getting students to identify and think about their own values, whatever they are. Thus, the problem of whose values are to be taught is sidestepped, since no particular values are promoted. Instead, educators now concentrate on the logical and analytical processes necessary for the students to make moral decisions based on their own values, whether derived from family, church, peers, or TV. Let us examine the purpose and characteristics of some of the leading values education processes.

Perhaps the first of a new breed of values educators who offered techniques other than those based on inculcation were Louis E. Raths, Merrill Harmin, and Sidney B. Simon, whose book, *Values and Teaching,* appeared in 1966.[1] The purpose of values clarification is to help students use rational thinking and become aware of their personal and social values. These educators devised numerous learning experiences which involve students in activities designed to help students discover their own values. During these experiences they resolve value conflicts by establishing a position on a simulated issue. Students are encouraged to act according to their own values and make choices in harmony with their personal system of values.

Lessons in values clarification make use of self-analysis worksheets which consist of drawings, questions, and activities which stimulate thinking about one's self. Also used are short stories or value dilemmas as well as creative tasks which stimulate reflection and awareness. The focus of the dilemmas developed for values clarification often are a simulated, real-life situation in which the student participates. The key question centers around, What should you do?

Values analysis has long been advocated by proponents of social studies. A process explicitly developed for values analysis has been demonstrated by Jack R. Fraenkel.[2] Values analysis helps students use logical thinking and scientific investigation procedures to deal with values; valuing is, thus, conceived of as a rational process.[3] It may include the use of a dilemma or a current happening described in a newspaper story, such as the Karen Quinlan case. Historical dilemmas can also arise from social studies, such as President Truman's decision in 1945 to drop the first atomic bomb. The values analysis approach can involve students in thinking about the content of social studies, science, health, or other subjects.

In analyzing the values involved in a difficult decision, the teacher leads students through a process involving clarifying the values question so that all students will understand the nature of the decision to be made. Students then gather evidence and identify all important details or facts leading up to the need for decision. Students are encouraged to look for possible alternatives: different actions or decisions that can be made by the principal character. Next the possible or probable consequences of adopting each alternative are projected. Fraenkel insists on the teacher taking a positive leadership role in carrying out these beginning steps thoroughly and completely so that students can learn the need for thorough identification and analysis of information before making rational decisions. However, the teacher's role throughout is one of facilitator, using an inquiry-type approach for eliciting information and ideas from students rather than supplying information and ideas. After listing the consequences, the teacher may break students into discussion groups for ascertaining the most desirable alternative. A rationale for choosing a particular alternative is selected by each of the groups. Consensus in the groups or class is neither necessary nor even desirable. A report by each group to the class may reveal a divergency of alternatives and differences in rationales among groups and also among the members of the groups. Such divergency should be accepted, even welcomed, by the teacher and no attempt at consensus should be made.

The objective of values awareness is to help students become aware of and identify their own values and those of others. A systematic method of doing this has been developed by Gus T. Dalis and Ben B. Strasser in the Dalstra Values Awareness Teaching Strategies.[4] This system involves the teacher in playing the role of facilitator, and in encouraging students to discuss values in a threat-free environment where they will not be ridiculed for either their comments or their values. To help teachers who may not be familiar with such a rule, Dalis and Strasser have identified categories of acceptable teacher and student comments. With some practice and a little help, teachers can learn to use the system and act as facilitators in the Dalstra image.

Basically Values Awareness Teaching Strategies involve the use of value-laden situations presented through written dilemmas, films, filmstrips, or role-playing. Group discussions and simulations can also be used. The students are asked to relate and empathize with the characters, making inferences about the values, thoughts, beliefs, feelings, and behavior of the characters, other people, and themselves.

Perhaps the newest form of values education to sweep the country is moral reasoning inspired by the research of Lawrence Kohlberg. Its purpose is to help students attain more complex patterns of moral reasoning. Kohlberg identifies six stages of moral reasoning: the individual in early primary school begins on the lowest level and progresses toward the higher stages. However, not all adults progress to the higher stages; some remain reasoning at various intermediate levels. The teacher may help students attain the higher stages of moral reasoning at the appropriate stage of development by exposing them to higher stages of reasoning through group discussions.[5] Several good interpretations of Kohlberg's ideas for the classroom are available.[6]

The procedure for moral reasoning involves presentation of value-laden situations or dilemmas. Leading students through a process of becoming familiar with the situation similar to the one used in value analysis, the teacher urges students to state a position regarding what the character in the dilemma should do. Students then develop a rationale for their positions. Next, the teacher divides the class into groups to discuss the various alternatives and the rationales for each. The teacher may also ask questions to test students' reasoning. Students are invited to reconsider their positions again individually after hearing others in group discussions. The hope is that students, being exposed to the higher-level reasoning of other students, will accept and adopt higher-level reasoning for their own use. In time students will begin to use by themselves higher-level reasoning when confronted with new but similar situations.

Teachers who wish to interest their students in a process of community involvement may use any of the new values education processes cited above in order to examine local issues. Then, after sufficient exploration of issues in the classroom, teachers may provide opportunities for students to engage in personal social action in support of their own values. If the teacher desires the arena of action to be limited, projects in the school may be used as the commitment component. If not, the whole community may be used as the laboratory for action. Thus students, choosing from various alternative community action projects, have an opportunity to clarify and restructure their own value systems in the light of conditions that exist in the larger world outside the classroom.

Upon analysis one can easily determine that there are a number of similarities among the new values education processes. All of them involve problem-solving and the problem can be contrived or real, drawn from the present or the past. All of them involve consideration of a difficult decision, usually made by an individual and include identification of the possible courses of action. Also involved is the development of a rationale for the decision made. Thus they all involve students' thinking about the problem.

All of the processes involve the student in self-evaluation (What should I do? What would I do?). They all must be conducted in an arena that is not risky to the student. There must be an accepting atmosphere where a student is not afraid of rejection or ridicule. In all processes the students listen to each other and not just the teacher.

This brings us to perhaps the most important similarity of them all. In all these processes, the teacher plays the role of facilitator, one who helps but does not dominate. The teacher's role is to help the students think, express themselves, and react unoffensively to one another. To teachers who play this facilitating role comes a rewarding and refreshing experience as their students' interest reawakens and their classrooms come alive with eager students.

SCHOOL AND SOCIETY: BARRIERS TO VALUES EDUCATION

Michael Silver, *formerly a classroom teacher and now a graduate assistant and instructor, Washington University, St. Louis, Missouri.*

Now that values education has become so prominent in the schools, there are good grounds to ask the question, "What are some of the existing barriers—social, political, cultural, and institutional—to the goals and outcomes of values education?" While there has been much discussion of the role of the teacher, the content and strategies, and the classroom atmosphere in which moral and values education should occur, values educators have almost completely ignored both the external (societal) values placed upon the school and the internal culture of the school. That the tensions between the goals and outcomes of values education and the existing sociocultural system of schooling have not been made explicit and understood is significant in light of the current emphasis placed upon values education in schools.

Schools are one part of a larger set of organizations, institutions, and processes that facilitate the development of children within the society. A careful analysis of the school as a source for values instruction suggests that attention needs to be directed not only toward the dimensions of the developing student, but also toward the processes occurring within the school as an organization, and the nature of the society of which the school and the student are a part. These three elements—student, school, and society—when considered both separately and interdependently, provide a tangled web of values, theoretical concepts, and empirical data.

As in all societies, formal education in America is the process of transposing an economic, political, and social ideology into an individual's personalized matrix of values. Galtung has studied this phenomenon and what significance it holds for the future. He has written:

> . . . schools are partly a reproduction, partly a reinforcement, of the social and economic structure of society at large. Of course, by being a reproduction, by mirroring macrosociety in the microcosm of the school, even of the classroom, reinforcement is already effected because the process of schooling is a way of getting acquainted with general social patterns, even to the point of internalizing them. But in addition, schools also serve the social order in a more direct manner. Thus two hypotheses link the fate of schools to the fate of society: the indirect one of reproduction and the direct one of reinforcement.[1]

Schools reflect issues in the economic or political arenas by implementing societal images of class distinctions, racism, sexism, and selfish aggrandizement. Hein[2] has demonstrated that school systems are essentially authoritarian organizations, with centralized power at the top and little of it lower down. Schools are also strikingly sexist institutions: there are almost no women superintendents of school districts in the entire country, although the population of teachers is predominantly female, especially at the elementary level. Bryant, Chesler, and Crowfoot[3] have recently written that curricular bias, racial imbalance between staff and student populations, tracking, or other forms of discrimination are similar to the domestic race and class structure and to the world situation that separates people with regard to life choices and access to knowledge. Teacher or administrator protection and abuse of unilateral authority adds additional stress to their roles as agents of law and order.

If we consider the roadblocks in the path of values education, surely none is so effectively obstructing as the manner in which our culture tends to regard competition. Sportsmanship within athletics is thought to be a value important for students to practice. However, sportsmanship is predicated on the belief that competition is good. The team should be supported by the students and the faculty. Team members must do what is best for all, and the leader makes key decisions which are not subject to question.

This type of "groupness" often works to the detriment of the individual. Jules Henry makes the following observation:

> In a society where competition for the basic cultural goods is a pivot of action, people cannot be taught to love one another, for those who do cannot compete with one another, except in play. It thus becomes necessary for the school, without appearing to do so, to teach children how to hate, without appearing to do so, for our culture cannot tolerate the idea that babes should hate each other. How does the school accomplish this ambiguity? Obviously through competition itself, for what has greater potential for creating hostility than competition?[4]

Admittedly, these characterizations are abstract and general, but they may be useful in picking out general thrusts within our society and understanding how educators do enforce the values that are widely held within society. Certainly it illustrates the tension between societal values and the aims of values education. The schools transmit the values and knowledge of the culture and its tradition and preserve the existing social order. This involves the socialization of children to conform, accept, obey, respect, and maintain the system. It means indoctrinating children to believe in the values, premises, and beliefs of the larger society and the immediate community.

Yet, as teachers often unthinkingly enforce dominant societal values through practices in the classroom, they are acting on the mandate to help parents and society in the inculcation of conventional moral norms. Beck has written about this conflicting moral outcome of schools:

> The final outcome of this whole process, which is subsequently supported by the very structure of the school, is a predominance of teachers who remain for the most part in the conventional stages (Stages 3 and 4) of morality. The emphasis on "law and order" in the school is important, but it inhibits some aspects of the educational process.[5]

But these same teachers, on reflection, will probably choose to continue these practices, not out of dogmatism, but as the necessary condition for maintaining the educational enterprise.

At the beginning of this century Dewey wrote two short monographs entitled *Moral Principles in Education*[6] and *The School and Society*.[7] His central thesis was quite simple—the social structure of the school and its latent processes rather than the formal curriculum are the major determiners of the socialization of young people. School lessons in morality and citizenship are trivial and inconsequential. Dewey characterized traditional schools as those with centralized authority, a curriculum fostering "absorption and mere learning," a focus on means rather than intrinsic ends, and routine recitational methods which demanded of each student individual competition in conforming to a single external standard. There was no opportunity for each student to work on something specifically her/his own through which she or he could contribute to the learning of others while he or she, in turn, participated in their activities. He argued that these schools did not produce "ultimate moral motives and forces" which are "social intelligence—the power of observing and comprehending social situations—and social power—trained capacities of control— at work in the service of social interest and aims."[8] Yet, after two-thirds of a century of social science inquiry in the schools, can we say that such a perspective is representative of schools in the 1970's?

Although we have more contemporary models and concepts which provide finer delineations of the structure of the school and which, perhaps, suggest a more complex set of interrelationships between school, student, and society, Dewey's perception of the influence of the school upon young people has been corroborated many times over. The actual structure and organization of the school are perhaps the greatest value-teaching elements in the school. One cannot discern or discuss the idea of moral education without some understanding of the purpose, content, and structure of the institution within which it is to be taught, since all institutions contain, or are informed by, many implicit assumptions and premises which can enhance or detract from a program in values education. In other words, no matter how well-meaning a teacher may be, many values are transmitted covertly, or indirectly, as a result of the institutional norms within which one works.

From a sociological perspective, one body of literature has addressed the manner in which the overall organization or structure of the school influences the moral development and values of students. Stated somewhat more broadly, the literature studies the institutional culture and the impress it leaves on the lives of institutional clients. Dreeben's analysis[9] of what is learned in school proposes that school experience is structured so that students acquire values and attitudes that facilitate their integration into the competitive, occupational, and political worlds of adults. Jackson's observational studies[10] of routine in elementary school classrooms document the major elements of school life: the crowds, the praise, and the power. Goffman's analysis[11] of mental hospitals and other total institutions stresses their potency in controlling behavior and changing values. Spady[12] has written that the schools' emphasis on formal achievement, interpersonal competition, and certification strongly suggests how it may act to select students for the occupational, economic, and prestige structures of the society.

Grannis[13] has pointed out that school in general could be classified into a rough typology: namely, family schools, factory schools, and corporation schools. The latter two models are by far the predominant mode for school in this country. The factory-school model is usually found in working-class (blue collar) neighborhoods. The organization of the school generally includes: students working on identical material at a uniform pace, a standard grading procedure, carefully prescribed assignments, and rote teaching. As Grannis puts it so well:

> Thus, the students in the factory school learn to think in terms of a crude standardization of products, effort and reward and . . . to expect an arbitrariness of the standards and . . . the necessity of repetition.[14]

By emphasizing the routine, the average, in an essentially paternalistic atmosphere, the messages that are transmitted to students in a factory school are clear and unambiguous. What they are really learning is the ability to take their place on a production line, to follow orders and to standardize output. These are the attributes that will be rewarded later.

In the corporation model the atmosphere is quite different. The buildings themselves are usually more up-to-date, with one-story sprawling construction and groomed shrubbery. Inside differences are noticeable too: modular scheduling, team teaching, multimedia instruction, and extensive evaluation procedures. In short, the atmosphere connotes specialization, efficiency, and elaborate equipment. "The whole attitude of the school is oriented toward planning and rationalization and toward the employment of specialized skills and technology."[15] The school has a highly differentiated adult bureaucracy and collective planning. The result, Grannis explains, is an atmosphere of depersonalization and a concomitant emphasis on individual achievement and competition. In this sense, the corporate school is a mirror image of the corporate life, suggesting that management training and/or junior executive development programs may indeed start quite early.

If the framework for values education is to have any meaning, we must see the school as an institution in this broad perspective. As schools present such organizational values as order, routine, output, authority, and efficiency within the lives of young people, they compete with human values. They lay too little emphasis on individualization, self-development, personal relationships, due process, justice, and equality. Unfortunately, in educational systems run on broadly authoritarian lines, the necessary relationship of mutual trust, respect, and cooperation among students and teachers is extremely difficult to cultivate. One may easily be forced into indoctrination by the authority structure within which one learns.

I have been focusing attention on what is called the "hidden curriculum" and its manifestations in schools. The hidden curriculum includes a wide range of learnings—attitudinal, emotional, moral, and social—of what is really learned from the ways in which the school environment has been organized. The hidden curriculum is in contrast to the overt, formal curriculum which consists of what goes on in formal class instruction. Beck has perceptively summarized the tensions and conflicts between the hidden curriculum and values education, when he states:

> Our experience in two high schools made us aware of the "hidden curriculum" discussed by critics of the school. We became much more sensitive to how the structure of the school can implicitly encourage a certain kind of morality—to be more specific, an authoritarian, conventional one. Many of the efforts of individual teachers to help students toward a postconventional (Stage 5 or 6) level of moral development are frustrated by a school atmosphere and organization which constantly emphasize lower-stage values and principles. Or to put the point more positively, a school atmosphere and organization which exhibit post-conventional features can greatly facilitate the development of students toward higher moral stages.[16]

What, then, does the school environment communicate to students in the everyday occurrences of school life? Obedience to the law, loyalty, respect for authority, and observance of school regulations are some of the values learned in this seemingly so but not really haphazard process. Beck[17] highlights the basic problem of stimulating moral development within a school atmosphere oriented toward authoritarian values and obsession with control and discipline. Students cannot be expected to progress at maximum speed toward higher levels of moral thought or values clarification when most of their daily experiences are at the preconventional or the lower conventional moral levels.

In short, the school environment is itself a prime focus for the continual exercise of moral choice. The everyday occurrences of a school life, as of life in general, require evaluation and decision. A teacher is often faced with the dilemma of choosing among the conflicting rights of individuals or between the rights of the individual and those of the institution and community. Mary and Theodore Sizer have characterized the hidden curriculum, thusly:

> Morality *is* put to the test every day in schools, and we teachers are often found wanting in it. While we doubt the value in giving grades, they're there anyway, often to the terror of the young. We put up with practices which we know are immoral because we don't want to get in trouble. All too often we don't really think through what is best for the young until pressured, and then we yield to that pressure. How can we expect them to understand this?[18]

The direction of this article has been toward developing an awareness of the political, social, cultural, and economic forces which affect the process of values education. Stewart[19] has recognized that in values education the planned and unplanned curriculum work against each other, with the planned curriculum largely negated by the more powerful and organic message of the hidden curriculum. Educators should be aware that values education leaves alone the overall structure and administration of the school. It does not touch the institutional processes and the hard realities of the school within which moral values are managed. The classroom situation typically suggests in powerful but unacknowledged ways the respectability of what Kohlberg calls the "bag of virtues"—honesty, willingness to defer pleasure, integrity, respect for elders, and so on, while at the same time, the teacher as a values educator may be exposing students to values clarification or higher patterns of moral reasoning. Thus, two curriculums can be expected to collide within the classroom and even to receive a certain legitimacy in their collision.

I have not wrestled directly with the major question of how one can alter, change, or improve schools to facilitate values education and moral development. It is clear that if change in values education is desired, the schools themselves will have to undergo radical transformations. Kohlberg has argued that "if you want to develop morality or a sense of justice in kids, you have to create a just school, a just environment."[20] Kohlberg describes the "Just Community School" as an attempt to engage students in democratic decision-making and stimulation in both moral reasoning and moral action within a just institution.[21]

Jencks writes that "until we change the political and moral premises on which most Americans now operate, poverty and inequality of opportunity will persist at pretty much their present level."[22] To this end, Scriven advocates that to implement moral education is to challenge the pluralism of societal values and "to face real-life problems—and that means controversy."[23] Efforts to change American values will require a major reform of all phases of life and commitment to a long social and political struggle as well as the cause of school reform.

This analysis does not imply that if one changed the schools everything would be fine with moral development. The success of values education depends upon the ability of educators to connect the teaching of values to the social reality of the school. Educators have neglected to recognize educational organizations as social systems. Educators have not examined school in terms of its formal and informal structures and the patterns of decision-making which arise within them. The major task of education has been to raise the kinds of questions which promote schools as places of humanistic instruction and vehicles for continuous social evolution. Clearly, it is a fruitful question to ask how and with what consequences the substantive content of social life in schools interacts with the formal content of values education.

CONFRONTATION, INSIGHT, AND COMMITMENT: MORAL EDUCATION AND THE TEACHER

David Purpel, *Coordinator of Field Experiences in Teacher Education, University of North Carolina, Greensboro*

Kevin Ryan, *Associate Professor of Education, the Graduate School of Education, University of Chicago.*

Moral education is an area where there is little consensus and, in fact, where there is a good deal of controversy. As educators we can react in a variety of ways. For example, we can ignore all responsibility, hoping the question will soon pass from public consciousness. Or we can wait for the theoreticians, researchers, and curriculum developers to resolve the issues and paradoxes in moral education. Or we might commit ourselves to implementing one of the several curricular approaches now available. None of these alternatives seems either fully adequate or fully responsible.

We certainly should not (and in a very real sense cannot) ignore this responsibility; to wait for the final resolution of critical problems is tantamount to indefinite inaction. However, we are convinced that the current available curricular models of moral education (as attractive, sophisticated, and imaginative as some are) raise serious and unresolved questions. We must, as usual, work within a context of insufficient data, inadequate research, and ambiguous social policy. But work we should, resisting the paralysis that can result from polemics and pedantry and filling the gaps in our knowledge and theory with common sense. This approach involves confrontation, insight, and commitment.

We need, first, to confront the inescapable reality that we are moral educators, that schooling is a moral enterprise, and that we are active participants in that enterprise. We must, also, confront the fact that we do not have many clear, valid models of moral education available to us. Lack of clear directions makes most of us tense and uncomfortable. But we must realize, too, that in taking on a most difficult problem we cannot be expected to have all the answers. We must reaffirm that our strength as teachers is not so much built on what we know but on our ability to pose the the most probing questions. We must honestly acknowledge the limitations of our knowledge without being paralyzed by them.

Second, we need to have special insights into and understandings of the complex dimensions of moral education. We need to be very well informed of the conflicting schools, knowledgeable about the inherent political and social considerations, aware of appropriate philosophical and psychological frameworks, and sensitive to the problems of classroom applications. We need to confront the questions of which issues to present to students. Original sin? The moral dimensions of the Vietnam war? The petty thievery in Miss Grundy's third-grade classroom? We also need to reflect on how students should deal with moral issues. With cold, hard logic? Empirically? Using intuition? With feelings? Most important, we have to face the issue of developing a set or sets of moral guidelines. Should they be situational? Developmental? Marxist? Judeo-Christian? Pragmatic? Relativist? Fortunately, we do not have to deal with such issues in isolation, since there is a vast, brilliant, and continuing tradition of serious scholarship in America on both basic and applied aspects of moral education. We need to become aware of this tradition and to participate in further rigorous inquiry.

Such inquiry should help us see in stark outline the quality and direction of the moral education that exists in our own schools. It should also aid us in bringing to the surface what we actually believe. While there is value in encountering the experts, what we ourselves believe is of particular importance. Once in touch with our own informed views, we can not only test these views with associates and through further readings, but we can begin to test them in the world of educational practice.

Third, we must deal with our commitment to both our own personal moral behavior and our role as moral educators. There seems to be little question that modeling is a powerful technique for moral education and that young people often take their cues from what adults do more than from what they say. We must therefore be aware of our own moral commitments by demonstrating to our colleagues and students what it means to act upon a meaningful, articulated, and informed moral viewpoint. As professionals we can combine our own moral development with our task of involving students in a mutual quest for moral insight. We need to pursue this quest rigorously, vigorously, and honestly, with the understanding that we will be doing so with insufficient knowledge. Our individual quests will be different, but they should all be aimed at helping students develop a commitment to the quest for moral understanding and an informed capacity for independent moral judgment. We must join them in the quest, since they are more than neophyte intellectuals or future adults and workers; they are now and will continue to be moral actors.

Education is simply not value-free. One cannot involve children in schooling from the time they are 6 until they are 17 or 21 and not affect the way they think about moral issues and the way they behave.

In Arthur Miller's *Death of a Salesman*, the worn-out Willy Loman describes the life of a traveling salesman to his two sons. They ask him, "Were you ever lonely, being on the road so much?" Willy answers poignantly, "Loneliness comes with the territory." Educators and the general public must realize that in our schools moral education is an unavoidable responsibility. It comes with the territory.

Part Two: Techniques

Editor's Note

The first ten articles in Part Two describe practical methods for developing values; the next eleven articles describe ways to apply these techniques to different subject areas. The final article by Senesh characterizes changes in our national values. This 200-page treasury should be sufficient for any teacher's particular needs.

Advances in values education, however, are not likely to come simply from proliferating new techniques, applying them to more subject areas, training more teachers, creating more Just Community schools. More is not necessarily an advance. Being clear about 100 disconnected values, instead of 50, is not sufficient. Each of us needs a dream of where all these values lead, an image of the good and honorable person each wants to become, a utopian vision of what it means to live in a Just Community. These larger ideals go beyond immediate choices in a particular situation. They prioritize our choices, clarify how values are related, provide additional incentives for action, and guide movement toward our utopia, even if it is ultimately unattainable. The heuristic value of these scenarios is conveyed by the word *utopia*, a pun by Thomas More on the Greek words "eutopos" (good place) and "outopos" (no place).

Teachers can help students create a vision of how they want to live, inductively, piece by piece, like a giant puzzle, from each value they clarify. This requires starting with issues that concern students and finishing with the implications of their choices for the future. It is absurd, of course, to expect first graders to articulate the details of a perfect society. It is appropriate, however, for teachers to assist young people, whatever their age, to see one step farther into the future.

Teachers can sabotage this grand purpose of values education by working on dead issues. Living values are won from the complicated, urgent problems students face. But if teachers choose topics solely according to the degree of existential heat, values education can become trivial. For example—Is it better to go out with Andy or Bobby? Which is the best rock group? Precious learning time should be devoted to questions significant to students now and over time.

To enlarge student perspectives, teachers need to be aware of those questions of continuing importance for the remainder of the millenium— such problems as allocating increasingly scarce resources; protecting our planet from pollution; protecting people from exploitation and fallout; emphasizing individual achievement or cooperative accomplishments; investing in military power or national strength through education, scientific progress, and economic development; establishing equity for all ethnic and minority groups. With this long-term view teachers can help students examine the implications of their choices regarding family life (conduct in dating relationships, time and conditions for beginning adult sexuality, whether to get married, pro-life or pro-choice response to the possibility of abortion), work and career (what career is best for the student; the importance of money, achievement, power, and family), drugs and alcohol (whether to use drugs from caffeine to cocaine, how to deal with an alcoholic, how best to manage consciousness). Whatever students choose to do about any of these significant issues, they create a bit of their futures.

What happens to us in the next twenty years will be caused, in part, by massive forces beyond our individual control. Nonetheless, at minimum, our choices have an impact on our own lives and on the lives of our families and friends. If no other single purpose were accomplished through values education, then, it would be enough to strengthen students' ability to create their lives and, thus, their futures.

A.S.A

ANALYZING VALUE CONFLICT

Jack R. Fraenkel, *Professor of Interdisciplinary Studies in Education, San Francisco State University.*

As students begin to identify and think about values, they will soon realize that values often conflict. For example, consider the hypothetical (but representative) case of Rob Smith. For as long as he could remember, Rob had heard his parents emphasize the values of honesty and loyalty. A "good" person was one who always told the truth and stood by a friend. One of Rob's friends, however, copied from Rob's paper during a history examination without Rob realizing it at the time. The next day the teacher asked both Rob and his friend to explain the fact that their two papers were identical, even to their having the same crossed-out words. Rob knows his friend copied from his paper and wants to be loyal to him, yet he also wants to tell the truth since he knows his teacher and parents will be disappointed in him if he doesn't. What should he do?

Value conflicts may be not only intrapersonal—within one person, as the above example suggests, but also interpersonal—between individuals. Arguments regarding capital punishment for murder are a case in point. Those who advocate the death penalty argue in terms of the value of retribution—repayment in kind, "an eye for an eye"—as a deterrent to murder. Those who advocate its abolition argue in terms of the value of human life—taking an additional life will not replace the life that was taken away.

Value conflict is a fact of life. It is realistic, therefore, for teachers to recognize (and to help students recognize) this fact and to realize that such conflict may often lead to inconsistencies in behavior. How can students be helped to realize that values often conflict? Here are some hypotheses for a values-education-inclined teacher to consider: Having students identify, discuss, and evaluate alternative courses of action, along with the consequences of these alternatives, may increase their awareness of value conflicts. Furthermore, such study (hopefully) will help students (1) to shift from supporting one value to supporting another one or others that they believe are more worthy of their support, (2) to realize that there are many different ways of dealing with a particular problem, and (3) to become more willing in the future to search for and consider a variety of possible solutions rather than insisting on only one as being "right" always and forevermore.

How might we test out these hypotheses in the classroom? We can start by presenting students with a value dilemma. A *value dilemma* is a situation, argument, or illustration in which one or more individuals are faced with a *choice* (this is essential) between two or more conflicting alternatives, each of which is desirable to some degree. An example of a value dilemma would be a police officer who is faced with deciding whether or not to allow a soapbox speaker to continue speaking before an increasingly hostile and menacing crowd. On the one hand, there is the physical safety of the speaker; on the other hand, there is the speaker's constitutional rights.

The following is an example of a value dilemma that might be used with secondary-level students. It is a fictionalized version of an actual incident a few years back on the east coast of the United States. I give my thanks to Peg Carter of Pontiac, Michigan, for writing the first draft of this story.

TIM COSBY'S DILEMMA

Tom Cosby arrived a few minutes early before the meeting. "Far out, far out," he thought. "Who would have thought that this many people would turn out for a Board of Education meeting? Well, here goes." He hurried down the aisle to his seat on the stage. Already present, he noted, were his principal, the president of the school board, Mr. Johnson, his social studies teacher, and a couple of other people that he didn't know. He also recognized many of the people in the front rows of the auditorium. His mom and dad were sitting next to the Reverend Sooners of Glide Episcopal Church. Mrs. Leibowitz, President of the Board of Supervisors, was there. Several union officials had shown up, along with the heads of the two teachers' associations. Many members of the Black community could be seen, and there was a pretty good sprinkling of other minority groups as well. There was Mr. Adams of the American Civil Liberties Union, too. He remembered Adams especially since he had liked what he said as a guest speaker in Civics I. "Outta sight!" he almost said aloud, "Old man Tabbett, the editor of the *Daily Express,* is here!"

Every year since 1945, the Plainsville Exchange Club had sponsored a visiting student from another country as part of an ongoing student exchange program. Tom, in fact, hoped he might be the student chosen from Plainsville to spend next school year— his senior year—in another country. Last year he had gotten to be pretty good friends with Alex Tomlinson, who had come to Plainsville from England. That guy could sure kick a soccer ball all right. He'd learned a lot from Alex, he thought. But this year—this year, things were different. This year the guest student was to be a white guy named Arthur Smith from a place called Windhoek in Namibia. Tom hadn't even known such a place existed. He was pretty shook when he found out where Namibia was. In Southwest Africa! He and several of the brothers in the Black Students Association were among the student leaders who had protested to the principal.

When he told his dad about it, the old man was just as angry as he was. He'd called several members of the Black community, along with some other friends, that very night. Tom could still see the article that appeared in the paper a few days later:

PROTEST DEVELOPS OVER ENROLLMENT OF EXCHANGE STUDENT IN PLAINSVILLE HIGH

September 21st

>Spurred on by protesting students at Plainsville High School, many members of the local community today picketed in front of the Board of Education to protest the forthcoming arrival and enrollment of Arthur Smith, an exchange student from Windhoek, Namibia, a territory illegally controlled by South Africa. Young Smith's invitation was part of the Student Exchange Program sponsored by the local Cultural Exchange Club.
>Protesters complained of the expressed governmental policy in South Africa of complete racial

segregation of whites, Blacks, and Asians and requested that Smith's invitation be rescinded and that another student, from a country which does not endorse segregation, be invited in his place. Neither the head of the Cultural Exchange Club nor the President of the Board of Education was available for comment on the matter.

Things really began to hit the fan then! The NAACP got into the act and publically denounced the invitation at the next meeting of the School Board. The Commander of the American Legion Post sent a strong letter to the editor of the paper protesting Smith's enrollment.

What had surprised Tom, however, had been the response of old man Tabbett, the editor of the paper. He had not agreed with the protesters. Some of the words of Tabbett's editorial of last week still stuck in Tom's mind:

> ... this is not an issue of government policy. Arthur Smith did not formulate and cannot be held responsible for the actions of his government. He may not be aware of all that such a policy implies. One thing, however, is certain. Arthur Smith will be unlikely to consider alternatives to such a policy unless he has the opportunity to experience other ways of dealing with people. How, we might ask, is he to obtain such an experience if he is denied the opportunity to meet and interact with others who perhaps think differently than he? His very enrollment in Plainsville High and his subsequent interaction with the many different types of students who make up the Plainsville student body would provide him with at least one such opportunity. Is this not a question of fair play and justice? Can a boy of 17 be blamed for a policy that was formulated and instigated before he was born?

Tom had to admit that much of what Tabbett said made sense to him. But what was "fair" in a case like this? How could he and his brothers in good conscience accept a student like this guy Smith from a country like that? South Africa was the place, after all, where even a champion tennis player like Arthur Ashe was not allowed to compete. It was a cinch that these white South Africans wouldn't accept him—Tom Cosby—as an exchange student in one of their own high schools!

Well, nobody could say that all this protesting hadn't brought results. "That's why we're here tonight," he thought.

The meeting was beginning. Mr. Johnson was talking: " . . . opposed to Smith's being enrolled for a year in Plainsville High. Under South Africa's policy of apartheid [which Tom now knew meant complete segregation of people of different races], it would be an implicit endorsement of segregation on our part. Forty percent of our student body would not even be considered for admission to South African secondary schools, let alone be allowed to enroll. The whites in South Africa are a minority who continue to occupy Namibia illegally, without the consent of the Black majority. It would be sheer hypocrisy on our part if we were to allow this student to enroll at Plainsville High."

The President of the School Board was next. "The official position of the Board," he declared, "was to accept any exchange student that any foreign government sends to Plainsville. The Board voted unanimously last night to reject the petitions of the NAACP and the various teachers' organizations that Arthur Smith not be allowed to enroll." A formal invitation had been issued on the part of the Plainsville School Board and endorsed by the Mayor. They could not, in good faith, go back on this invitation.

Phyllis Ramires from the State Human Rights Commission spoke next. She spoke in favor of Smith's enrollment. She mentioned such things as the rights of the individual, equal opportunity for all, fair play, and justice as fundamental aspects of American society. "We should not hold this boy responsible for the actions of his government," she said. "This might be just the opportunity he needs to gain an understanding of what this country stands for, and to open his eyes to the rest of the world."

Now it was Tom's turn. He hadn't been sure what he wanted to say. But now he knew. He stepped to the podium and started to speak: "Ladies and Gentlemen, I . . .

What should Tom say? What would you say if you were in Tom's shoes? The situation in which Tom finds himself is the kind of situation that all of us are likely to be in at one time or another. Perhaps not exactly like Tom's, but quite possibly something fairly similar. How can a teacher proceed in order to help students determine for themselves what Tom should do? Here are some guidelines to consider:

- Clarify what the value conflict is about, then
- Ask for facts
- Ask for conceivable alternatives
- Ask for possible consequences of each alternative
- Ask for evidence to support the likelihood of each consequence occurring

- Ask for an evaluation of desirability of likely consequences
- Ask for a judgment as to which alternative seems best, and why.

Here is a set of questions organized along these lines:

1. What is this incident about? (What is Tom's dilemma?)
2. What might Tom do to try to resolve his dilemma? (What alternatives are open to him?)
3. What might happen to him if he does each of these things? (What might be the consequences of the various alternatives?)
4. What might happen to those who are not immediately involved? (What might be the long- as well as the short-range consequences?)
5. What evidence, if any, is there that these consequences would in fact occur?
6. Would each consequence be good or bad? Why?
7. What do you think Tom should do? (What do you think is the best thing for Tom to do?) Why?

Question 1 asks students to *sort out and identify what the value conflict or dilemma is about*—what is the disagreement? Is the conflict one of means—that is, a disagreement over how to attain an end or goal that all parties to the conflict regard as desirable—as worth attaining? Or is it a conflict between different ends, with each of the parties to the conflict desiring that a different goal be attained? It is important for everyone involved in the conflict to be clear as to what the conflict is about. Unless there are some agreed-on goals, the discussion cannot proceed.

Once the dilemma has been identified, the facts of the situation must be determined. This is the purpose of Question 2. Students are being asked to describe what has happened in the incident. This asking for facts is extremely important, for it provides students with a solid factual base from which to draw their later conclusions.

Question 2 asks students to *identify alternatives*. It is helpful here to form the class into small groups of five to six members each. Choose one person in each group to jot down members' ideas and another person to act as chairperson to keep the discussion focused on the task at hand. Brainstorm here. Encourage students to think of as many things as they can that Tom might possibly say in this situation. Each chairperson should encourage members to suggest ideas, with any and all ideas being welcomed, no matter how far fetched or unusual they may seem at the time.

The next step (Questions 3 and 4) is to have the class *predict consequences.* What might happen if the alternatives (recommendations that are suggested) were to become reality? Who would be affected and how? What about effects on future generations?

Take each alternative that has been suggested (or as many as the class is able to handle without getting tired, bored, etc., depending on their age, ability, etc.), and again have the class engage in brainstorming, this time about the possible consequences of each alternative—that is, the possible things that might happen were Tom actually to pursue this alternative.

It is helpful at this point to prepare a values-information chart on the blackboard (or have students prepare such a chart individually in their notebooks). Figure 1 below illustrates one example of a chart that can be used for recording information about a value dilemma.

FIGURE 1

A Values-Information Chart for Recording Information About a Value Dilemma

FACTS	ALTERNATIVES	CONSEQUENCES			
		Short-range		Long-range	
		Self	Others	Self	Others

When students can think of no further consequences, then begins the search for evidence to support or refute the likelihood of the consequence occurring. Question 5 is intended to *encourage students to search for data*—reports, photographs, eyewitness accounts, newspaper articles, etc.—which describe what happened in similar situations in the past. Once such evidence has been collected, its truthfulness and relevance should be assessed. Is the data that has been collected accurate? Does it refer to situations like the one under consideration?

When students can find no more evidence, they need to consider whether they would want each consequence to happen or not. They should also be encouraged to discuss why they think certain consequences are more desirable than others. Question 6 will help students ascertain *whether each consequence is good or bad.*

It is necessary at this point, therefore, to make sure that students understand the concept of criteria. A criterion is the characteristic or set of characteristics which makes a consequence (or anything else) desirable or undesirable (or somewhere in-between) to someone. Criteria are essential for intelligent, reasoned ranking. Value objects (ideas, policies, individuals, etc.) are often rated quite differently by people because they are using different sets of criteria. The development of criteria is an extremely important task, for it not only gives students a yardstick or guideline by which to measure things (e.g., consequences) in order to determine their desirability or undesirability, but it also enables other students to understand the reasons for the rating, whatever the rating may be.

Students must do the determining, however. It does not help a student to think about which criteria are important if the teacher simply tells the student which ones to use. But the teacher can and should expose students to a wide variety of criteria so that students do not look at consequences from only one point of view. Thus, various criteria should be identified and their meaning discussed with the class. Such criteria include the:

- Moral criterion (To what extent would the lives and dignity of human beings be enhanced or diminished?)
- Legal criterion (Would any laws be broken?)
- Aesthetic criterion (Would the beauty of something be increased or reduced?)
- Ecological criterion (Would the natural environment be harmed or helped?)
- Economic criterion (How much cost would be involved? Are sufficient funds available to pay these costs?)
- Health and safety criterion (Would the lives of human beings be endangered in any way?).

These are only some of many possible criteria students can use. Students should also be encouraged to suggest additional criteria for consideration. It is important to realize, however, that any sort of reasoned, intelligent rating of consequences (or any-

FIGURE 2
VALUE-ANALYSIS CHART

ALTERNATIVES OPEN TO TOM	CONSEQUENCES	DESIRABILITY FROM VARIOUS POINTS OF VIEW							RANKING
		Moral	Legal	Aesthetic	Ecological	Economic	Health & Safety	Etc.	

thing else) in terms of desirability/undesirability is impossible unless some criteria are used. To help students analyze consequences from several different points of view, a value-analysis chart can be used. Figure 2 is an example of one.

When class members have finished discussing the desirability of each consequence and have both stated their reasons and listened to the reasons of others for considering certain consequences as either desirable or undesirable, the choices open to Tom Cosby can be ranked from most desirable to least desirable. This can be done by using the last column on the right in the value-analysis chart. At this point Question 7, *What do you think Tom should do?* can be answered.

Everybody in the class should now be able to discuss the following: Why did they rank the alternatives as they did? Which alternatives seemed most preferred? Why? Would the reasons given for thinking a particular alternative as most desirable in this situation hold true in others as well? Why? Why not?

Underlying this strategy is the assumption that through realizing, discussing, and evaluating various courses of action along with their consequences and the evidence to support or refute the likelihood of their occurring—

1. Students will become more aware that all people hold values that conflict some of the time.
2. Students will realize that there are many different sets of criteria that can be used to evaluate a consequence.
3. Students, hopefully, will become more willing to evaluate the consequences of differing courses of action that they have now been exposed to from several points of view.

STRATEGIES FOR CLARIFYING THE TEACHING SELF

Stephen J. Taffee, *doctoral candidate in the area of curriculum and instruction, Michigan State University, East Lansing.*

Not too long ago, I was a brand-spanking-new teacher who couldn't wait to get into the classroom. I had studied my major and minor areas in college thoroughly, I thought, and had had an exciting, if short, student-teaching experience. All in all, I felt I was as ready as I would ever be for my first year.

I was wrong.

And so I turned to my colleagues, the seasoned veterans, for advice. This is what I heard:

> "Just be strict with them. Discipline—good, quiet discipline is what counts to the administrators around here."
>
> "Follow the teacher's manuals. That's all you need to do."
>
> "Don't try anything new or rock the boat—not until you have tenure."
>
> "Sounds like a good idea to me. Let me know how it works out."
>
> "Don't join the union. They're just a bunch of troublemakers."
>
> "You better join the union, or the others will think you're funny."

Copyright © 1976, Stephen J. Taffee

All of my colleagues were trying to be helpful.
They failed.
They failed because what I needed was to become clearer about my ideas, not hear just their ideas. No one asked me how I felt about things. No one asked me if I had considered alternatives, or if I had considered the possible consequences of my actions. No one asked me if I felt good about what I was doing.

Fortunately, however, as I continued to teach, I was able to go to conferences and workshops where people did ask how I felt, and slowly, sometimes painfully, I became clearer and more resolute about myself as an educator.

Our world of education is full of confusion and conflict. Little help is offered to the beginning teacher, or the pre-service teacher towards clarity and conflict resolution. Phrases and words, such as behavior modification, values clarification, competency-based learning, accountability, dyslexia, open classroom, integrated day, career education, humanistic education, confluent education, are tossed about in lounges and journals, often with little agreement on meanings. If veteran teachers are confused about these things, pity the novice.

There is a methodology, however, for working in these areas of confusion and conflict, which is both practical and theoretically sound.

Borrowing heavily from John Dewey, several contemporary educators have endeavored to formulate a theory of values and the valuing process.[1] They believe that values are formed by way of the following processes:

1. Feeling (being in touch with one's affective side)
2. Thinking (thinking critically, logically, and creatively)
3. Communicating (sending clear messages and interpreting information, asking clarifying questions)
4. Choosing (from among alternatives, choosing freely, and choosing after thoughtful consideration of foreseeable consequences)
5. Acting (on your values, acting with some consistency).[2]

Within this framework, a number of practical teaching strategies could be employed, aimed at encouraging the use of one or more of the valuing processes. Such teaching strategies could, in the case of preservice teachers, be used as a portion of their methodology classes, or even as a special class entitled "Clarifying the Teaching Self." In the case of the beginning teacher, the strategies could be used by a principal, counselor, or another teacher in regular rap sessions or meetings for beginning teachers and interested veterans.

Here are a few examples of five possible strategies:

Ten Memorable Teachers[3]

List the names of ten memorable teachers in your life. They may or may not have been professional teachers. They may be living or dead, real or fictional, positive or negative influences, but who, nonetheless, have had great impact on your life.

	A	B	C	D	E	F	G	H
1.								
2.								
3.								
4.								
5.								
6.								
7.								
8.								
9.								
10.								

A. Put an "X" next to those who probably know that they are on your list, that you consider them to be a memorable teacher.

B. Put a "5" next to those who probably would not have been on your list five years ago.

C. Put a "T" next to those who were teachers of yours in an actual school.

D. Put an "M" next to those who have benefited from your own teaching.

E. Put a "*" next to the five most important teachers of the ten listed, those five who are most memorable to you.

F. Next to the starred names, write a key word or phrase summing up what memorable thing it is that the teacher has given you or taught you.

G. Next to those items, put a "!" if you feel you have gained for yourself what your memorable teachers were trying to teach.

H. Finally, put an upward arrow "↑" next to those items which you are still working on and getting more of. Put a downward arrow "↓" next to those items you may wish you had less of in your life.

This activity may then be processed by the use of sharing trios, or a large group discussion, or both. It should be emphasized that there are no right answers, and the leader should avoid any tendencies to moralize in this or in any of the other strategies.

Continuums

How do you stand on:
The Use of Drugs to Control "Hyperactive" Children
. . . .
strongly approve   strongly disapprove

Explanation (optional):_____

The leader can ask people to rate themselves on the continuum, and then ask for volunteers to share where they stand and why. As in all activities, however, the right to pass must always be respected. An alternative method for using the continuum would be to designate different sides of the room in which you are meeting as the ends of the continuum, and ask people to stand in a place which represents their beliefs. Discussions can then take place between those standing next to each other, or you can ask those at opposite ends of the continuum to explain their positions.

Other possible topics for continuums may include: behavior modification, teacher strikes, re-instatement of prayer in public schools, grading, sex education, compulsory school attendance, corporal punishment, tenure, behavioral objectives, year-round school, sexism, busing, or even such things as study halls, smoking in bathrooms, snowball fighting, and how school funds should be spent.

Rank Orders

Rank order the following items from most important to least important:

In my classroom: ___discipline   If budgets have
                  ___creativity   to be cut: ___athletics
                  ___skills   ___library
                                                  ___salaries

Rank orders can also be used with people, but only with caution. For example, the following sample strategy requests that the candidates for a principal's position be rank ordered. The descriptions of the individuals are general and stereotypical. In processing such an activity, some attention must be given to stereotyping, its effects upon our feelings and thinking, etc.

Rank order these candidates for the position of principal in your school:

___ 1. Former athletic director, somewhat traditional, but committed to a good school.
___ 2. A fellow teacher, has been taking administration courses and has aspirations to join the central administration, is liked by most administrators in the district and would work hard at pleasing them.
___ 3. Female. No previous administrative experience, but known as a hard worker who expects the same from those around her. Goes by the book.
___ 4. Female. Has a reputation as a feminist and will not tolerate sexism. Seen as a very innovative person, but lacks credibility within the community.
___ 5. Male. Near retirement. He has been with the system for many years, is well liked and respected.
___ 6. Female. Former union negotiater. Levelheaded, practical. Not perceived as a very effective classroom teacher, however.

Unfinished Sentences

Unfinished sentences can be used in a number of ways. They may be part of a journal kept by the teacher, in which case the same ones could be repeated several months later to see if anything different has emerged. They may be processed in small groups, posted individually for others to see. They may be used a number of times to encourage deeper reflection. Here are some examples of unfinished sentences:

A good teacher....
People learn....
The single most critical issue facing education today is....
As a result of my students coming into contact with me, I want them to....
The hardest thing for me to do is....
You know, I'm really very good at....
One thing I have learned from kids is....

Environmental Descriptions[4]

This activity is an extended strategy designed for continuing use. In its final form, it resembles a comprehensive statement of educational beliefs and how those beliefs can be put into practice. This strategy may possibly be most effective only after considerable thought has already been given to some of the issues surrounding education. It may be used again and again to assist in clarifying just what the beginning teacher or preservice teacher values. Collectively, the two parts of this strategy form a written description of the educational environment the teacher would like to create.

1. "Towards an Environmental Description." This preliminary activity deals with much of the same information contained in an environmental description, but in a less formal manner. In it, unfinished sentences are used, much in the same way as described above:

   As a college student (or as a beginning teacher), I have been in different classrooms for many years. The one thing I wish more teachers would have remembered about me as a student is. . . .

   The one thing I'm going to make sure my students learn is. . . .

   If I could have an ideal classroom, it would contain. . . .

   If my principal really wants to help me be a better teacher, he/she should. . . .

   The three most important things kids need are. . . .

   And so to help them get those three things, I am going to. . . .

   The most frustrating thing about teaching so far has been. . . .

   I can tell I have really done a good job of teaching when. . . .

   Other sentence stems could also be used, but should always deal with structure, evaluation or philosophy, and purposes.

2. "An Environmental Description." This strategy asks that the teacher, using a somewhat standardized format, answer certain questions in an effort to define his or her position clearly.

Structure
A. How are decisions going to be made in your classroom? Will you, as the teacher, be making all the decisions for kids, or just some of them? What decisions might you reserve for yourself? Do you want to be in total control, make decisions cooperatively, or allow students to make all decisions themselves? Why?
B. How do you plan to utilize the space in your classroom? Will you use learning centers? Desks all in a row? Will students be allowed to put things on the walls? Will you have a couch in your room? A quiet area? An off-limits area? How about carpeting? Etc.
C. How do you plan to use and/or provide resources in your classroom? Will you use a textbook? How about other supplies? Will students be encouraged to bring things from home? What about human resources? Will community people be utilized? What other resources are available for use? Etc.
D. How do you plan to structure time in your classroom? Will you decide when everything happens in your classroom? How much time should be spent on particular subjects? Why?
E. What restraints will be a part of your classroom? Are you next door to the library, thus requiring less noise? What rules will your classroom have and why? How will discipline be handled?

Evaluation
A. How will you evaluate your students? Is there a grading policy you must follow? How will you evaluate within your classroom? Contracts? Performance objectives? Normal curve? Narrative statements? Student self-evaluation? Etc.
B. How will you evaluate your classroom? How will you check to see that this environmental description accurately reflects what is happening in your classroom?
C. How will you evaluate yourself? How will you know when you are doing a good job? Will you ask for feedback from your students? Your principal? Parents? Colleagues?

Philosophy and Purposes
Some find this easier to do at the end of an environmental description rather than at its beginning. Either way, its purpose is to serve as a guidepost for the remainder of the document. Overall, what is the general philosophy operating in your classroom? What

do you believe about kids, learning, and teaching that leads you to construct your classroom in such a way?

Many other strategies could be created to focus upon education. Clear beliefs and values do not occur overnight, and certainly lack of clarity is not confined just to preservice or beginning teachers, and the strategies described above would probably be of benefit to veteran educators also. But perhaps the biggest beneficiaries from these activities will not be the teachers who have used them, but their students and, after all, isn't that why all of us are in the game?

FROM INCULCATION TO ACTION: A CONTINUUM FOR VALUES EDUCATION

Julia Bell, Sarah Bennett, and James Fallace, *teacher education candidates, Grinnell College, Grinnell, Iowa.*

As prospective teachers, it is difficult to predict what we would actually do with values education in the classroom. It has a rightful place, but the present procedures seem inappropriate and inadequate. Students come to school with values from home, friends, church, and society; but they often do not know what their values are, how they acquired them, or how they should express them. It is not the teacher's place to explain or lecture on student values. This would just present another source serving to impart arbitrarily more values to students. Students must actively explore their values for themselves. Teachers, however, seem at a loss with the present choices of value schemes that promote active student involvement. Teachers too often focus on one approach for classroom use without utilizing valuable aspects of other schemes. Having reached a point of uncertainty regarding further direction, the teacher might recognize the limitations inherent in concentrating a values education program on one isolated approach.

We see the various processes of values education as a taxonomy. Presented separately, each system isolates a particular level of thought or process of inquiry and is, therefore, inadequate for the student and teacher. Our scheme is a continual process that combines inculcation, clarification, analysis, moral reasoning, and action learning. Each scheme is a process supporting a continuum in values inquiry.[1] While our discussion and examples will involve only the present values encountered by students, the continuum is equally applicable to the development of future values.[2]

Inculcation occurs before students enter school. Students bring unquestioned values with them which are presented as facts, constantly reinforced and accepted as givens or absolutes. In this sense, inculcation is the first step in our process.

Inculcation does not stop upon entering school. Many values are reinforced and actively expressed in schools by the present nature of these institutions and through the presented content matter. Among other values, schools enforce conformity, competition, and obedience. These often are not the school's goals, but through the interpretation and application of educational philosophies, they have become incorporated into the school system. Dress codes prescribe a certain dress form for students and teachers; written tests which assume only one correct answer stifle creativity; grades encourage competition, cheating, and learning for extrinsic rewards; rules and regulations control attendance and students' behavior; the teacher's authoritarian role and disciplinary power demand obedience and docility. In other words, the school promotes its own hidden curriculum. It is often not acknowledged, but evident just the same.

Most of these values are reflected by the society at large, substantiating the traditional role of schools as the transmitter of culture. Although the transmittance and continuation of our culture is necessary, students have a right to learn how to discriminate between the values and the factual content of subject matter. Today, values are often presented as facts. For example, it is common for students to learn from the curriculum or teachers that democracy, our form of government, is the best government. As James Barth and Samuel Shermis have pointed out, students learn in traditional social studies classes that although capitalism was marred by exploitation, it is superior to all other economic systems. The attitude is that if students succeed in equating capitalism with democracy, no real harm is done for both ideas are good.[3] This is a value presented as a fact, but students do not learn to discern values from facts and schools should not present values in this way.

Given the omnipresence of inculcation in the school system, the problem becomes one of identifying an acceptable position. Values should be dealt with openly and systematically. The intent should not be one of indoctrinating students into specific value systems, but rather inculcating an attitude toward values that will lead to more autonomous, independent individuals.

To counter inculcation, students in the early grades should begin to recognize, analyze, organize, and act upon their values within a consistent framework. This process of values clarification is often postponed or never initiated. But most importantly the basis for any values inquiry is the present values system of the student. Inculcation has already occurred; the school's role is to carry values education further.

Values clarification is an attempt to help students become more aware of their values. The approach utilizes activities which stimulate individuals to think about themselves. For example, Sidney Simon and his colleagues offer a wide range of activities for the classroom teacher to use in many subject areas. It is argued that through such activities, students will become more clear, purposeful, and consistent.[4]

The clarification approach has achieved such popularity among educators that it is often treated as a panacea. While clarification proponents specifically state that the approach should not be treated as a panacea, they have a tendency to overstate the merits of clarification. For example, Simon states that clarification helps people to be more purposeful and productive, to sharpen their critical thinking, and to have better relations with one other.[5] In our opinion, clarification techniques provide only one step in a larger process required to realize these goals. Educators must realize that values clarification is not the only technique required for values education; however, clarification can initiate a series of approaches to make values education more complete and comprehensive.

A basic objective of values education is to help students determine their actual values. Students are often confused when they attempt to identify what they value. Clarification writers have established a seven-point criteria which must be met before something becomes a "value." Values must be chosen (1) freely, (2) from alternatives, (3) after thoughtful consideration of the consequences, and an individual must (4) cherish, (5) be willing to publicly affirm, (6) act on the value, and finally (7) act on it repeatedly.[6] These criteria are not sufficient to define a value because the element of a rational, analytic examination is absent. That is, a belief may fit all seven criteria and still not be a value.

Assume a student completes a values continuum exercise concluding that democracy is the best form of government and that capitalism is the best economic system.[7] To be absolutely sure that these are true values, the student should not stop the clarification effort at this point. It is possible that these values were chosen freely, chosen from alternatives, and even acted upon repeatedly. Still with additional information, three important considerations have been omitted. All supposed values must be examined further because the seven-point criteria do not examine (1) the origins of a value, (2) the possibility that this value may change with additional information, and (3) the value in relation to other personal values.

Acting upon a value is an important criterion for judging commitment to the value but the individual must examine the possibility of having been misguided or even unknowingly pressured by parents, other adults, or peers. The student who is convinced that democracy is the best form of government must ask "When did I first begin to feel this way about democracy? Are there serious flaws in the American form of democracy? Have my parents and teachers permitted criticism of our democratic system?" These questions attempt to examine the origins of one's belief, setting the stage for moving beyond clarification into analysis. Next, the student must gather relevant information concerning democracies and other possible forms of government. In doing so, it is necessary for the student to be sure of having a clear understanding of the concepts involved in the value judgment. At this fact-finding stage, the student must assess the truth of the purported facts and be able to express points of view that are in opposition to his or her own. Some facts may support or illustrate strengths of a democratic form of government, other facts may indicate its weaknesses. In this way the student becomes more rational in future decision-making. The student must also consider any qualifications that might alter the original value statement, for example, the student may conclude that a totalitarian form of government is preferred if the collective intelligence of the people is insufficient. Finally, students must examine a fact's potential value in relation to their other personal values. Such a conflict in values necessitates further examination of students' perceptions of their own values. If we again extend the example of a totalitarian government to include the type of economic society one values, further critical discrimination results. The student begins to recognize that the capitalist system has shortcomings as well as strong points in its relation to principles of a democracy. Similarly, socialism for the first time may be seen as compatible with democracy.

Values clarification has merits, but we see a need to complement it with a values analysis approach. If students are to understand more clearly what values they hold, educators must follow clarification exercises with analytic situations. Analysis deals with the source of values, their consistency within a values framework, and their dependence upon varying conditions. Moral reasoning adds a new dimension to values education.

In discussing his six stages of moral reasoning, Lawrence Kohlberg states that each stage defines what the student values (clarification) and the reasons for valuing it (analysis). Through the presentation of a dilemma, the student is exposed to conflict. Discussion of hypothetical solutions to these dilemmas may result in the student's dissatisfaction with the particular approach to the dilemma. Kohlberg exposes the student to the six states of reasoning to stimulate the student's movement to the next higher stage.

We maintain that at the first four stages the individual is acting largely on the basis of inculcated values. Cultural rules are unquestioned and accepted as absolutes. At stages 1 and 2, rules are right or wrong depending on the subsequent punishment or reward for the individual. As Kohlberg adds, "Avoidance of punishment and unquestioning deference to power are valued in their own right, not in terms of respect for an underlying moral order supported by punishment and authority."[8] With movement into stages 3 and 4, the emphasis shifts to a faith in the social order. The individual supports the social order because of a felt responsibility or duty to do so regardless of the consequences. The individual's loyalty to the social order is perceived as valuable in its own right; however, the social order and its cultural rules are accepted as givens without critical consideration of their sources.

Although values up through state 4 are inculcated, the individual can clarify specific values and may be aware of particular values that conform to cultural expectations and the social order. Clarification can assist the individual in recognizing the values that determine his or her own behavior.

As one moves along Kohlberg's hierarchy, elements of analysis can also be identified. Through analytical discussion of dilemmas, an individual may become dissatisfied with his or her present level of reasoning. Realizing this, the individual will be more inclined to progress to the next higher stage. However, at stage 5 analysis adopts a broader dimension. Cultural standards and individual rights now come into question. The individual begins to examine critically the sources of these standards and regulations. Laws, no longer absolutes, are open to change by appealing to rational considerations and procedural rules. What results,

Kohlberg claims, is an emphasis upon the legal point of view but with the possiblity of changing law in terms of rational considerations of social utility.[9]

Up to this point, Kohlberg's approach has added nothing substantially different from inculcation, clarification, or analysis. However, two points should be stressed which distinguish moral reasoning from the other three approaches. First, Kohlberg's dilemmas are designed to clarify the structure or framework of the individual's values, not specific values as such. Whereas values clarification only attempts to elicit awareness of values, Kohlberg's approach fosters the individual's movement toward principled stages (5 and 6) of reasoning. The discussions of dilemmas are aimed at helping all students see inadequacies in their particular stages of reasoning or system of thought. Resulting dissatisfaction is intended to stimulate movement to the next stage of reasoning.

The second distinguishing factor in moral reasoning is the highest stage. At stage 6, moral reasoning assumes an existential quality not found in preceding stages. Moral reasoning is based on an appeal to abstract universal principles that are applicable to all people. Not only are these principles universal, they are also self-chosen. Reasoning goes beyond mere application of an external abstract principle. In being self-chosen, the principle becomes internalized and personal. As the existentialist would remark, moral reasoning is uniquely right as it encompasses Kohlberg's logical comprehensiveness, as well as an internal feeling for its adequacy.[10] At this stage, intellect and emotion are inseparable in reasoning—in the current language of educators, the cognitive and affective are merged. In existential terms, moral reasoning is founded in a highly individual, informed passion.

At a stage 6 level, what effect does moral reasoning have on value judgements? Returning to the example of democracy, it can be seen that moral reasoning adds a new dimension to the process. As discussed earlier, analysis yields information on the strengths and weaknesses of a democratic society. A judgment may be reached by examining critically the pros and cons of the concept. However, upon reaching stage 6, reasoning revolves around an internalized conception of democracy as a process that best serves the potential of humankind and affords a better quality of human experience. In discussing the democratic society, John Dewey states that "the principle of regard for individual freedom and for decency and kindliness of human relations" will ultimately lead to a "higher quality of experience on the part of a greater number" of people.[11] The individual's perception of the human conditon is one in which people not only have the right but also the capability to govern themselves. The universal principle of individual freedom concerns the individual's potential for action and subsequent personal responsibility for that action.

Proceeding further, in judging between a democratic capitalist and a democratic socialist system, reasoning may focus on the degree to which one better complements this conception of human nature. Depending on one's interpretation of the evidence (analysis), a student may conclude that capitalism provides greater opportunity for individual freedom or independent decision-making. However, one is just as likely to decide that greater individual potential may be realized under a socialist system of shared wealth. Regardless of the decision, the reasoning process involves an internalized conception of universal principles.

A possible dilemma on this theme would involve students deciding the best form of government for a new community. Students would have information concerning the location of the community and access to resources, the background of the inhabitants including their knowledge and skills, and their purpose in forming the community. In addition to choosing a government, students could determine how production decisions are to be made and how the wealth is to be distributed, i.e., choosing between a capitalist and socialist economic system.

Generally, then, the dilemma is a classroom technique for identifying reasoning levels at which students operate and for stimulating thought at higher levels. Inasmuch as Kohlberg's approach emphasizes exposure and thought, it is inadequate if removed from the continuum. What remains is for values to be expressed through overt action.

All previous approaches, inculcation through reasoning, direct attention to the internal change within systems of thought. Overt behavioral change is inferred. Action learning, the final step in the continuum, adds the culminating dimension of directing thought into outward action.

Clarification exercises, role playing, and dilemmas are useful to the extent that they provide an opportunity to assume hypothetical value positions. But as Charles Silberman points out, "Talking about morality, honesty, or kindness in no way insures that people will act morally, honestly, or kindly."[12] An awareness of particular values, an understanding of their sources, a realization of their appeal to underlying reasoning processes are limited objectives of values education. In other words, mere knowledge is not the goal, but action. Not until individuals are confronted with conflict which necessitates an actual decision can individuals determine what their actions will be. The school cannot create these situations. Rather, it becomes the teacher's role to assist and encourage the student, not only by utilizing all strategies discussed, but by shifting the learning outside of the school where values action can be authentic.

CONDUCTING MORAL DISCUSSIONS IN THE CLASSROOM

Barry K. Beyer, *Associate Professor of History and a member of the Staff of the Education Center, Carnegie-Mellon University, Pittsburgh.*

Research by Lawrence Kohlberg and his associates suggests that individuals at any given stage of moral development* exhibit three characteristics which have important implications for education. First, most individuals can comprehend reasoning about moral issues at the next higher stage of reasoning above their present stage, but at no stage higher than that. Thus, for example, a person reasoning predominately at Stage 2 probably comprehends Stage 3 reasoning, but not reasoning at Stages 4, 5, or 6. Second, individuals prefer reasoning at the highest stage they can comprehend, because higher stage reasoning offers a way to resolve moral issues which cannot be resolved as satisfactorily at a lower stage. Finally, when individuals examine reasoning about moral issues repeatedly, they tend to move up to the next higher stage.

If these findings are accurate, then it is reasonable to assume that educators can devise classroom activities to help their students move from one stage of moral reasoning to the next.[1] Recent classroom experimentation supports this assumption, for moral discussions in classrooms have facilitated cognitive moral development.[2]

A moral discussion consists of a purposeful conversation about moral issues. Most moral discussions are triggered by moral

---
*See "Definition of Moral Stages" on p. 20.

dilemmas which present situations for which the culture supplies some support for a number of actions which the protagonists could take. Discussions of these situations focus on the moral issues involved in a dilemma and the reasoning used to justify recommended actions.

Perhaps the best way to illustrate the nature of a moral discussion is to examine a transcript of a portion of such a discussion. In the dialogue that follows, junior high school students discuss Sharon's dilemma. This dilemma involves the following situation:

> Sharon and Jill were best friends. One day they went shopping together. Jill tried on a sweater and then, to Sharon's surprise, walked out of the store wearing the sweater under her coat. A moment later, the store's security officer stopped Sharon and demanded that she tell him the name of the girl who had walked out. He told the storeowner that he had seen the two girls together, and that he was sure that the one who left had been shoplifting. The storeowner told Sharon that she could really get in trouble if she didn't give her friend's name.[3]

The students are discussing whether or not Sharon should give Jill's name to the security officer. The excerpt begins mid-way in the class discussion.

> GEORGE: Jill could say "I don't even know her. I just walked in the store off the street, and I don't even know where she lives. I just met her."
> TEACHER: So what she ought to do is lie for a friend, Right?
> GEORGE: Yah.
> TEACHER: What is going to happen to all of us if everyone lies whenever they feel like it, whenever it suits their convenience? What kind of life are you going to have? Peter.
> PETER: If everyone goes around shoplifting, if someone goes and steals a whole bunch of things from somebody's store, then you go back to your store and see everything from your store missing, do you know what kind of life that would be? Everybody would just be walking around stealing everybody else's stuff.
> TEACHER: Mary Lu, do you want to comment about what he said?
> MARY LU: Yah, but everybody doesn't steal and everybody wouldn't, and the thing is that the

storeowner probably has a large enough margin of profit anyway to cover some few ripoffs he might have.

GEORGE: But the store can't exist if everybody is stealing, there are so many people, and it is getting worse and worse every day. It said in the story, they can't afford to stay.

MARY LU: I'm not sure I believe the storeowner.

ROLAND: I am saying so what? It is like stealing from the rich and giving to the poor. It just doesn't work, you know.

TEACHER: Why doesn't it work, Roland?

ROLAND: Because it is exactly what Dan said. Mary Lu can say everybody does not do it, but the only thing that holds it together is the government, and you don't have government if everybody does not follow the rules. Well, we'll have government, but we won't follow the rules....

(After more discussion, the teacher utilized reports from small groups which had developed reasons why Sharon should or should not tell and had written them on the chalkboard.)

TEACHER: Let's look over on the board for a minute where the chairpersons from the small groups wrote the best reasons the groups could think of for giving Jill's name and for not giving it. The first reason the "should nots" gave was friendship. Will you explain what you mean by friendship?

IRENE: The thing is, friendship is like a person matters more than a rule and that you have someone's friendship. The rules are upstanding when you need them; they are there. But the thing is you are going to go by them most of the time. But you've got a friend, and I at least would value a lot higher a friend and somebody who I could talk to, a lot higher than a sweater, than something material. There is absolutely no comparison between emotions and material things.

TEACHER: I think you have explained what you mean by friendship very well. Let's get the other group to explain "Thou shalt not steal." Perry?

PERRY: Well, you shouldn't steal. I said it once before; it is just not fair if everybody steals; you can't live if everybody is stealing.

TEACHER: Perry, what about the whole matter of these two reasons. "Thou shalt not steal" is one reason, but your friendship is another one. Which is more important to you?

PERRY: I say that if you steal and you don't tell on your friend, you will probably keep your crummy friend who left you in the store and is really a liar and all that, but even if you lose your friend and you tell, somewhere along the line you will get some other friends, because I am sure that one or two people in this world are straight.

Four characteristics of this discussion should be noted. First, the students evidently feel free to air their opinions; they do not seem to think that they will be censured or embarrassed for what they say. Second, the discussion centers on moral reasoning—on why Sharon should or should not tell—not on what action she should take. Third, most of the conversation takes place among students who comment on and challenge each other's reasoning. Finally, the teacher facilitates discussions of reasoning at contiguous stages of the Kohlberg scale by involving students who reason at adjacent stages, using questions which stimulate one-stage-higher reasoning, and focusing discussion on arguments at different stages. The following analysis of goals, materials, strategies, and teacher competencies will clarify the use of moral discussions such as this one as a vehicle for facilitating cognitive moral development.

The goals of moral discussions should not be defined too narrowly. By becoming an integral part of a course, these discussions can contribute to the realization of existing overall course objectives as well as bring new objectives to the learning situation. Among the general educational goals which can be reached by using a program of moral discussions are the following:

1. *Improving learning skills.* Moral discussions can help students to develop listening skills, skills of oral communication, and the ability to participate constructively in group discussions.

2. *Improving self-esteem.* Properly conducted, moral discussions can improve a student's self-esteem if teachers and students focus classroom dialogue on the substance of student remarks, accept statements and points of view as given, and treat each other and each other's ideas with respect.

3. *Improving attitudes toward school.* Most students find moral discussions fascinating and look forward to these discussions in class. Hence, school can seem a more interesting and relevant place to them.

4. *Improving knowledge of key concepts.* Moral discussions often involve key concepts which students understand in stage-

related terms. For example, definitions of justice relate to stages of moral reasoning as follows: Stage 1: Justice is getting rewarded for something I do. Stage 2: Justice means that you will do something for me later if I help you now. Stage 3: Justice means doing what all the people in the group approve of. Stage 4: Justice comes about when everyone follows the rules on which we have agreed. Stage 5: Justice means that people get their basic rights for which government was originally founded. By reasoning at increasingly higher moral stages, individuals can develop a more sophisticated understanding of basic concepts that underlie the structure of the society in which they live.

5. *Facilitating stage change.* Stage change takes place slowly, as the article about research findings points out. Hence, a realistic goal in this area might be stated in the following terms: As a result of several years of moral discussions as an integral part of social studies classes, the typical high school student who began as a freshman thinking in a mixture of Stage 2 and 3 terms will think predominately at Stage 4.

Students will be more likely to achieve objectives derived from these five sets of goals when teachers establish a non-judgmental classroom climate that reflects trust, informality, and tolerance. To help create such an atmosphere students can sit in a large circle so that everyone can face and clearly hear each other. By joining this circle, a teacher can take a role as a discussant and leader or mediator rather than as an authority figure who has established a separate teacher space. This type of class arrangement helps teachers to listen to what students say and to guide the discussion in response to their cues. The resulting classroom atmosphere encourages exchange and interaction, two keys to effective moral discussions.

Moral discussions can be best initiated by considering a moral problem or dilemma. Dilemmas are stories which present a central character in a problematic situation for which there are several possible responses and in which a number of moral issues come in conflict. To be most useful, a moral dilemma should meet four criteria. First, it should be as simple as possible. The dilemma should involve only a few characters in a relatively uncomplicated situation which students can grasp readily. Complicated dilemmas confuse students who are then forced to spend time clarifying facts and circumstances rather than discussing reasons for suggested actions. Second, a moral dilemma should be open-ended. It should present a problematic situation to which there is no single obvious right answer.

Third, a dilemma should involve two or more issues that have moral implications. Among the key issues Kohlberg has identified are punishment, affectional relations, authority, contract, property, life, civil liberties, and personal conscience. In Sharon's dilemma, for example, Sharon's affectional relationship with Jill conflicts with both authority and property. Sharon faces the prospect of being punished herself if she fails to give Jill's name or of bringing punishment on Jill if she does tell her name. At the same time Sharon faces the possibility of losing Jill's friendship if she tells or of losing the affection of her own family if she becomes a party to the shoplifting.

Finally, an effective dilemma must offer a choice of actions and pose the question "What should the central character do?" Note the use of the word *should*. This word focuses thinking on moral reasoning, for it asks students to decide what is the right or correct or good thing to do. "Would" questions, on the other hand, are predictive and do not necessarily generate moral reasoning.

Dilemmas may be derived from three main sources. Life in our society abounds with moral dilemmas. Should a terminally ill patient be allowed to die or be kept alive by a life support system? Should police officials use force to capture criminals who are holding hostages? The life experiences of students also offer sources of dilemmas. Should a student let another student copy examination answers? Should a child tell parents that a brother or sister did something he or she had been told not to do? Such dilemmas may be used as they are found or recast as hypothetical incidents involving fictional characters, such as in Sharon's dilemma.

Course content can also serve as a major source of moral dilemmas, especially in social studies classes. Such dilemmas may be based on actual incidents (Should Thoreau have gone to jail rather than pay taxes to support a war of which he disapproved?) or on imaginary incidents or characters which are true in general to historic fact (Should Private Black follow orders to shoot the Indian women and children in the cavalry attack on Sand Creek?). Dilemmas that fit naturally into a course enable teachers to engage students in moral reasoning while at the same time they add to student knowledge of and feeling for the subject under discussion. Literature, history, and the problems of modern society provide many dilemmas that can trigger moral discussions.

Dilemmas may be presented to students in many ways—for example, in the form of short readings, or via a film, filmstrip, recording, or sound filmstrip. Dilemmas may also be presented orally by the teacher or as a role play or simulation. Regardless of the media used to present the dilemma, however, it is the way in which a dilemma is used that makes the ensuing classroom activity an effective moral discussion.

To facilitate cognitive moral development most effectively, a moral discussion must be carefully organized. One tested approach for conducting moral discussions requires that the teacher help students engage in sequence in five distinct activities: (1) to confront a dilemma; (2) to recommend tentative courses of action to resolve the dilemma and to justify these recommendations; (3) to discuss their reasoning in small groups; (4) to examine as a class their reasoning and the reasoning others use as they justify recommended solutions to the dilemma; and (5) to reflect on this reasoning as they bring temporary closure to their discussion.[4] A brief analysis of teaching techniques useful in conducting each of these types of activities follows.

Presenting the Dilemma. To launch a moral discussion, teachers or students present a dilemma to a class. It is sometimes useful to precede presentation of the dilemma with comments or questions designed to prepare the students for the kind of situation or character described in the dilemma. For example, before introducing Sharon's dilemma to a class, a teacher might point out that crimes involving property are a major type of teenage crime today and that shoplifting losses represent a significant portion of the price paid for retail items in stores. The teacher might also ask if students have ever heard of anyone actually stealing something from a store or if they have known of someone who once had to decide whether or not to tell on a friend. After students hear or see the dilemma, the teacher should ask questions in order to help students to clarify the circumstances involved in the dilemma, define terms, identify the characteristics of the central character, and state the exact nature of the dilemma and the action choice open to the central character. Little more than five minutes need be devoted to this part of the strategy.

Dividing on Action. Once students have stated the dilemma, each individual should take a tentative position about what action he or she thinks the central character should take. This can be done by asking students to reflect briefly on the situation facing the central character and then to state tentatively whether the character should or should not take a certain action, usually answered in terms of a written "Yes" or "No" response to an action alternative. This phase of the lesson usually requires about four or five minutes.

Organizing Small Group Discussion. From this point on, the students can engage in small group and large group discussions about the reasoning used to justify the actions they recommend. However, in order to conduct a meaningful discussion, the teacher must first find out what action positions were taken by the students. A good dilemma usually generates a division within the class on the action that the central character should take. A significant number of students should favor one course of action, while others should favor another. A fairly even division over action generates the kind of confrontation that motivates a critical evaluation of moral reasoning. In order to know how to proceed, therefore, the teacher must determine whether there has been a split about action and, if so, what proportion of students has selected each alternative action. Students can indicate by a show of hands how many support each position. When students divide on action on at least a 75-25 basis, discussion can begin.

The teacher must next focus the discussion on the moral issues of the dilemma. Teachers sometimes ask for several volunteers to state reasons for the positions they have taken. This opportunity usually stimulates a number of students to state their reasons or to criticize reasons they have just heard. Teachers can use the interest thus generated to embark on the discussions that should follow.

The most productive moral discussion involves small group discussions followed by a discussion involving the entire class. Approximately a third of a regular class period ought to be devoted to each of these two activities. Small group discussions maximize student-to-student interaction, generate thinking about a variety of reasons for supporting a particular position, create a supportive feeling within each group, and set up the larger class discussion that follows. Students feel comfortable in small group situations because all members of a single group have often made the same action decision. Students also tend to feel comfortable because such groups maximize the opportunity for them to contribute to the group discussion with relatively little apparent risk of failure.

Any of several different grouping strategies may be used. Where the class division on action is uneven, groups of from four to six students can be created in which all members of each group hold the same position. The students in a group can list all the reasons they have for their position, choose the best of these reasons, and then state why this reason is the best one. With a fairly even class division about action, the teacher can organize groups in which an equal number of students represent opposing positions. The group members can discuss their positions and reasons in order to make a list of the two best reasons for each position represented. Students should feel free to switch from one group to another if, in the midst of a group discussion, they decide to change their position on action. When these group tasks have been completed, students can then convene as an entire class to continue their discussion.

While students meet in small groups, the teacher should move from one group to another, helping students to focus on the assigned tasks, to clarify their reasoning, to avoid arguing about the facts of the dilemma, and to list questions to ask of those who took an opposing position. But when the class reconvenes, the teacher assumes a quite different role.

Conducting a Class Discussion. A discussion with the full class gives students a chance to report the reasoning which supports their positions and to hear reasons given for other positions or different reasons given for the positions they have taken, to challenge these reasons, and to hear their own reasoning challenged. This process of examining moral reasoning critically lies at the heart of an effective moral discussion. The process of stating, challenging, being challenged, defending, explaining, criticizing, and comparing highlights the existence of a gap between one's own stage of reasoning and the reasoning at the next higher stage. In time, students become conscious of this gap and move to close it.

Class discussions may follow various formats. Recorders from each group can report the positions and reasons given in their groups while other students challenge what they hear. Or various groups can pose questions to those who took an opposing view and attempt to persuade them of the validity of their own positions and reasoning. Students can list reasons on the chalkboard, and members of the class can then choose the best reason for each position. As students discuss the merit of one reason over another, they engage in the type of thinking that facilitates cognitive moral development.

In a class discussion, teachers have two main tasks—to promote student-to-student interaction and to keep the discussion a moral discussion. Student interaction can be promoted by the way student seating is arranged, by the classroom climate, and by using questions or comments to draw students into the discussion. For example, silent students can be asked to paraphrase a comment, react to a statement, summarize points already made, or take a stand regarding a particular statement.

Teachers can use three techniques to keep the discussion focused on moral issues. First, they should short-circuit substantive diversions—arguments or comments about the facts and circumstances of a dilemma. Instead of permitting speculation about facts and circumstances, teachers can simply state what the facts are and return the discussion to reasoning. Second, they should (at least ideally) encourage discussion between students who argue at contiguous stages of the Kohlberg scale, perhaps by calling on a person who has made a comment representing Stage 3 reasoning to respond to a Stage 2 comment. Alternatively, inviting comments on reasons at contiguous stages from lists on the chalkboard will accomplish the same goal. Finally, the teacher should use probe questions to help students examine issues they had ignored or to think about reasoning at a higher stage.

Any of five types of probe questions can be used.[5] A clarifying probe calls on students to define terms they have used or to explain a comment which does not convey reasoning. For example, if a student says "I think that stealing is immoral," the teacher might respond with a clarifying probe, "What do you mean by immoral?" An issue-specific probe encourages students to examine their thoughts about one of the nine major issues which Kohlberg argues provide a focus for moral reasoning. In discussing Sharon's dilemma an example of such a probe question might be "What obligations do you owe to a friend?" This question gets at the specific issue of affectional relations. An inter-issue probe encourages students to think about what to do when a conflict occurs between two separate issues: "Which is more important, loyalty to a friend or the obligation to obey the law? Why?" A role-switch probe puts the students in the position of someone else involved in the dilemma in order to get them to see another side of the problem. Such a question might be "From the point of view of Jill's parents, should Sharon tell?" Finally, a universal consequence probe asks students to consider what might happen if such a position or such reasoning were applied to everyone. For example, "Is it ever right to tell on a friend?"

Probe questions play a crucial role in guiding a moral discussion. These questions require students to do a number of things which seem to facilitate movement from the lower to the higher stages of moral reasoning—(1) to think increasingly in more generalizable terms, (2) to develop an increasingly broad societal perspective, (3) to develop an ability to see and empathize with more than one side of an issue, and (4) to focus increasingly on the larger moral issues implicit in a moral dilemma. Without specific efforts to help students develop these abilities, discussions are unlikely to facilitate cognitive moral development.

Closing the Discussion. The final activity involved in a moral discussion consists of helping students bring the discussion to a close. This task usually occupies the final few minutes of a class. Students can be asked to summarize all the reasons given for the positions being considered and then choose individually the reason they now find most persuasive. Public declaration of the results is neither necessary nor desirable, for doing so might imply that there is a correct answer, an assumption antithetical to this entire strategy. Alternatively, a teacher may choose to extend the lesson beyond the class period. Students can be asked to write an essay about their solution to a dilemma. They could describe a similar dilemma and its resolution or question their peers or parents about how they would respond to the dilemma discussed in class. Students can also be assigned to find dilemmas in newspapers, television shows, textbooks, or other sources involving issues similar to the class dilemma. Finally, in succeeding weeks students can discuss other dilemmas that involve similar issues and compare their reasoning across all these dilemmas.

Figure 1 on the next page illustrates the basic elements of the strategy described here. The five activities listed down the center of the diagram in boxes represent what the teacher does. The activities listed at either side represent what students do as they engage in the core activities.

The strategy described here aims to point up the gap between an individual's stage of reasoning about moral problems and reasoning at the next higher stage. It attempts to force individuals to confront consciously the inadequacies of their present stages of reasoning so that they will become dissatisfied with them, recall other reasons that suggest more adequate solutions, and move toward the next higher stage of reasoning. In short, the approach creates cognitive dissonance and uses that dissonance to generate cognitive development.

Many variations of this basic strategy can be employed. For example, instead of asking students to identify a single course of action that should be taken, students can be asked to brainstorm courses of action that the central character could take. The class can then attempt to identify the possible consequences for each course of action. When these consequences have been listed and examined, students can choose the course of action they think should be taken, state their reasons for their choice, and launch a class discussion.

114 ♦ VALUES CONCEPTS AND TECHNIQUES

FIGURE I

A STRATEGY FOR GUIDING MORAL DISCUSSIONS

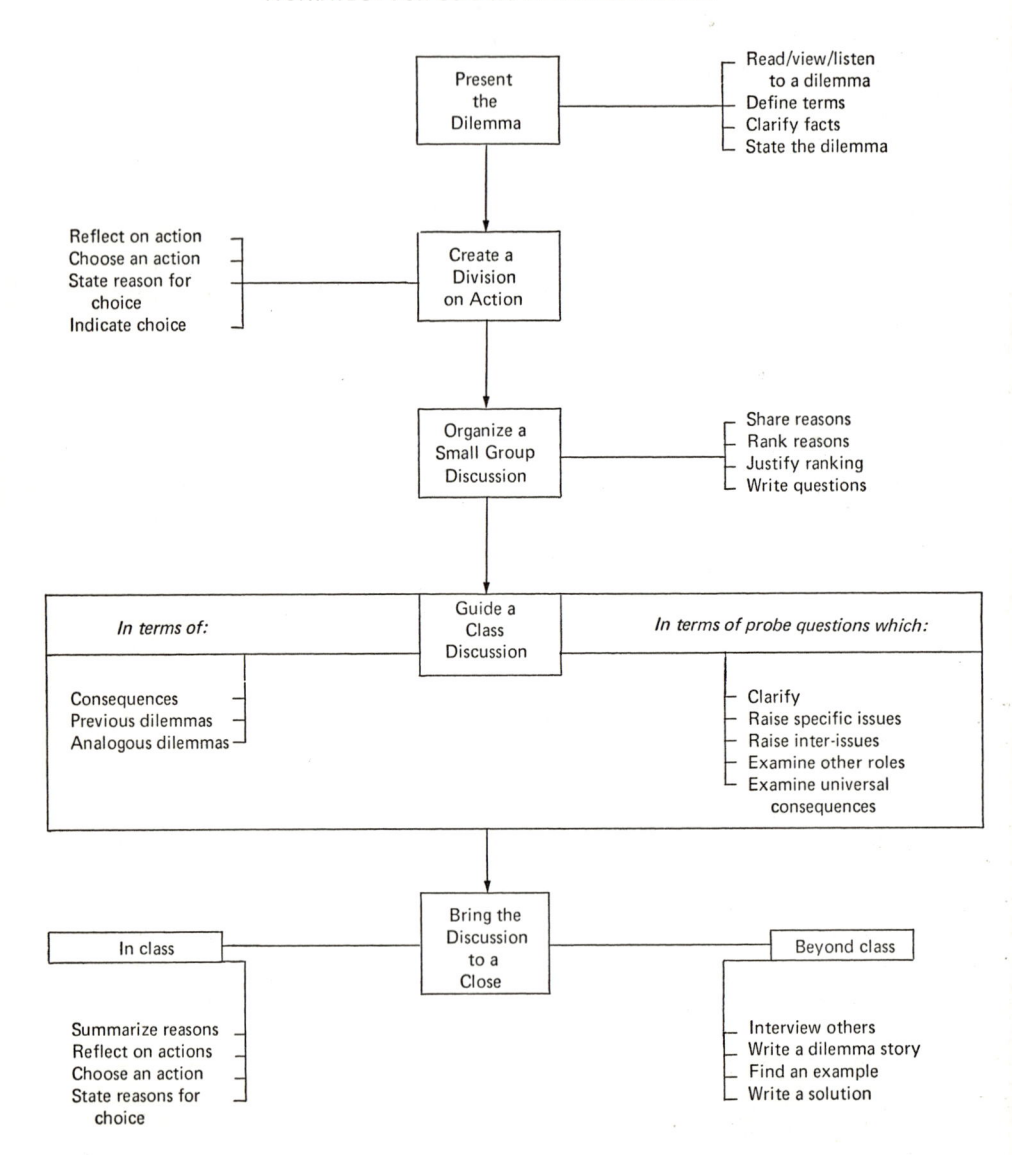

Present the Dilemma
- Read/view/listen to a dilemma
- Define terms
- Clarify facts
- State the dilemma

Create a Division on Action
- Reflect on action
- Choose an action
- State reason for choice
- Indicate choice

Organize a Small Group Discussion
- Share reasons
- Rank reasons
- Justify ranking
- Write questions

Guide a Class Discussion

In terms of:
- Consequences
- Previous dilemmas
- Analogous dilemmas

In terms of probe questions which:
- Clarify
- Raise specific issues
- Raise inter-issues
- Examine other roles
- Examine universal consequences

Bring the Discussion to a Close

In class
- Summarize reasons
- Reflect on actions
- Choose an action
- State reasons for choice

Beyond class
- Interview others
- Write a dilemma story
- Find an example
- Write a solution

Regardless of the specific techniques used in conducting a moral discussion, however, the processes of confronting a dilemma, taking a tentative position, and examining and reflecting on the reasoning behind various positions remain essential activities. Crucial, too, are the student-to-student interaction, the constant focus on moral issues and reasoning, and the emphasis on a supportive, trusting, informal classroom atmosphere. The extent to which the teacher can direct the entire process without assuming an expository or authoritarian role largely determines the success of a moral discussion.

Chances of success in using this strategy may be even further enhanced by being alert to some of its many nuances. For example, teachers need not devote an entire class period to every moral discussion. Students often tire of a discussion technique when it is used to excess. Varying the amount of time devoted to discussions can provide variety and heighten interest. Sometimes moral discussions arise spontaneously as part of a lesson whose major goals are acquisition of knowledge or the development of skills. In such cases moral dilemmas embedded in the content of a course can serve as take-off points for discussions of perhaps ten or fifteen minutes duration. A lesson about the underground railroad, for example, can lend itself to discussing the morality of breaking a law in order to help slaves. A teacher can introduce the issue orally and without elaborate preparation: "Do you think people were justified to break the law in order to help slaves escape?" The class as a whole can then discuss this issue without dividing into small groups, hearing reports, or carefully identifying best reasons.

Three developments may impede a discussion at the point where students are called upon to make a decision upon action in a dilemma. Sometimes all or most members of a class take the same position on a choice of action. When they do so, the teacher can pose an alternative to the original dilemma—a twist to the story that alters some of the circumstances without changing the characters involved or the central issues. For example, if an entire class agreed, in responding to Sharon's dilemma, that Sharon should not tell on Jill, the teacher could suggest this twist to the original story: "Suppose that earlier Jill had told their teacher that Sharon had cheated on an examination. What should Sharon do in this case?" Such alternatives prepared in advance for just this type of situation often generate an appropriate class division.

Three other options may also be used when a class fails to divide on an action. First, the class can be divided into groups with half the students being assigned to defend their original positions and the other half to defend the opposite position as they imagine those who might take such a position would argue. After each group picks its best reasons, the class can reconvene and proceed, using one of the class discussion formats outlined above. Or, without any disagreement about action, students can be divided into groups. Each group can then share and rank the reasons given for its position. These reasons can be listed on the board so that the class can discuss the top two or three reasons. Finally, if no division occurs it may be that the students fail to perceive a dilemma in the story. In this case, students can be asked "Why isn't this a dilemma? What would have to exist to make it a dilemma?" Most students are eager to respond to such questions and are quite frank in their replies and suggestions. Once students have responded, the teacher can note their suggestions for latter use in revising the dilemma and suggest that the conditions introduced by the students be assumed to exist in this case. The class can then proceed to a division and subsequent discussion.

A second obstacle to continuing a moral discussion sometimes arises when students refuse to take a position on a dilemma until they have more facts about it. For example, in discussing Sharon's dilemma, they may want to know how much the sweater which Jill stole was worth. Many students want to weigh the cost of the item stolen against the possible consequences of stealing it. Attempting to determine the value of the sweater, however, will divert attention from moral issues. To avoid this development, the teacher can ask students why they need this information. Why is stealing a valuable article worse than stealing one which costs little? In this way, a request for more data can be used to refocus a discussion on moral issues.

A third obstacle to a discussion sometimes appears when some students cannot make up their minds about an appropriate action in a dilemma. The teacher can group such undecided students together and give them an active role in the discussion. They can be asked to list the major reasons why they are undecided, and the subsequent class discussion can then be focused for a time on their report of these reasons. Undecided students can also serve as an audience for a debate between the pro and con groups who try to win them over to one set of reasons or another. Or undecided students can be encouraged to question individuals who have taken positions about the reasons they give to justify their actions.

Two final points remain. Guiding moral discussions successfully requires special efforts to avoid "putting students down."

There is often the temptation to interview students—that is, to interrogate a single student with a rapid-fire series of questions. This tendency should be avoided, for it tends to intimidate students and it gets in the way of student-to-student interaction. A second potentially threatening situation can occur when a teacher wishes to have certain students attend to stage-higher remarks. Here attention must be called to a particular statement without threatening the speaker. The extent to which a teacher can support a student in this situation will go far toward turning an exchange into a valuable learning experience.

Teachers need not be able to identify the stages of reasoning their students use in order to be able to lead moral discussions. Unless a class is extraordinarily homogeneous, it will usually contain students who think at at least two and often three stages. For example, most eleventh-grade students probably use Stage 3 thought predominately, but many will reason mainly at Stage 2 or Stage 4. Teachers who learn to encourage students to respond to each other can usually engage them in arguments at contiguous stages. With experience and with re-reading reports of Kohlberg's research, teachers eventually can become more skilled at identifying the stages at which their students reason. They can then use probe questions more skillfully and encourage student-to-student interaction with a higher probability of success.

The teaching plan which follows illustrates how the five basic activities comprising this strategy can be used to guide a moral discussion of Sharon's dilemma. Teachers can devise similar plans for any moral dilemma which they create.

Teaching Plan for Sharon's Dilemma

Part I—Presenting the Dilemma
Distribute the handout which describes Sharon's dilemma. Make sure that the students understand any difficult terms or phrases in the dilemma. Have the students clarify the facts of the situation. Have a volunteer state and explain the nature of the moral dilemma Sharon faces.

Part II—Dividing on Action
Ask the students to think for a moment about what they think Sharon should do. They should then write their recommendation and reason for their recommendation on a sheet of paper. Determine by a show of hands or in some other way how many students think Sharon should or should not tell her friend's

name to the security officer. Have a volunteer representing each position explain the reasons for their positions.

If the class fails to divide satisfactorily, use the following alternatives as appropriate:

If the members of the class agree that Sharon *should* tell:

1. Suppose Sharon knows that Jill is on parole and will be sent back to a reformatory if she is caught stealing. What should she do in that case?
2. Suppose that Jill has done Sharon many favors and that Sharon knows that she will lose many of her friends if she tells on Jill. What should she do in that case?

If the members of the class agree that Sharon *should not* tell:

1. Suppose that on a previous occasion, Jill had told their teacher that Sharon had cheated on an examination. What should Sharon do in that case?
2. Suppose that instead of being a friend, Jill was only an acquaintance whom Sharon knew casually. What should Sharon do in that case?

If the alternative dilemmas fail to provoke a division, have students role-play different sides of the dilemma or have them revise the dilemma and then take positions. Then have a volunteer representing each position explain the reasons for their positions.

Part III—Small Group Discussions

When the class divides with no less than one-quarter of the students on each side of the issue, organize a small group discussion in which students can share their reasons, choose those reasons they think are best for the position recommended, and decide why these reasons are their "best" reasons.

Part IV—Class Discussion

Reconvene the class in a large group. Have students from each small group report the group decisions or list their decisions on the board. Encourage students to discuss the merits of the reasons given by each group. Use some of the following probe questions where appropriate to focus the discussion:

1. What is a "best friend"?
2. Does Sharon have an obligation to Jill? the storeowner? the law? herself? Why or why not?
3. Which set of obligations, to Jill, to the storeowner, or to the law, are most important? Why?

4. From the point of view of Jill (of the storeowner, of Sharon's parents) should Sharon tell? Why or why not?
5. Is it ever right to tell on a friend? Why or why not?

Part V—Closing the Discussion

Have the students who feel that Sharon should tell summarize all the reasons given by those who argued that Sharon should not tell. Have the students who said Sharon should not tell summarize the reasons given by those who argued Sharon should tell. Then have the students think about what they have heard, choose again what they think Sharon should do, and write their choice and a reason for their choice on a piece of paper. Do *not* collect the papers.

In order to lead moral discussions, a teacher should be able to use the following curricular skills:

- identify suitable places in a course to conduct moral discussions
- locate appropriate, already-prepared moral dilemmas
- prepare new moral dilemmas
- use prepared lesson plans or write new lesson plans for moral discussions

A teacher should also be able to employ the following teaching skills:

- establish and maintain a supportive classroom atmosphere
- involve students in moral discussions
- ask questions which do not threaten students
- encourage student-to-student interaction
- identify and cope with substantive diversions

Many teachers lack some of these competencies. In order to acquire them, they need knowledge of Kohlberg's research findings and supervised practice in conducting moral discussions. Teachers can embark on a self-directed study of the research findings by consulting the relevant literature.[6] Programs of self-study will be doubly effective if several colleagues embark on them simultaneously and hold periodic discussions. Teachers can also begin to lead moral discussions using the techniques outlined in this article. Working with colleagues who agree to critique classes will increase the effectiveness of this learning process. But in addition to self-study, many teachers will benefit from assistance from experts in techniques of conducting moral discussions. This assistance is now available in two forms.

First, publishers are bringing out two teacher training programs. We have not yet seen either program in final form, so we cannot comment on them at firsthand. Each one, however, is being developed by people with extensive experience with the problems of applying Kohlberg's research to the classroom.[7] For maximum effectiveness, teachers should probably use these materials in groups in which they can discuss ideas and practice techniques, preferably with the leadership of a trained educator.

Second, in-service consultant help is available from educators who have worked extensively with the Kohlberg group. They offer three major types of in-service assistance. The first type presents a basic introduction and is primarily informational in nature. This introduction requires about three hours and consists of a demonstration moral discussion in which the teachers participate, an analysis of the teaching strategy, a presentation of the basic elements of Kohlberg's research findings, and an analysis of the place of moral discussions in a social studies program.

A second and more extensive in-service program requiring from six to twelve hours helps teachers learn more about moral discussion techniques and should precede a decision about whether or not to make a major effort to inaugurate a program of moral discussions in a school system. The first three hours parallel the shorter introductory program described above. The program can also include a detailed study of teaching skills through the analysis of a videotaped class, demonstrations of moral discussions using local students, the presentation and analysis of alternative teaching strategies, an introduction to writing original moral dilemmas, and an analysis of appropriate classroom observation techniques.

Schools that wish to make a program of moral discussions an integral part of a curriculum require an even more intensive teacher preparation program. It might begin with a six or twelve hour workshop such as the one described above. But it also requires on-going activities with a specialist extending over a period of at least a year. These activities should include workshops directed to specific objectives such as writing original moral dilemmas, evaluating moral discussions through interaction analysis, analyzing videotaped lessons, conducting moral interviews, or studying additional research findings. Such a program, combining study with immediate application to the classroom, can help to bring about the changes in teacher behavior upon which a successful program of moral discussions depends.

THE DEVELOPMENTALISTS' APPROACH TO ALTERNATIVE SCHOOLING

Peter Scharf, *Assistant Professor of Social Ecology, University of California, Irvine.*

Democratic socialization in school has been assigned primarily to the social studies. While there have been notable, effective classroom efforts to teach the logic of constitutional democracy, they have not had significant effect in producing citizens who can grapple with the problems of democratic life.[1] Even in expertly taught courses, students often emerge with an abstract understanding of democracy. Students may understand the names, titles, and underlying ideas of democratic institutions, but they usually acquire little feel for democracy's power or potential abuses.

As a possible way to remedy this gap between the requirements of democratic society and its educational institutions, three democratic school projects were initiated, each using Kohlberg's theory of moral education as its ideological and psychological base. Each of his stages* offers a more comprehensive notion of society and its relationship to individual rights.

At Stage 1 there is an orientation towards punishment and obedience. Law is conceived as the force of the powerful to which the weaker submit. At Stage 2, right action becomes that which satisfies one's own needs. Law is conceived of in terms of the rules of expedience or a naive rational hedonism. Stage 3 offers what we

---
*See "Definition of Moral Stages" on p. 20.

call the good boy/good girl orientation. Law becomes associated with collective opinion. One obeys the law because that is what others expect. At Stage 4 there is a shift towards fixed definitions of law and social duty. The law is justified in terms of its order-maintaining function. "Without law, the entire fabric of society would crumble." Stage 5 is a legalistic-contract orientation. Law becomes the agreed-upon contract among social equals with duties of state and individual clearly defined and regulated. At Stage 6 Kohlberg argues that there is a rational basis for ethical decision-making. Here, the law is a repository for broader social principles and is subordinate to justice when the two conflict.

The rate and extent of development are closely linked to the institutions with which one comes into contact. Broadly speaking, social institutions encouraging social role-taking and productive moral dialogue are associated with rapid and complete moral development. In terms of reasoning about specific legal issues, important experiences are with what Kohlberg calls the secondary institutions of society, e.g., law, economy, education, etc.

It has long been established that participation in democratically organized institutions is associated with rapid social development. Charles Cooley and George Mead have both suggested that democratic groups offer possibilities for interdependence and mutual sharing not found in authoritarian groups.[2] Kurt Lewin suggests likewise that ideological change occurs more rapidly in democratic groups allowing for a shared sense of control and for opportunities for dissent.[3] Chris Argyris similarly observes that democratic groups facilitate more mature ego structures than do coercive organizations.[4]

In addition, Kohlberg argues that individuals placed in "an institution-maintaining perspective" tend to develop more rapidly than do individuals in an obedience perspective. Thus he observes that gang-leaders show higher stage thinking than do gang-followers.[5] Similarly, in traditional schools, student leaders show higher stage thinking than do regular students. As well, preliminary evidence from Kibbutz youth indicates that the collective-democratic structure of the Kibbutz youth-group stimulates adolescents towards principled thought more rapidly than do the best American suburban educational environments.[6]

Three democratic schools have adopted somewhat similar orientations. In the Cambridge, Massachusetts, Cluster School, the Brookline, Massachusetts, School Within a School, (SWS), and the Irvine, California, SELF School, there is a common effort to turn over as many issues as possible to the student community. The schools hold a weekly or twice-weekly community meeting where major issues are posed, debated, and resolved. Each school has oriented its curriculum to include intensive offerings on political problems and dilemmas. Finally, in all three schools there is a conscious effort to pose dilemmas, occuring within the school, as moral, as opposed to simply practical issues. Thus a pot-smoking offense is dealt with as a conflict between community and individual rights, rather than an issue of school law and order.

The schools differ in several respects, though. The Cambridge and Brookline projects contain roughly 70 students each and exist as sub-units of larger high schools. The SELF School has nearly 250 students and is housed in a warehouse apart from the main high school. Both the Cluster School and the School Within a School use a direct democracy format with almost all issues raised before the entire student body. The SELF School operates as a representative democracy with students being elected at-large to what is called the Rep Council.

During the first year of operation, some surprisingly similar issues emerged in each of the three schools; the issue of drugs became an immediate concern in each school. The three programs established drug rules and enforced them. Problems of "AWOL's," "Skips," and "hooks" were similarly met by students' formulating appropriate attendance standards and penalties. As the three schools prepared for a second year, admissions procedures became a critical question in the democratic alternative. In the Cluster School, the student town meeting voted to accept 16 Black students to balance the school racially. The California SELF School decided to randomize admissions. The Brookline School Within a School voted for students to interview their incoming peers.

To illustrate this process of democratic decision-making, let me offer an example from a recent meeting at the Brookline SWS project. The students in the school had come to feel that staff were plotting town meeting strategies at their weekly staff meeting and were better prepared than were the students. They demanded to have students present at staff meetings. In the following conversation, Barb and Bill are the teachers:

   Ellie: I really know that you (teachers) are not doing anything bad in there to us, but I feel that we should be able to come to your meetings.

   Tom: That's right. SWS is supposed to be a family. When you are in your house, you can go wherever you please. Why not here?

> Betsey: I agree with Tom; but in a family, parents have a right to meet together sometimes. Like, let's say they are talking about paying the bills, or a vacation; can't they meet by themselves before they present it to the kids?
>
> Peter (Consultant): I hear two models here. One, a family model, the other, a power model. Do you really think the teachers and students are like a family, or do they really have different interests?
>
> Barb: I feel there isn't really an issue. In 90% of our meetings we just talk about "dippity-do." It isn't worth coming to, especially at eight in the morning.
>
> Sue: We can get up. As to Peter's question, I think they have their needs; we have ours. It's not that we don't trust them, though.
>
> Bill: How about if the students find a time in the day to plot about (teacher) community meetings. Then they will be prepared, too.
>
> Leslie: But you have "A-block" reserved: When could all the students meet?
>
> Betsey: I still think we don't have a right to come. They should be able to meet without us.
>
> Bill: I don't know about all this. We have a bunch of things that don't concern you. Don't private groups have a right to meet privately?
>
> The group eventually voted, by a small margin, to allow teachers to meet privately.

The key to the town meetings is that conflicts are dealt with explicitly as moral conflicts. The issue of staff privacy is a good moral issue for Stage 3 and Stage 4 students. The Stage 3 position that Tom offers (SWS is a family and kids/students can go wherever they please in the house/school) conflicts with Betsey's stage 4 notion that the parents and teachers have a special privilege to meet privately. This type of debate might be expected to produce moral change if conducted seriously and continually.

These efforts in democratic education may be contrasted with both traditional comprehensive high schools as well as with alternative schools with laissez-faire ideologies. In traditional high schools there is little role or encouragement for most students to become involved in important school policy decisions. While there might be a student council, important decisions are made by administrators often with little faculty or student involvement. As well, a rotating schedule (i.e., first period: Math; second period: Social Studies; etc.) mitigates against the creation of even the most superficial forms of school community.

Alternative education in the past 10 years has made some inroads into the hegemony of the traditional comprehensive school. As Charles Silberman observes, most alternatives are based on the "open-classroom" model with an ideology of free-choice and individualized instruction.[7] Reacting to what is seen as the lockstep of the traditional high school, students are offered opportunities, often free from formal evaluation by teachers or peers, to choose learning activities.

This laissez-faire model differs from the democratic approach represented by the SELF, SWS, and Cluster experiments. In most laissez-faire schools students are given a choice of attendance. It is assumed that if attendance is not required, then students will gradually choose to attend school and will perform out of intrinsic interest, rather than from a fear of being punished or downgraded.

This contrasts with the approach used at SELF, SWS, and Cluster schools where the issue of attendance is seen as a conflict between group and individual to be resolved by the student-teacher community. In the democratic alternatives, for example, students agree to a contract requiring attendance. This is enforced by the Rep Council or Discipline Committee. Similarly, democratic schools emphasize group projects and learning activities. This contrasts with the free-choice learning contracts found in most open alternatives. Finally, in most laissez-faire alternatives, teachers are loathe to act as disciplinarians. In contrast, in democratic alternatives, discipline is removed from the unilateral hands of the faculty and is transferred to the student-faculty community. In this new form, it is seen as a positive educational and social issue for group debate.

Initial research has focused on student perceptions of the justice of decision-making in the new democratic alternatives. It has been assumed by Kohlberg that school environments perceived as just will tend to encourage optimum moral development. This assumption (clearly critical in the approach) is now being carefully researched in a study being conducted by members of the Center for Moral Education at Harvard University.[8] This research program will measure the degree to which moral change among students correlates with independent measures of school moral atmosphere.

As an initial step to understand the relationship between school moral atmosphere and moral change, we decided to compare student perceptions of democratic, traditional, and laissez-faire schools. The author interviewed 12 students (selected randomly) in the SELF School, in a traditional school in a nearby school district, and in a self-defined open, laissez-faire, alternative school in a nearby Orange County school district. The traditional school was selected as it appeared quite typical of small (1,000 students), comprehensive schools. The laissez-faire school was selected as seemingly typical of open, free-choice schools in the area, and because teachers appeared content with the definition of their approach of emphasizing the laissez-faire ideology.

A new method of scoring environmental perceptions, called the Moral Atmosphere Scoring System (M.A.S.S.), was developed by the author of this study. The instrument involves an hour-long interview probing student perceptions of program goals, rules, student and teacher roles. Fixed criteria were developed for each aspect of moral atmosphere to determine if the student accepts, rejects, or is ambivalent towards a particular aspect of moral atmosphere. This represents our first effort to describe and evaluate perceptions of school climates in developmental categories. A similar system had been piloted in our work in a Connecticut prison where we were able empirically to relate shifts in prison atmospheres to innate moral change.[9]

Trained interviewers were used in gathering the data for the study. The interviewers were University of California (Irvine) students with no affiliation with the experimental project. Interviews were hand-written, and trained scorers, who scored each interview without knowledge of the interviewee, analyzed them. An interjudge reliability of .85 was achieved among Moral Atmosphere raters. Qualitative analysis was conducted after ratings were established.

Clear qualitative differences were found in the perceptions of "rules and authority" in the three schools. The SELF school's democracy was accepted by most of the students interviewed in the school, and almost all of the students (10 out of 12) perceived themselves as being authors of the school rules. One student offered:

> We made the rules in here. Jack (the school manager) made suggestions, but we agreed, and we proposed our own. It was a group thing. That's what the first two monthly meetings were about, making rules, like the pot rule.

The student believed that the rules were generally necessary. One student commented that, "You need these rules for the school to survive." Another suggested, "that though some rules conflict, they are genuinely needed." Where the students were critical of the SELF rules structure it was because either "we should enforce the rules stricter" or because "Some kids in here don't understand the rules yet." Overall, the SELF students feel a high degree of ownership of both school and rules. Students were surprisingly critical of both themselves and others for failing in the school. For example, one student commented:

> Things get screwed up, but we can go to the town meeting and propose things.... If other kids agree then the Rep Council does something it can change. The problem is not that many kids really care.... It's just a few in here, but that could change if kids could be changed.

The traditional school perceptions revealed a great perceived distance from the rule-makers and students. Of twelve students, eight perceived the school-board as making school rules. Two students suggested the "teachers made them." The two remaining students felt that the principal created the rules.

The rules were generally seen as arbitrary:

> Like the late pass thing. It's just a thing for the convenience of the school secretary. Even if you got an important thing it's, "Go get a late pass."

The students usually blamed the principal, or the personalities of the teachers, for failings in the rules. A few students (4 out of 12) thought that the principal was generally fair in his decisions: "Mr. X usually is fair to you. He listens and then makes a decision. He doesn't yell or nothing." The most striking difference between the democratic and traditional school perceptions was the lack of sense of control students perceived in changing school rules. One student perceived that "it was up to the principal." Another suggested simply that "the school's rules don't change."

The laissez-faire school's rules presented a somewhat ambiguous portrait. Most (8 out of 12) students perceived the student body as making rules. An equal number, however, perceived rules as totally inadequate. One student suggested, "They're too lenient and not enforced." Another, when asked if they are fair, said,

"Generally, they are fair towards the students but not fair towards [this school]." Another offered:

> No, the rules aren't strict enough. People get away with too much in here. It kind of sets a contempt for the rules since people know they aren't going to have any consequences... they should have mandatory attendance... it would be neat if people did things with other people besides their friends.

Strangely enough (or predictably enough) the laissez-faire school was characterized by a high degree of perceived helplessness in terms of the student's ability to change the rules. One student characteristically offered:

> You got to do something. If they had some rules then people would at least get something done.... If they made classes mandatory, kids would feel like they belonged to something...but it probably won't change. No organization....

The few students who approved of the rules, as they existed, offered justifications much like those articulated by the teachers. One student commented:

> No rules are good rules. People should be self-disciplined and regulated. The people who participated in the rule-making think they are fair. Those that didn't participate are now bitching.

Summary coding of evaluation of fairness indicated there were significant differences among the three schools. A chi-square test indicated that the distribution of rating was significant at the .01 level.

These differences should be understood as merely preliminary indications that students actively evaluate settings in terms of their perceived justice. The more critical test is the link between these perceptions of moral atmosphere and the development of moral thinking. This we noted is our current research problem.

Student Rules Perception

Type of school	Accepts	Ambivalent	Rejects
Democratic (self)	10 (83%)	1 (8%)	1 (8%)
Traditional school	2 (17%)	4 (33%)	6 (50%)
Laissez-faire alternative	5 (42%)	3 (25%)	4 (33%)

The just community ideal represents, in my view, the most significant application of moral development theory to education. It suggests that while classroom discussions may affect the adolescent's ethical understanding, such efforts may be ineffective in creating a citizenry capable of grappling with the tasks of constitutional society. Critical to this effort is a conceptualization of the school's moral climate. While we have made preliminary steps to evaluate settings in terms of student perceptions of justice, we will need to make conceptual and methodological progress before we can genuinely categorize school moral atmospheres and meaningfully link them to changes in ethical reasoning.

HUMANIZING THROUGH VALUE CLARIFICATION

Mary M. Yanker, *Chairperson, Division of Social and Behavioral Science, Aurora College, Aurora, Illinois.*

As teachers search for ways to humanize their classrooms, a focus to be considered should be value clarification. To be more fully functioning humans, students of all ages need help in understanding and developing their own value systems. If this is to occur, more humane learning environments must be created. Value clarification is one tool that may be used to achieve both these goals.

Alvin Toffler has made us all more aware of the tremendous value bombardment we face in living in our world of future shock. He alerts us to the many concurrent revolutions in our society—sexual, racial, economic, generational and technological. Each of these revolutions pulls us in new value directions with unchartered courses. How different is the world of present-day students from the one their parents knew as adolescents? Of course, previous generations had value problems, but if one were looking for stability, there was some refuge of legitimacy—home, church, school or country. Our current American scene has left many with little faith in such institutions, and, indeed, today's students cannot remember a period when any of these institutions was not under attack. Often students find the values expressed in each of these important elements of their daily existence in conflict with each other. They will also find value diversity among various peer groups.

The school's answer to their multiplicity of values has too

often been to ignore the value dilemma faced by students. Is it any wonder that many students find that school has little relevance? Even when school personnel have sensed the problem, they have often felt confused and helpless when searching for solutions. After all, would they not offend some segment of the school population by taking a value stand in any given direction? Teachers themselves are not a homogeneous group with regard to "which values to teach," and thus the student finds himself with little consistent help in developing a set of values by which to live.

Social psychologists underscore the importance of developing a firm set of values since they see our values as the prime determinant of our behavior. To be fully "in charge" each individual needs to know these determinants of behavior and since the external world offers few consistent models, each needs to look at other sources, namely internal sources. The role of the teacher becomes one of helping students discover and clarify their own values rather than one of "teaching" a prescribed set of values.

A theory and a set of classroom techniques have been advanced to help teachers and students clarify their values. These value clarification theory and techniques were introduced in the mid-sixties by Sidney Simon, Merrill Harmin and Louis Raths. Simon and Harmin were graduate students of Raths and the two students found their teacher to be challenging to their own self-analysis and development, but always accepting and non-judgmental of their ideas. Recognizing their own growth with such a teacher, they tried to capture his teaching style in the book, *Values and Teaching*. Since that book, a number of other books have been published giving teachers practical tools for putting the Raths-Simon-Harmin theory into classroom practice.

Value clarification theory recognizes the multiplicity of values in American society. The theorists believe that when students are faced with conflicting sets of values, an individual value crisis may occur which could produce confusion, apathy, hostility or other negative results which are destructive to personal growth and the teaching-learning process. The basic theory focuses on seven processes of helping students toward developing and clarifying their own values. These seven processes are: choosing freely, choosing from alternatives, choosing after consideration of the consequences, prizing one's choice, publicly affirming these choices, acting on choices and incorporating these choices into a pattern of life. Classroom techniques for clarifying values have been developed to help students learn and use one or more of these seven processes. A popular technique, "Twenty-Things I Love to Do" can illustrate some of these processes.

In "Twenty-Things," the teacher asks students to list quickly twenty things they love (like) to do. After the listing, students are asked to categorize the list by using various symbols. The categories and accompanying symbols can include many ideas such as: $ for items that cost more than $3 to do, "A" for items usually done alone, "O" for items preferred with others, "M" for items that might be on Mother's List, "W" for items done this week, "N5" for items that would not have been on such a list five years ago or a circle around the five most important items. Then students are asked to complete the sentence, "I learned that I . . . ." This is followed by a class sharing of "I learned" statements and discussion about what the exercise helps people to discover about themselves: "Have I changed in the last few years?" "Do I need money to enjoy life?" "Am I similar to my parents?" "Am I really doing the things I most enjoy?" "What could I do to improve the quality of my life?" This technique involves giving students the chance to go through the valuing processes of choosing, prizing, and it even questions the acting aspect of their lives.

Teachers can adapt techniques such as "Twenty-Things" to add a new dimension in subject matter areas. For example, a home economics teacher may ask students to list all the foods they like to eat. Then the teacher has the students categorize the items into food groups and also uses personal categories, such as, "food that make me feel good." The writer uses this technique in a college curriculum class. The students list their fondest memories of high school. The categories include items from the list which were usually done with friends, those which would have been on the principal's list of school purposes and items which could be considered as part of the school's curriculum. The discussion which follows centers around the implications this "Learning" has for the potential teacher. The class usually discovers that few members list items which would be included as a part of the school's curriculum. Further discussions about curriculum theory take on a deeper significance after this personalized experience.

The numerous value clarification techniques can be personalized and/or made relevant in content areas for all students at all levels of instruction. But more important, the teacher that uses and creatively integrates these techniques into lesson plans discovers a way to humanize instruction. The techniques give the teacher a new method for approaching all instruction. The techniques require an open, accepting, non-judgmental, and caring attitude on the part of the teacher and a psychologically safe learning atmosphere for students. Teachers who initially find resistance among students in using the techniques, usually find, upon self-examination, that they are neglecting one of the above attitudinal ingredients. Continued use of the techniques not only makes the teacher more conscious of these important teacher-attitudes, but the techniques themselves help create a more humanistic classroom environment. The application of value techniques is a way of helping the teacher become more aware of himself in relationship with students and also builds this humanistic relationship. The teacher who continues to use the techniques discovers that they soon become "second nature" and it becomes automatic to plan for the value dimension in teaching content. The techniques become one means to the end of establishing a more personalized, humanistic style of teaching.

Through a funded values project, the writer has worked with public and parochial school teachers in helping them develop proficiency in incorporating value and practice into their classrooms. The feedback from these teachers illustrates the benefits for teachers and students.

> In every classroom situation and interpersonal relationship, the opportunity exists to raise questions concerning values. Programs like values education serve to make participants aware of these opportunities and suggests methods for taking advantage of every opportunity. The ultimate responsibility lies with each teacher and individual to convert this awareness into conscious practice on a continuing basis.

> The excitement that these values activities generate is just great! The students have thoroughly enjoyed every values activity that we have done. I feel that this is a very exciting program that is very rewarding and I truly hope that other teachers will see its value and initiate it into their curriculum also!

> The greatest thing that comes from values clarification is the responses I've gotten from the students when I've used the techniques. Students that rarely speak up in the regular classroom really shine here. The student that is sometimes a troublemaker responds in such a way that you can understand some of his problems.

> I feel that if students learn that they do not have to think and act like everyone else in the group and that this behavior is accepted by the group—later they will feel more confident about not going along with

the group if it means getting in trouble, trying drugs, for example. Peer pressure may not exert as strong an influence.

This year my rapport with students and their rapport with classmates is unusually strong, and I attribute this in large part to a kind of openness which value techniques helped to establish.

After working with value education, I feel there is a two-fold benefit for the students. First, there is their immediate reaction—delight, enthusiasm, and interest. Second, there is the beginning of a process of prizing, choosing, and acting which is just starting to grow, hopefully will continue to be nurtured, and finally will blossom forth in meaningful life values.

I want you to know how optimistic I am about the future of values education. The teachers who implement the program will benefit in two ways. For those to whom the philosophy and approach come rather naturally, values education will provide a well organized set of techniques which are readily accessible and easily used. For others, it will provide the background and structure within which the warm atmosphere most conducive to learning can be achieved.

Value clarification is not a panacea but it is one valid method for increasing opportunities for student and teacher introspection The teacher searching for such opportunities will wish to explore value education, and successful application will need to be evaluated by individual teachers through their own experience. Teachers interested in helping students develop a set of values to serve as guides of behavior and in helping students toward independence will wish to explore value theory and practice through value clarification techniques. At the same time the added benefits of a humanistic, personalized approach to teaching will be fostered.

VALUES CLARIFICATION vs. INDOCTRINATION

Sidney B. Simon, *Professor of Humanistic Education, University of Massachusetts, Amherst.*

Whatever happened to those good old words we once used when we talked of values? Remember how comfortable it was to say *inculcate?* It was a nice, clean, dignified, closely shaved word if there ever was one. Then there was the old standby, *to instill*—usually followed by "the democratic values of our society." Doesn't anyone instill anymore? And what about the word *foster?* In schools, not so very long ago, we used to "foster" all over the place. But nobody does that much anymore. What has happened to the old familiar jargon of value teaching?

What happened was the realization that all the inculcating, instilling, and fostering added up to indoctrination; and despite our best efforts at doing the indoctrinating, we've come to see that it just didn't take. Most of the people who experienced the inculcation, instillation, and fostering seem not the much better for it. They appear to play just as much hanky-panky with income taxes as anyone else and concerned letters-to-the-editor are not written by them in any greater profusion. They pollute and defoliate; move to the suburbs to escape integration; buy convertibles with vinyl tops that collapse in roll-over accidents; fail to wear seat belts; and commit all kinds of sins even while they are saying the very words that have been dutifully inculcated, instilled, and fostered in them. It is discouraging.

At this point, one might ask: "Is it all that bad?" "Aren't they also among the good people who go to the polls in November, read the current events weeklies, and pay their BankAmericard charges on time?" Yes, of course. But in these troubled, confused, and conflicted times, we need people who can do much more than that. We desperately need men and women who know who they are, who know what they want out of life, and who can name their names when controversy rages. We need people who know what is significant and what is trash, and who are not so vulnerable to demagoguery, blandness, or safety.

The indoctrination procedures of the past fail to help people grapple with all the confusion and conflict which abound in these baffling days. For example, in values clarification, we apply a strategy which is deceptively simple. We ask students to spend some time listing the brand names in their home medicine cabinets. Just think of your own medicine cabinet as you are sitting reading this. What's in it? How many creams, ointments, and salves have you been sold? Do you use a brand-name, buffered product instead of plain old aspirin? How did you get started on that? What about the spray cans? How many are in your aerosol arsenal? What did you use before the product you now spray? How did all those brand names get there? Who bought them? What was the motivating force? How did you learn what to value as seen in your medicine cabinet? As long as you have the door to your cabinet open, why don't you pull out the cosmetic tray? How vulnerable are you to avoiding the hysteria surrounding all of us about getting a wrinkle? Getting old has become such a negative value. Who are the people who fear it?

In place of indoctrination, my associates and I are substituting a process approach to the entire area of dealing with values in the schools, which focuses on the process of valuing, not on the transmission of the "right" set of values. We call this approach values clarification, and it is based on the premise that none of us has the "right" set of values to pass on to other people's children. Yes, there may be some things we can all agree upon, and I will grant you some absolutes, but when we begin to operationalize our values, make them show up in how we live our days and spend our nights, then we begin to see the enormous smugness of those people who profess they have the right values for others' children. The issues and hostility generated around hair length and dress and armbands are just the surface absurdity.

More dangerous is the incredible hypocrisy we generate when we live two-faced values and hustle the one right value to children.

Think about the hundreds of elementary school teachers who daily stop children from running down the halls. I close my eyes and I see them with their arms outstrectched, hands pressing against the chest of kids who put on their "brakes" in order to make the token slowdown until the teacher ducks into the teacher's room for a fast cigarette before all the kids get back to hear the cancer lecture. Think of those teachers preaching to children about the need to take turns and share. "We wait in lines, boys and girls, and we learn to share our crayons and paints in here. And, I don't want to see anybody in my class being a tattletale—except in cases of serious emergency, naturally." The words are all too familiar. I have used them in the old days. I have also seen myself cut into the cafeteria lunch line ahead of third graders. (Take turns? Well, not when we have so few minutes for lunch and always so much to do to get ready for afternoon classes.)

The alternative to indoctrination of values is not to do nothing. In this time of the anti-hero, our students need all the help we can give them if they are to make sense of the confusion and conflict inherited from the indoctrinated types. Moreover, we all need help in grappling with the chaos of the international scene, with the polarization of national life—not to mention the right-outside-the-door string of purely local dilemmas that confront us every day.

An approach to this problem is to help students learn a process for the clarification of their values, which is a far cry from indoctrination. The theory behind it can be found in *Values and Teaching* (Louis E. Raths, Merrill Harmin, and Sidney B. Simon, Columbus: Charles E. Merrill, 1966). In the remainder of this chapter, I will describe some of the strategies we are presently using to help students learn the process of values clarification and begin lifelong searches for the sets of personal values by which to steer their lives.[1]

Five Value-Clarifying Strategies and Their Use

Strategy 1—Things I Love to Do

Ask students (teacher does it with them) to number from 1-20 on a paper. Then suggest they list, as rapidly as they can, 20 things in life which they really, really love to do. Stress that the papers will not be collected and "corrected," and that there is no right answer about what people should like. It should be emphasized that in none of values strategies should students be forced to participate. Each has the right to pass. Students may get strangely quiet; and, at first, they may even be baffled by such an unschool-like task as this. Flow with it, and be certain to allow enough time to list what they really love to do. Remember, at no time must the individual's privacy be invaded, and that the right of an individual to pass is sacrosanct.

When everyone has listed his 20 items, the process of coding responses can be started. Here are some suggested codes which you might ask the students to use:

1. Place the $ sign by any item which costs more than $3, each time you do it.
2. Put an *R* in front of any item which involves some risk. The risk might be physical, intellectual, or emotional. (Which things in your own life that are things you love to do require some risk?)
3. Using the code letters *F* and *M*, record which of the items on your list you think your father and mother might have had on their lists if they had been asked to make them at your age.
4. Place either the letter *P* or the letter *A* before each item. The *P* to be used for items which you prefer doing with people, the *A* for items which you prefer doing alone. (Stress again that there is no right answer. It is important to just become aware of which are your preferences.)
5. Place a number *5* in front of any item which you think would not be on your list 5 years from now.
6. Finally go down through your list and place near each item the date when you did it last.

The discussion which follows this exercise argues more eloquently than almost anything else we can say for values clarification.

Strategy 2—I Learned That I. . . .

This strategy fits in with the one above. After students have listed and coded their 20 items, the teacher might say, "Look at your list as something which tells a lot about you at this time in your life. What did you learn about yourself as you were going through the strategy? Will you please complete one of these sentences and share with us some of the learning you did?"

>I learned that I. . . .
>I relearned that I. . . .
>I noticed that I. . . .
>I was surprised to see that I. . . .

I was disappointed that I. . . .
I was pleased that I. . . .
I realized that I. . . .

The teacher must be willing to make some "I learned that I. . . ." statements, too. And they must not be platitudinous, either. Every effort is made for the values-clarifying teacher to be as honest and as authentic as possible.

"I learned that I. . . ." statements can be used after almost any important value-clarifying strategy. It is a way of getting the student to own the process of the search for values. It should be clear how diametrically opposed "I learned that I. . . ." statements are from indoctrination, although it is possible to misuse this or any clarification strategy to get kids to give back the party line. On the other hand, using this strategy can begin to build that lifetime search for personal meaning into all of our experiences.

Strategy 3—Baker's Dozen

This is a very simple strategy which teaches us something about our personal priorities. The teacher asks each student to list 13, a baker's dozen, of his favorite items around the house which use PLUGS, that is, which require electricty.

When the students have made their lists, the teacher says, "Now, please draw a line through the three which you really could do without if there were suddenly to be a serious power shortage. It's not that you don't like them, but that you could, if you had to, live without them. O.K., now circle the three which really mean the most to you and which you would hold onto until the very end."

It should be clear that again there is no right answer as to what "good" people should draw lines through and circle. The main thing is for each of us to know what we want and to see it in the perspective of what we like less.

Strategy 4—"I Urge" Telegrams

The teacher obtains blank Western Union telegram blanks. Or simply has students head a piece of paper with the word Telegram. He then says, "Each of you should think of someone in your real life to whom you would send a telegram which begins with these words: I Urge You to. . . . Then finish the telegram and we'll hear some of them."

A great many values issues come out of this simple strategy. Consider some of these telegrams:

To my sister: "I urge you to get your head together and quit using drugs." Nancy. (All telegrams must be signed. It is our affirmation of the need to name your name and to stand up for what you believe in.)

To my Sunday School teacher: "I urge you to quit thinking that you are the only person to know what God wants." Signed, your student Rodney Phillips.

To my neighbor on the North Side: "I urge you to see that we have no other place to play ball and that you not call the cops so often." Signed, Billy Clark.

One of the things that students working with values clarification learn to do is to find out what they really want. "I urge telegrams" help do that. Just think of the people in your own lives to whom an "I urge telegram" needs to be sent. The second thing students working with values clarification learn to do is to find alternative ways of getting what they need and want. Take the case of Billy Clark's neighbor. The class spent some time brainstorming ways of approaching that neighbor. They talked about how to negotiate with a grouch, and how to try to offer alternatives in your drive to get what you want.

"I urge telegrams" are used several times during the semester. The students keep them on file and after they have done five or six, they are spread out on the desk and "I learned statements" made from the pattern of the messages carried by the telegrams.

Students also learn to use the "I urge you to. . . ." model to get messages across between student and student and between student and teacher.

An assignment I like to use, related to the "I urge telegram," is to have each student get a letter-to-the-editor published in a magazine or newspaper.

Strategy 5–Personal Coat of Arms

Each student is asked to draw a shield shape in preparation for making a personal coat of arms. The teacher could go into the historical significance of shields and coats of arms, but the exercise is designed to help us learn more about some of our most strongly held values and to learn the importance of publicly affirming what we believe, that is, literally wearing our values out front on our shields.

The coat of arms shield is divided into six sections (see Figure 1). The teacher makes it clear that words are to be used only in the sixth block. All the others are to contain pictures.

He stresses that it is not an art lesson. Only crude stick figures, etc., need be used. Then he tells what is to go in each of the six sections:

1. Draw two pictures. One to represent something you are very good at and one to show something you want to become good at.
2. Make a picture to show one of your values from which you would never budge. This is one about which you feel extremely strong, and which you might never give up.
3. Draw a picture to show a value by which your family lives. Make it one that everyone in your family would probably agree is one of their most important.
4. In this block, imagine that you could achieve anything you wanted, and that whatever you tried to do would be a success. What would you strive to do?

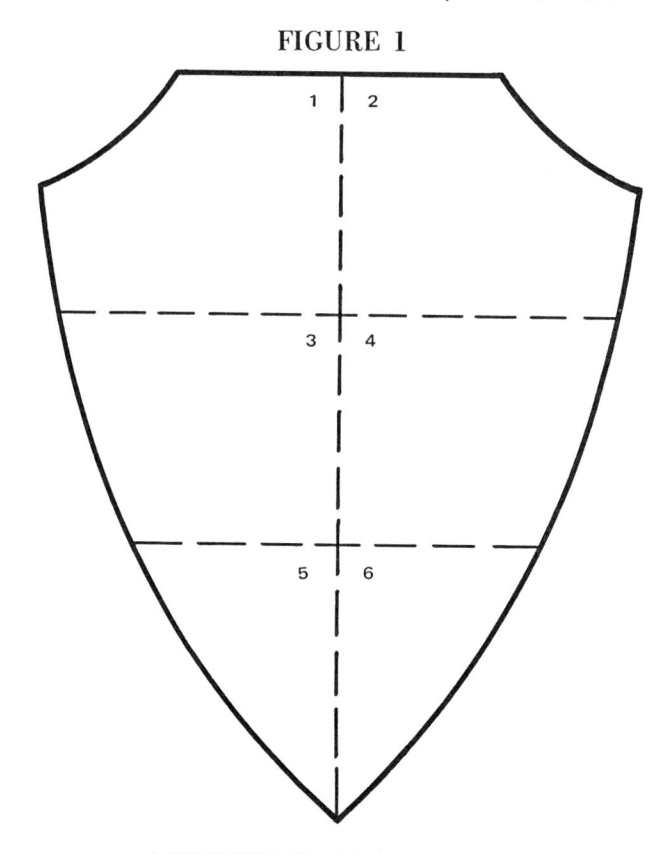

FIGURE 1

A PERSONAL COAT OF ARMS

5. Use this block to show one of the values you wished all men would believe, and certainly one in which you believe very deeply.
6. In the last block, you can use words. Use four words which you would like people to say about you behind your back.

The teacher can do several different things at this point. He can have the students share among themselves in little trios or quartets. He can also get the pictures hung up on the walls and get people to take each other on gallery tours to share the coats of arms. A game could be played which would involve trying to guess what the pictures represented. The class might try to make a group coat of arms to represent their living together in that classroom. In any case, the value expressions elicited in this nonverbal way are very exciting and lead to discussions which range far and wide. Incidentally, this strategy is a good one to use with parents to illustrate to them the power of the values-clarification methodology. It makes a meaningful exercise for an evening PTA meeting.

The Coat of Arms strategy illustrates quite well some things common to all of the values-clarification strategies. The teacher sets up an interesting way of eliciting some value responses. He establishes that there is no right answer. The strategy is open-ended and allows students to take the exploration to whatever level they want to take it. Finally, there is a chance to share with each other some of the alternatives that emerge from our searching. This whole process allows each student to focus on areas where he has some work yet to do in order to keep growing. The Coat of Arms can be done several times during the school year and the various shields compared and seen as measures of a student's search.

The five strategies used as illustrations of what values clarification is must raise some serious questions in the minds of readers who have more conventional views of what the social studies should be. For one thing, I have used no standard subject-matter content, there is no history, no geography, etc. Yet, if one thinks through what the outcomes of a course will be making use of the five strategies, he will see the student emerging with a deeper sense of who he is, what he wants, what is precious, and what is of most worth in his and others' lives. Has the social studies ever done more than that?

Values clarification demands that we take a new look at what we have been calling the social studies. I feel more and more strongly that the most severe problem facing all of us is how to get people to look at the lives they are leading. How can we get fathers and mothers to see that high college-entrance scores are not the end of a high school education? How can we get people to see that getting a high-paying job is not the final reward of a college degree? How can we get men and women to take on some larger share of their personal responsibility for the rampant racism in our nation? Or for allowing a senseless war to continue indefinitely? When will educators make a contribution towards helping people examine the headlong pursuit towards accumulating more and more material possessions and enjoying them less? Or what can we do about keeping our students from making drab and dreary marriages or being trapped into pointless jobs which they hate to go to each morning? It boils down to a concern for values, and yet we must not fall into the trap of believing that if only we could give boys and girls the right set of values to believe, they would avoid the mistakes of the rest of us. Nonsense!

Indoctrination is not the answer. The only thing that indoctrination did for people in the past was to help them postpone the time when they began the hard process of hammering out their own set of values. Values simply can't be given to anyone else. One can't value for other people. Each individual has to find his own values. One can memorize all the platitudes he wants, but when it comes to living and acting on the values, he needs to carve them out of carefully reflected experience. The skills necessary for doing this can be learned in values clarification.

Perhaps when the reader and author acknowledge how little help they received from their own education about making sense out of life, maybe then they will be willing to help other people's children learn the process, a lifetime process, of searching for a viable set of values to live by and perhaps even to die for.

The author is convinced that he can leave his own children no greater inheritance than the gift of knowing how to negotiate the lovely banquet of life ahead of them. That is indeed something of value.

VALUES CLARIFICATION: SOME THOUGHTS ON HOW TO GET STARTED

Joel Goodman, *Assistant Director, Program Development and Consultation Services, National Humanistic Education Center, Saratoga Springs, New York.*

The past decade has witnessed an incredible amount of growth and interest in the emerging field of values clarification. There has been a proliferation of books and workshops in this field throughout the country. Many people who have participated in workshops and who have read books often carry away a great deal of excitement and hope from such experiences. Unfortunately, the school environment does not always welcome this excitement and hope. Fellow teachers and administrators may feel threatened by new ideas, students may become puzzled by a new orientation, and you may become disheartened by the roadblocks you encounter. This article is designed to speak to some of the ethical and implementation issues you may face.[1]

Based on thousands of teachers' experiences, I offer the following guidelines on how to get started in values clarification. Of course, not all the ideas listed below will apply to your situation. In fact, this is the first guideline!

- Remember that values clarification is an ongoing process. Don't expect to flick a magic wand and obtain a panacea.

Copyright © 1976, Joel Goodman

- In the same light, be aware of others who expect values clarification to be a cure-all. This often manifests itself when they are disappointed that values clarification used in one health course didn't "cure" the school's "drug problem" in one semester. Values clarification is a preventive, proactive approach, not a reactive bandaid.
- Try to create a safe classroom environment, one in which students (and teacher) have a right to pass, one in which their statements are accepted. It is crucial that we respect others' space and privacy. Try to avoid moralizing, and imposing or deposing others' values. Attempt to expose your values whenever appropriate.
- Try to experience values clarification as much as possible yourself by reading and participating in workshops and in classroom activities with the students. It is important that you be willing to take the same kinds of risks which you ask your students to take. The more personal experience you have with values clarification, the easier it will be for you to make professional applications.
- Start by using values activities, clarifying responses, and/or third-level lessons with which you feel comfortable.[2] Be flexible. There is no one recipe for being a values clarification facilitator.
- Remember that values clarification can be fun, but that it is not for fun. Other people in your environment may not have this perspective. You may choose to communicate it to them in some way.[3]
- Diagnose the students' needs and interests. Build your activities and lessons to speak to them.[4] Later, call upon the students to help generate new strategies. Ultimately, it would be wonderful for the students to have an active part in developing their own emerging curriculum.
- Examine continually your role and values as a teacher. This is crucial both in terms of your personal growth and your professional development.[5]
- Focus your curriculum on the development of skills in these areas: (1) Cognitive—choosing freely (e.g., dealing with peer pressure), choosing from among alternatives, choosing with an awareness of the consequences of one's choices, being aware of patterns in one's life, thinking critically (analyzing, synthesizing, drawing inferences), thinking divergently. (2) Affective—identifying and acknowledging feelings as one data source

in making decisions, legitimizing one's intuition as another possible data source, focusing on what one prizes and cherishes. (3) Active—acting on one's choices (moving from insight to behavioral change), goal-setting, achievement motivation, culling out the inconsistencies between what one would like to do and what one is likely to do. (4) Interpersonal—publicly affirming one's choices where appropriate, sending "I" messages, empathic listening, resolving conflict situations, asking clarifying questions, community-building (building on commonalities, respective differences), validating (focusing on the positive in self and others, avoiding killer phrases). In this way, the activities, clarifying responses, and third-level lessons will be given direction and purpose. In fact, many teachers use the skills to delineate their curriculum objectives.

- Beware of the effects of grades and what Sid Simon calls "the red pencil mentality."[6] Avoid grading students on their values.
- Start with lower risk activities. Provide opportunities for differing levels of risk. Alternate the arenas in which participation occurs, e.g., individual reflection, journal writing, small group sharing, large group discussion.
- Be ready to discuss what values clarification is not, since people often have some strong and misguided understandings. For instance, values clarification is not: (1) Sensitivity training (values clarification has safety guidelines in its process—e.g., the right to pass). (2) Therapy (although it may be therapeutic in a sense). (3) A bunch of gimmicks, fun and games (again, it may be fun, but it is not for fun—it seeks to help people develop the skills mentioned above). (4) Behavior modification (in fact, values clarification is at the other end of the continuum—it seeks to help people internalize the locus of decision-making). (5) Space-killer, time-killer (it is not to be used only to fill in the five minutes before the bell rings or to be used on the day before vacation because "the students won't do anything else").
- Establish the norm of unfinished business in the classroom: there may be times when students feel like they have not completed their reflection or sharing around a particular values issue. You may want to suggest that

they take responsibility for themselves and identify a time, place, and way in which they would like to bring closure, e.g., outside of class or in class the next day.
- Encourage students to keep an ongoing class journal which is private. This can help them (and you, if they choose to share it with you) inventory their growth over time and note the cumulative effects of the values clarification approach.
- Solicit feedback and encourage feedforward from students. Students can be of vital support to you in evaluating values clarification and in prescribing what next steps to take in the classroom.[7]
- Initially, you may find security in drawing from the multitude of structured values clarification activities, but try to wean yourself away from them. Develop your own activities, move toward spontaneity, and avoid falling into the humanistic technician trap of "cranking" students through exercises.
- Stay awake to the danger of the "100 Things I Love to Do" syndrome. This often occurs when more than one teacher in the building is involved with values clarification. What happens is that during the first period, students in English class do the inventory "20 Things I Love to Do in Life." When second period rolls around, the social studies teacher hits them with the same inventory. And so on through the five periods of the school day. It is important for teachers to talk with one another (intra- as well as inter-departmentally) and to develop short-range and long-range goals for integrating values clarification in the classroom.
- Related to this it is so crucial that teachers be sensitive to the needs and readiness of students. What may work in one class might fall flat in another. Stay tuned to your students.
- Seek support from colleagues and friends. Many people realize the value of support and have moved on to formalizing support systems for themselves.[8]

VALUE DECISIONS AND THE ACCEPTABILITY OF VALUE PRINCIPLES

W. Keith Evans and Terry P. Applegate, *Bureau of Educational Research, University of Utah,* and *Research and Development Consultants, Inc., Salt Lake City, Utah.*

Value questions in the social studies, in our personal lives, and elsewhere are unavoidable. The question is not whether educators and other individuals will address values questions, but how they will address them. The question of how to teach students to handle value questions is itself one of the most important value questions facing educators today. Alternative ways are available. An educator can teach students particular answers to particular value questions, or an educator can teach answers to particular value questions but give the students reasons for the answers. The approach we take is neither of the above.

Our approach has its conceptual roots in the 1971 NCSS Yearbook[1] and its practical roots in the work done over the past four years in high schools.[2] The approach can be characterized as a process approach. Instead of teaching students particular answers to particular value questions, we teach students a process whereby they can arrive at their own answers to make their own value decisions. Our process is based on making sure that students meet four standards of rationality whenever they are attempting to make a value decision. The closer the student comes to meeting

---

Copyright © 1976, W. Keith Evans and Terry P. Applegate

these four standards of rationality when making a value decision, the more rational will be that decision. The further away one gets from meeting the four standards of rationality when making a value decision, the less rational will be that decision. The four standards of rationality are:
1. A wide range of factual claims should be considered before making a value decision.
2. The factual claims must be true or well-confirmed by evidence.
3. The factual claims must be genuinely relevant (have valence) to the person making the value decision.
4. The value principle implied by the value decision and the reasons for the value decision must be acceptable to the person making the value decision.

We have developed materials[3] in the form of programmed units and handouts which give students ways of meeting these four standards of rationality when making a value decision and have tested these materials in high school classrooms.[4] In general, the results show that students trained in using our materials score significantly higher than control classes on measures of values reasoning and intelligent question-asking.

Making Rational Value Decisions

Our step-by-step procedure for making a rational value decision is as follows:

Step 1. Make sure students clarify important terms in the value question. For example, in the value question, "What is the best way to stop inflation?" the terms "stop" and "inflation" should be defined. Does "inflation" mean an increase in the consumer price index above a certain level, or what? Does "stop" mean reduce to zero, or what? In order to go on to the next steps, these crucial terms in the value question should be defined so that everyone knows what they mean. Sometimes, after attempting to define crucial terms in a value question, the value question is best rephrased. Instead of using the term "stop," the term "reduce" might be more appropriate. The purpose of this first step is that the students understand as clearly as possible the meaning of crucial terms in the value question.

Step 2. Make sure students consider a wide range of factual information (standard of rationality no. 1). This means making sure that the students consider both the pros and the cons of the issue as well as a number of areas of concern. There are usually many. Some of the more common areas of concern are: the health and safety aspect, the religious aspect, the moral aspect, the legal aspect, the personal aspect, the social aspect, and the political aspect. If the students consider many aspects of the value issue, including the pros and cons, then they are more likely to base their value decision on a wide range of factual claims.

Step 3. Make sure students have qualified, unbiased sources to back up their factual claims (standard of rationality no. 2). Many considerations are involved in determining the validity of sources. First of all, the person making a factual claim should be qualified in a field relevant to the content of the factual claim. We normally want to hear from an expert chemist when facts about chemistry are being discussed and not, say, an expert in art crticism. In addition, we want to watch out for possible bias. If a person has something to gain by making a statement, then that statement might be suspect even though the person is highly qualified. A statement becomes more acceptable, of course, when many qualified and unbiased persons agree on it and few, if any, disagree. We should keep in mind, however, that expert testimony can be wrong and often is.

Step 4. Make sure that each factual claim that a student uses to make a decision has valence for the student (standard of rationality no. 3). The student should be able to assign either a positive or negative valence to every factual claim used in deciding a value question. Suppose that someone were trying to answer the value question, "Is capital punishment desirable?" and looked at the following array of factual claims:
1. Capital punishment is a deterrent to crimes like murder and kidnapping.
2. Capital punishment can execute an innocent person.
3. Capital punishment was introduced into America through English law.

Usually, people think of number one as having positive valence and number two as having negative valence. Number one, by itself, would probably lead most people to a value decision of "desirable" and number two, by itself, a value decision of "undesirable." But what about number three? When trying to decide whether capital punishment is desirable, what valence would this have? Would number three, by itself, lead one to a decision of "desirable"? Would it lead one to a decision of "undesirable?" Probably neither. If a factual claim, by itself, does not lead to either a positive or a negative value decision, then it is probably not relevant to the value decision.

Step 5. Make a tentative value decision based on the first four steps above. The decision should be made on the basis of weighing a wide range of well-confirmed, relevant facts.

Step 6. Make sure the value principle, as implied by the value decision and the reasons to support it, is acceptable. To test the value principle, one should write a value principle which incorporates both the value decision and the reasons used to support the value decision and then test this value principle to determine whether it is consistent with one's other values.

First, of course, one has to be able to write a value principle. Let's look at an example:

Value Decision		Reason
Legalization of abortion is intolerable	because	it involves taking a human life.

The value principle implied by the value decision and the reason for it is: Things that involve taking human life are intolerable. This value principle is constructed from the person's own value decision and the reason given for making that value decision. The person, therefore, is committed to this value principle.[5]

Let's look at another example:

Value Decision		Reason
Capital punishment is desirable	because	it is a deterrent to crimes like murder and kidnapping.

In the following space try to write a value principle based on the above value decision and its reason:

_____

_____

How did you do? Let's see. Your value principle should look something like this: Things that are a deterrent to crime like murder and kidnapping are desirable. If you don't quite get the idea, try some more. Make up your own value decision and reason, and then try to write a principle.

Once you have written a value principle, the acceptability of the value principle can be tested in a number of ways. We have used two tests of principle acceptability: New Cases Test and Subsumption Test.

New Cases Test

In brief, the New Cases Test involves determining which other value issues the value principle can be applied to and then determining if the same value decision would have been made. There are five steps:

Step 1. Write a value principle. Let's look back at the value principle we wrote for legalizing abortion: Things that involve taking human life are intolerable.

Step 2. Think of other values issues (new cases) the value principle can be applied to. Once we think about it, there are a host of other things that involve taking human life. Some are: particular wars, capital punishment, mercy killing, defending ourselves from attack by others, murder, suicide, and so on.

Step 3. Determine whether there are inconsistencies in value decisions which fall under the same value principle. In order to be consistent, we would have to evaluate as intolerable all of these ways of taking life because they all fall under the value principle. The value principle is consistent with value decisions, such as, murder is intolerable, suicide is intolerable, or mercy killing is intolerable but is inconsistent with others. As written most people would have to reject the value principle because it would lead them to some inconsistent value decisions. In rejecting the value principle, it is necessary, then, to reject the original value decision on abortion. The following are examples of inconsistencies which might occur: A lot of people believe that legalization of abortion is intolerable but that capital punishment is desirable. In addition, many people believe it is right to defend oneself from attack even if it involves killing another person, but that legalization of abortion is intolerable. However, before we reject the value principle and the value decision, we must make sure that these new cases are really the same as abortion. Is capital punishment really the same as abortion? There is at least one significant difference. Abortion involves taking an innocent human life while capital punishment, we hope, does not.

Step 4. Determine whether the value principle can be qualified so as to do away with inconsistencies. Recognizing this distinction of an "innocent" life, if we alter our value principle to be: Things that involve taking innocent human life are intolerable, then the value principle would apply to abortion but not to capital punishment. We could similarly alter our value principle to exclude self-defense: Things that involve taking innocent human life with the exception of self-defense are intolerable. We should continue this process of qualifying our value principle until it reflects what we really believe.

Step 5. If you cannot do away with the inconsistencies, you should reject or at least seriously question the acceptability of both the value principle and the original value decision. In the process of testing the acceptability of the value principle related to abortion, we have been involved in clarifying that part of our value system related to taking human life. Testing the acceptability of our value principle could only take place after clarifying our values in relation to taking human life.

Subsumption Test

The Subsumption Test involves determining whether the value principle can be justified by other value principles that we can accept. The following example is taken from an actual classroom experience:

Value Decision		Reason
Abortion is wrong	because	it causes the destruction of a human soul.

Step 1. Write a value principle based on your value decision and the reason for your decision. The value principle for the above value decision is: Things that cause the destruction of the human soul are wrong.

Step 2. Give a reason why you believe the value principle.

Step 3. Write a second value principle based on the original value principle and the reason why you believe the original value principle. For example:

Value Principle		Reason
Things that cause the destruction of a human soul are wrong	because	it goes against what the Pope says to do.

The second value principle is: Things that go against what the Pope says to do are wrong. You will notice that exactly the same procedure is used for writing the second value principle as for writing the original one. The only difference is that the second value principle is based on a more general value principle rather than on a specific value decision.

Step 4. Determine whether you can accept the second value principle. If you cannot, then you must reject or at least seriously question the original value principle and the value decision which is subsumed under it. If you can accept the second value principle, then you can continue the Subsumption Testing process.

As you might have guessed, what you do next is to give a reason why you believe the second value principle and then construct another value principle based on that reason:

Value Principle		Reason
Things that go against what the Pope says to do are wrong	because	you are going against God's will.

The third value principle is: Things that go against God's will are wrong. Again, you now must decide whether you can accept this third value principle. If you cannot, you must reject the previous two value principles and the value decision which is subsumed by these previous value principles. If you can, then you can continue with the Subsumption Testing process.

You might, at this point, be wondering where the process can be terminated. In the example given, the process was terminated after it was determined that the person could accept the third value principle. The idea behind the Subsumption Test is to determine whether less general value principles are consistent with more general value principles. Thus, judgment must be used to determine how general an acceptable value principle must be before the Subsumption Testing process is terminated. Hopefully, a person can trace his or her original value decision back to a very general, basic value principle, such as, "Killing is wrong," or some constitutional value concerning freedom of the press, of religion, etc. In the above example, the value decision on abortion was consistent with an overriding, religious value principle ("Disobeying God is wrong") that was part of the person's own value system.

Below is an actual example which shows how a student couldn't accept a general value principle based on his original value decision. The original value decision and reason were:

Value Decision		Reason
Students should give grades to teachers	because	the students see the teacher every day and know what they are like.

The value principle was: People who see the teachers every day and know what they are like should give the teachers grades. This student then gave the reason why he believed the value principle and constructed a second value principle based on that reason:

Value Principle		Reason
People who see the teachers every day and know what they are like should give the teachers grades	because	we might get rid of teachers who are too strict and make trouble for kids.

The second value principle was: We should get rid of teachers who are too strict and make trouble for the kids. This student was asked whether he could accept the second value principle, and he said yes. However, after some discussion it was pointed out that some teachers who are strict and make trouble for kids actually help kids out in the long run and under his own value principle, he would have to get rid of the helpful teachers along with the "bad" apples. The student then decided he didn't like that and couldn't accept the second value principle. He, therefore, rejected his original value decision that students should give teachers grades. His value decision had led him to a value principle he couldn't accept.

Again, as with the New Cases Test, a person is involved in clarifying his or her value system as regards a particular area. In the abortion example, it was a religious area. In the grading-teachers example, it was an educational area.

Role Exchange Test

The Role Exchange Test is one test of value principle acceptability that differs from the New Cases and Subsumption Tests in two ways: (1) you don't have to construct a value principle to use it, and (2) it is applied only to value decisions involving an action. However, as with the other tests, if the person cannot accept his or her value decision, then the value principle implied by the value decision must be rejected or seriously questioned.

Let's work through an example of the Role Exchange Test:

Value Decision	Does the value decision involve an action?
We should do away with the welfare system in the U.S.	Yes___ No___

Step 1. The Role Exchange Test can only be applied when the value decision involves an action. In the above case, it does. In some value decisions, it is not immediately apparent that the value decision involves an action. Take, for instance, a value decision like, "Capital punishment should be reinstated." This value decision may not seem to involve an action at first, but when you think about it, capital punishment is killing, and killing is an action. So before you decide that the Role Exchange Test cannot be applied to a value decision, make sure that you determine whether an action is embedded in the definition of terms in the value decision. Here we can see the importance of clarifying the value question by defining crucial terms, which is step one in the overall procedure for rational value decision-making.

Step 2. Determine the consequence of the action in the value decision.

Step 3. Determine from the consequence who would be the most adversely affected person:

Value Decision	Consequence	Person Must Hurt
We should do away with the welfare system in the U.S.	Drastic reduction in the number of welfare payments	Children of a family on welfare who get their welfare payments stopped.

Step 4. Exchange roles with the person who would be most adversely affected by the action. Then describe the person's predicament in detail, including his or her thoughts. Essentially, this involves empathizing with the person. You must really "get into" the role. Let's empathize with the "children of a family on welfare who get their welfare payments stopped":

> They would probably be hungry and have the attendant feelings of hunger pangs, weakness, etc. They would feel even more inferior because of their clothes. They might even be cold in the winter and get sick more often than kids not on welfare. Despair would probably always be with them. They would have very little hope for the future. Their relations with parents would probably be very frustrating. Constant worry would be evident. They would probably live in dingy, decaying quarters, and their surroundings would be depressing.

Once you have gone through the empathy experience, then you

must again weigh the pros against the cons and determine whether your value decision would still be the same. If your value decision is the same, then you may want to determine another adversely affected person and go through the Role Exchange process again. If your value decision is different, then as with the New Cases and Subsumption Tests, you must reject or question seriously the value decision.

Universal Consequences Test

Sometimes the effects of an action are not, by themselves, significant. In this case, the Role Exchange Test would be difficult to apply. We can, however, apply another test—the Universal Consequences Test. Like the Role Exchange Test, you don't have to construct a value principle to use it, and it is applied only to values decisions involving an action. For instance, when somebody decides to throw a cigarette package or an orange peel out of a moving car because he or she doesn't have any place to throw it at the time, this single action would not be of very great consequence. It would be difficult, if not virtually impossible, to make a case for a most adversely affected person. However, if all people threw cigarette packages or orange peels out of moving cars when they couldn't find anyplace else to throw them, these actions might be of very great consequence. The consequences would be unsightly piles of cigarette packs and orange peels on the side of virtually every road. The county and state governments would probably, at the very least, have to spend more money to clean up. You might be able to think of other consequences.

Let's discuss an actual example of a Universal Consequences Test. One of our students made the value decision, "I should be allowed to take any class I choose because that way I would get the classes I liked." Obviously this action by itself would not upset the system very much, and thus the Role Exchange Test was not of much use. However, the student was asked to name the consequences of everybody taking only the classes he or she choose to take—and no others. The student listed some of the consequences that might follow:

> Some classes would be dropped along with some teachers. Scheduling of classes would be next to impossible until after all the choices had been made. Some of the teachers would have huge classes and others very small classes, creating bad feelings among the teachers.

After going through the Universal Consequences Test, the student decided to reconsider his original value decision. As with the other types of tests, if you cannot accept the consequences of an action, then you should reject or seriously question the value decision.

Curricular Applications

The six-step procedure for making rational value decisions can be used in the classroom in at least two distinct ways. The first way is to teach the procedure itself as a course in sound value decision-making. The objectives of such a course would be to teach students a procedure for making sound value decisions, and the particular value issues addressed would be used as vehicles for teaching the six steps of rational value decision-making. The second way involves using the procedure as a method for teaching actual course content. The objective of this would be to teach particular course content using the six-step procedure as one of the methods of teaching. Virtually all our experience is with the second way. We have integrated the procedure into one-semester courses in the following areas: world history, world problems, U.S. history, sociology, psychology, and American problems.

The general strategy for integrating our materials into the courses is as follows: Students study materials related to a particular topic area of a course (e.g., the topic area "family" in a course on sociology). From that topic area, a specific value question is chosen for analysis (e.g., "Is mandatory restriction of family size desirable?" in relation to the topic area "family"). During analysis of the first value question, the first three steps of the procedure are taught, and during analysis of the second value question, the last three steps are taught. For analysis of all value questions, thereafter, all six steps in the procedure are used. Usually, six value questions are analyzed during any one semester, and we have found that analyzing six value questions gives the students sufficient practice to learn the procedure. We are currently adapting the six-step procedure for use in elementary and junior high school grades. In addition, the procedure is being integrated into career choice programs, drop-out education and prevention programs, and an economic history program.

When the procedure is used, the total amount of course content covered in a semester may not be quite as extensive as with traditional teaching methods. However, we have found that in using the procedure, students learn specific areas of course content in more depth. This is the strength of a process approach.

EXPLORING SOCIAL ISSUES: A VALUES CLARIFICATION SIMULATION GAME

Judith Kirkhorn, *Curriculum Specialist and Instructor, Division of Education and Research, College of Allied Health Professions, University of Kentucky, Lexington*

Patrick Griffin, *Instructor, Community Education Department, School of Education, University of Wisconsin, Milwaukee.*

In education settings the ubiquitous discussion group is a tool used to explore a variety of issues as well as to analyze and solve problems. These discussion groups may take many forms. One form can be brainstorming sessions that involve all group members and generate an extensive number of ideas and solutions to a problem by suspending criticism and evaluation until a later processing session. But typically, for a variety of reasons, discussions—perhaps more accurately termed lectures or debates—can involve only a relatively small number of individuals in the larger group. It is clearly important to create a psychologically safe climate in which all group participants can actively experience increased self-awareness, self-acceptance, and acceptance of others. Simulation games, we believe, encourage involvement by all group members and expand possibilities for experiencing or viewing reality both rationally/analytically and emotionally/dramatically. All participants in simulation exercises actively focus on a problem or situation representative of a real or imagined reality. Thus, we are suggesting that simulation, and in particular the model we have developed, offers an interesting and pedagogically useful alternative to discussion of issues.

The chairperson of Chicago's City Planning Commission said recently that the two major obstacles to the growth of middle-class communities in the city were unsafe streets and inferior and dangerous public schools. He was recognizing the obvious fact that public education is a broadly significant urban issue. Even beyond that, education is an issue of importance to the entire society, especially at a time when the schools are being challenged by increasing demands.

The educational setting includes a variety of issues and is in many ways defined by these issues, as surely as education is defined in some respects by current educational issues. Among these current educational issues are: the debate over the uses and abuses of behaviorism, the equality or inequality of races, various administrative and pedagogical philosophies, accountability, free schools, and all the rest.

The list of issues we wish to define in the educational setting includes sexism, racism, marriage, the problems of the aging, the varieties of alienation. We assume that we must utilize a multi-disciplinary approach, though it is helpful to break down issues into disciplines for the purposes of simulation. Furthermore, we assume that players will readily see relationships between the various disciplines. They may, in fact, perceive the disciplines as arbitrary structures and may suggest more adequate ways of viewing or assessing social issues.

To distinguish between simulation and games Klietsch and Wiegman define the two frequently interchanged terms:

> "A game is a system in which participants voluntarily allow their fate to be, in part, based on chance events, and, in part by personal skills or direct control. A simulation is also a system, but one designed to replicate essential aspects of reality, for the purpose of finding ways of managing, controlling, solving, and ultimately, agreeing upon a problem's optimal solution."[1]

The necessity of doing away with the often harmful separation between theoretical (abstract thought) and practical (concrete action) knowledge is inherently recognized in simulation, which stresses integration of knowledge and experience. Through vicarious experience in the complexities of political, economic, and social systems the learners will be exposed in a humane, honest, and truthful way to their natural and social worlds. Their senses will be extended with glimpses of new or ultimate realities. The importance of an individual's perceptions of self and the world, conceiving of life as she/he perceives it to be, is emphasized and clarified in simulation games. Simulation, for example, may illustrate human bondage or lack of freedom because of societal myths or dehumanizing attitudes or practices. Through an alleviation of the remoteness of abstractions or facts from their own life experience, game participants are accorded opportunities for increasing internal and external awareness, extending their phenomenal world, and realizing and critically analyzing their capacity to influence life. As Erich Fromm has said:

> "...only a sense of identity based on the experience of his own powers can give strength, while all forms of identity experience based on the group, leave man dependent, hence weak. Eventually, only to the extent to which he grasps reality, can he make this world *His*, if he lives in illusions, he never changes the conditions which necessitate these illusions."[2]

Simulation games can reshape and transcend society's normative environment. With new insights into the underlying structure of daily occurrences, Erving Goffman contends, we become game players:

> Games seem to display in a simple way the structure of real-life situations. They cut us off from serious life by immersing us in a demonstration of its possibilities. We return to the world as gamesmen, preparing to see what is structural about reality and ready to reduce life to its liveliest elements.[3]

Role-playing, one aspect of simulation design, permits groups to explore, try on, and invent variations of roles in a psychologically safe environment. Feelings can be expressed, aesthetic perceptions and spontaneity are welcomed, and reactions and beliefs of others are valued. The learners who feel unsure begin to trust their own feelings, their means of self-expression, and their values during simulation because of the trust and acceptance they experience during the interaction sequence. Throughout this basically noncompetitive role-playing the compelling uncertainty of the game or exercise is one of identity—"Who am I?" and not conflict—"Who will win?" Individuals can, through intimate interaction with others, obtain a better sense of how they are perceived by others. In addition, they may discover personal skills, abilities, fears, weaknesses, that weren't apparent before. Thus, through role-playing, participants become aware of their own conscious and unconscious values and are thereby in a position to modify their values.

Perhaps Neil Postman and Charles Weingartner most thoroughly describe the process of questioning as a means of creating knowledge. They suggest that certain standards, also stated in the form of questions, must be used in evaluating questions:

> Will your questions increase the learner's *will* as well as his capacity to learn?
> Will they help to give him a sense of joy in learning?
> Will they help to provide the learner with confidence in his ability to learn?
> In order to get answers, will the learner be required to make inquiries? (Ask further questions, clarify terms, make observations, classify data, etc.?)
> Does each question allow for alternative answers (which implies alternative modes of inquiry)?
> Will the process of answering the questions tend to stress the uniqueness of the learner?
> Would the questions produce different answers if asked at different stages of the learner's development?
> Will the answers help the learner to sense and understand the universals in the human condition and so enhance his ability to draw closer to other people?[4]

In the simulation we have designed, participants or learners will pose questions from a given perspective. The perception of the players regarding what is and what is not relevant will undoubtedly be extended.

> There is no learning without a learner. And there is no meaning without a meaning maker. In order to survive in a world of rapid change there is nothing more worth knowing, for any of us, than the continuing process of how to make viable meanings.[5]

The Simulation Model

The simulation we have developed provides systematic mechanisms to examine various social issues, particularly in terms of their implications for education. It also provides a construct in

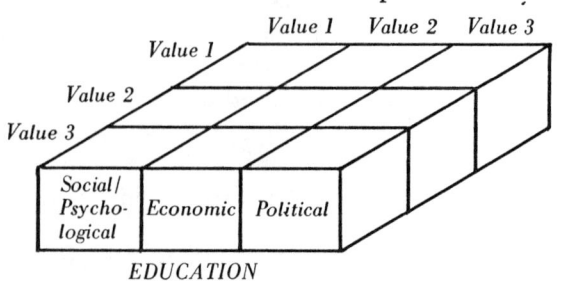

EDUCATION

which questions can be raised (and possibly answered) regarding specific disciplinary perspectives and general value orientations. The following taxonomy portrays some perspectives from which a social issue may be viewed.

For the purposes of the model and the process, we have chosen education as the larger context in which to explore the issue. However, if you examine the taxonomy you can easily see how one might interchange any one of the three perspectives given across the front of the diagram with *Education.* This, of course, would refocus the process; participants would examine the same issue, but the emphasized larger context might be *Economics* instead of *Education.* The assigned roles with their implicit value orientations would then examine the economic implications of the social issue and raise the questions in terms of society/psychology, education, and politics.

The disciplines that we have chosen reflect the areas which we feel are most pertinent to many social issues and to education. But other perspectives could be included or interchanged with any of those suggested. An example of an alternative might be historical, and/or anthropological perspectives. Our primary reason for limiting the number of perspectives is to provide a process that can be thorough as well as manageable within a limited amount of time. We have intended the suggested disciplines to be used as frames of reference, but it is possible that they could be more specifically defined and adapted to the needs of a particular group.

In our model we define *Education* as the process in which an individual or group comes to know something that they did not know before. This could range from formal, institutional processes on the one hand to the informal process experienced by an individual in meditation on the other.

We have included *Economics* as a perspective to stimulate questions regarding the financial aspects of the education process in terms of the social issues. This category could include questions about financial aspects of programming as they apply to the financial or economic loss to a society if no education were provided in the given social issue.

Social/Psychological is actually two perspectives that we have combined to expedite the process of the model. It is very likely that these perspectives could be used separately—depending on the nature of the issue—but for our purposes we will continue to treat them as one.

Questions from this perspective might include the social and psychological implications of educational programming for a given issue—that is, how does it or how would it affect our social institutions and, consequently, ourselves? Or how have the existing assumptions in education affected the present status of the issue? How should the issue be treated educationally, or should it be treated at all?

The *Political* perspective is probably the most diffuse of them all. It is probably also the most inclusive. However, the political reality is rarely the same as the theoretical reality of a situation. Questions addressed under this category might typically include the following: What causes this type of situation? Why wouldn't sophisticated research from the various disciplines provide the information upon which policy decisions would be based? Given an individual value, what are the dimensions that really influence decision-making? Which has the stronger influence: economic structure or political ideology? How should education respond to such possible dichotomies? Does education make a difference?

The Simulation—*Exploring Social Issues*

Since 1900 the National Historical Association of the United States has sponsored an annual Futurists Conference in various cities throughout the country. Participants, randomly selected from all parts of the nation, are asked to submit one or more questions that address dilemmas and concerns about social issues during that calendar year. At the annual conference individual participants will present their questions and explain the process by which they answered (partially or completely, inconclusively or conclusively) the question. While it is conceivable that participants will agree about which question or questions to ultimately submit for each of this year's crucial social issues, the NHA is hopeful that the contributions of selected participants will reflect the diverse perceptions and points of view prevalent in American society. Each year's list of questions generates new questions and enhances awareness of probable and possible futures. The NHA publishes the proceedings and results of each conference and tentatively plans—in the year 2000—to place questions about social issues from 1900 to 2000 in a time capsule designated to be opened in 3000.

The _____ Futurists Conference is scheduled to meet in
_____ _____ on _____ , at the _____ .
City   State   Date

You have been selected to participate in this year's Conference. Please submit a question about *sexism* from a *political* perspective. You may phrase a question that reflects either your personal experience or information gained through reading, reflection, conversation, media, movies, etc. Your attempt to answer the question and/or emphasize the importance of the question you have posed may take many forms: written statement, poem, poster, graph, tape recording, music, etc.

The National Historical Association sincerely believes that your personal participation in and contribution to this conference will also contribute to a creative conception of knowledge about social issues.

Directions for Playing the Simulation Game, *Exploring Social Issues*

Goals: To provide a stimulating, lively context in which to explore various social issues, their implications for education, and diverse perspectives and value orientations.

To integrate theory and practice in an educational setting.

To provide participants with opportunities, through role-playing, to try on and/or invent variations of roles and thereby become aware of their own values.

A. Pre-Simulation Experiences

   1. Assign a role and a perspective from which to view a chosen issue, such as sexism, racism, marriage, the problems of aging, the varieties of alienation. (These assignments may be made a week ahead of time.) Distribute the scenario.

   2. Instruct participants to pose a question, taking into consideration their role, perspective, and value orientation. For example, a player may be assigned a *romantic* value orientation and be asked to ask a question about the issue of *sexism* from a *social/psychological* perspective.

   3. Stress that players should respond to the question they pose in any way they choose, in a manner that recognizes both their own experience and their perceptions of the role they are playing.

4. If the number of players exceeds nine (the number of roles described in the model), additional roles may be defined or two individuals may work together to interpret a role and to suggest a question.

B. Simulation Exercise

1. Players meet together to present individual questions and responses. Each participant must respond to questions asked by members of the group according to the role she/he has been assigned. That is, if one player questions another about the validity of her/his submitting a poem as an answer to the question she/he has raised, the individual being questioned responds in terms of the role assigned the previous week.

2. After each player has presented her/his question and creative response, the contributions may be placed in a real or imitation time capsule. In a classroom, for instance, this process could continue periodically throughout the year, with individuals assuming a different role each time a new issue is discussed.

Notes: With some slight modifications in the simulation exercise, larger groups could present questions and responses simultaneously. A group might conceivably be asked to submit only one or two questions for the time capsule about a given issue. This would necessitate their reaching a consensus.

C. De-Briefing
1. Players should have sufficient time to explore the feelings that emerged during the pre-simulation experiences and the exercise itself.

2. Obviously, this portion of the simulation game will vary depending on goals and follow-up or repeat exercises. Participants may suggest directions or refinements in the process for a sequel to the exercise.

Value Orientations

We have attempted to design roles that would reflect three general value orientations. The roles are not a pure example of a

given value orientation, but rather reflect inconsistencies that will better approximate reality. It is hoped that the inconsistencies will stimulate questions that will address these discrepancies.
1. The first general value orientation is the *Humanistic Rationalist*.

The following three characters are the randomly selected participants in the project.

Bonnie Virginia Morrison
Married 15 years. Bonnie is a school teacher from Boise, Idaho. She has three children, a girl 14, a girl 12, and a boy 9. Her husband is a colonel in the Air Force and did a tour of duties in Viet Nam.

Harrold Urus Gust
Harrold is a professor of international law at Harvard Law School. He is married and has no children. His wife is an associate professor of English at Amherst. Both were very active in the anti-war movement in the 60's. It has even been insinuated that their resort homes on Cape Cod and in the Bahamas were used to harbor fugitives of the same movement.

Louis Oliver Vine Eagle
Louis is the third son of a prominent Oglaha Sioux chief from Pine Ridge Reservation, South Dakota. He was the only son to leave the reservation to attend college at the University of Colorado at Boulder. There he pursued his interests in education and recently secured a master's degree in early childhood education. He is presently responsible for program development for all Bureau of Indian Affairs schools on the Pine Ridge Reservation. He was on the reservation when the seizure of Wounded Knee occurred. He is obviously in full sympathy with the Indian movement but believes the Indians must begin to help themselves and that violence is certainly not one of the means to employ.

In addition to the implicit values defined in the roles given, all three of the aforementioned individuals held in common the following value positions:

Humanistic institutions vs. crass impersonal institutions
Humanistic technology vs. reckless development and employment of technology
Help those who are willing to help themselves

Purposeful creativity
Freedom is responsibility, not a license
Practicality

2. The second general value orientation is the *Scientific Rationalist*.

The following three characters are representatives selected to participate in this project.

Beatrice O. Masterson
Beatrice is an atomic physicist employed at the Rockefeller Institute. She is 38 years old and has been married three times. She has two children, one from each of her first two marriages. She is a Christian Scientist and firmly believes each must find their own way. She feels that the Women's Liberation Movement is an irrelevant and emotional effort. Given the advanced development of technology and determination, any woman can do just about anything she wishes. Beatrice believes the true leaders of this country and society will emerge through this process.

Peter E. Weatherbee
Peter is the young heir to the Weatherbee Doorknob fortune. He is a recent graduate from law school and has just returned from a 6-month tour of South America. He does not plan to practice law but rather intends to apply practically his newly-acquired knowledge to the expansion of his family's firm. He is rarely seen wearing anything but a three-piece suit except at poolside. He takes great pride in his family's reputation; years ago he personally donated $3,000 to the Nixon campaign.

Shirley Roosevelt
Shirley is a 53-year-old Black woman from Jamaica, Queens, New York. She has been serving as congresswoman from that area for 16 years. She has been married for 21 years and has 4 children, one in Princeton and another just entering Yale. The youngest two are away at boarding school in Hartford, Connecticut. She attributes her success to hard work and to being a fierce competitor. She is an ardent supporter of the "Boot Strap Theory" in cooperation with technology to bring Black people to the level of Whites. She is also cool to national movements primarily because of their emotional elements.

The other value positions these three people hold in common are:

>Social directed vs. aimlessness
>Conservatism
>Logical vs. emotional
>The world is made up of objective truth
>Scientific methods are paths to truth
>Technology will be the savior of man

3 . The third general value orientation is the *Romantic.*

The following three characters are the representatives selected to participate in this national project.

>**Francine E. Ellis**
>Francine is from Camden, New Jersey. She has been a secretary for the past three years. She enjoys cooking, sewing, reading, painting, and being alone. She rarely sees men but has a few close female friends. She was raised a Lutheran but hasn't attended church services for five years. She has never voted and doesn't intend to do so. Although she has been a sympathizer with Civil Rights movements, she has never actively participated. She works to earn money and expects no personal satisfaction. She would very much like to have a mountain cabin to go to so she can do those things she likes best. She doesn't know why she was selected to be a part of this project.

>**J. Jesse Solez**
>J.J. is an ex-migrant work from Texas. For fifteen years he has worked in migrant camps, ever since he was 13 years old. He never finished elementary school but is a brilliant writer, particularly of poetry. He has spent the last three years wandering around the Southern and Eastern part of the United States writing and giving poetry readings. Recently he published a collection of his revolutionary poems dedicated to the migrant workers of America. He has also just received a contract from a communist publishing house in Seattle for another collection of his prose and short stories. He recently announced to friends and associates that he is homosexual; he supports no movements but his own.

>**Linda Olezenki**
>Linda is a 45-year-old woman who left her husband and family four months ago. She states that she loves to dance, read, and design and decorate home

interiors. She claims that being married and a mother did not allow her to do any of these. She is presently a waitress in a bus depot and is living in a furnished room on the East side of Milwaukee. She teaches modern dance at Milwaukee's Free College and is writing a novel/autobiography of her life. She loves her family but feels she will not grow as an individual if she returns home.

The other value positions these three individuals hold in common are:

Defiance vs. submission
Self-expression vs. conformity
Privacy
Shallowness of work ethics
Institutions are inherently corrupt
Revere the past
Technology is a tool of the devil

DEVELOPING VALUES AWARENESS IN YOUNG CHILDREN

Alan J. Hoffman, *Assistant Professor of Education, Georgia State University, Atlanta*

Thomas F. Ryan, *Chairperson of Teacher Education, Western Michigan University, Kalamazoo.*

A first grade teacher in Bay City, Michigan, was concerned about her children's apparent lack of consideration for each other, for her as a teacher, and for the school. She sought to use "Be Kind to Animals Week" as an entree to deal with caring. She prepared and carried out these activities:

One day the teacher arrived in class with a kitten and a bag of lollipops. She stated she had found the kitten on the way to school, that it apparently had no home. She explained that since she had an infant daughter at home, she could not care for the kitten. She asked the 26 children to decide whether or not they wished to care for the kitten. Those who chose not to would receive a lollipop. The children were asked to explain their choices briefly. (Teacher recorded the responses.)

Interestingly, the class split with 14 children electing to care for the kitten and 12 selecting the lollipop. She was interested in why children selected lollipops. These reasons stood out:

"My dad's allergic to furry animals."
"Because I don't feel good and my mom knows it."
"Because when I was a child, a cat scratched me."

The children were allowed to care for the kitten during the next two weeks. During that time several of the lollipop group asked if they might help with the kitten. The teacher accepted their request but reminded them they had made a decision and would have to stand by it. Surprisingly, the "class bully" took a leadership role in planning and supervising the care of the kitten.

On Monday of the third week, the teacher's husband and their baby daughter visited the class. The teacher reviewed the process of decision-making used in the kitten incident. She pointed to the real choice the children were forced to make. Then she asked them to consider a new situation and to use the same process to make a pretend decision.

Referring to her baby, the teacher asked the children to consider whether they would choose to care for the baby or to receive one of a list of material objects. Again the class chose and gave reasons. This time the group split 25 to 1 in favor of caring for the child. It was not possible to analyze precisely why the choices were made. Undoubtedly, some children played a game where they gained by behaving in an expected manner.

One child voted for the "object." His reason: "There are six kids in my family and each one takes care of himself. Nobody takes care of me and I can't take care of anybody else. That's the way it is."

Later the teacher admitted to her class that she had purchased the kitten and it really didn't need a new home. A few children expressed displeasure, "You were just fooling us." But one child responded, "No, she wasn't! She was just trying to see what we would do."

In this lesson the teacher made a decision regarding a personal value disposition. Her belief that caring is important led her to develop a learning experience in which the children in her class faced the question, "What do I care about?" The experience was based upon several assumptions:

1. The affective dimension of a child's education deserves specific planned attention.
2. The children and the teacher must trust each other before a lesson on feelings or values can be attempted.
3. The level of cognitive as well as affective development of pre-school and primary grade children makes them somewhat dependent upon the teacher to structure the learning situation.

Our first grade teacher had previously worked with the children in a straightforward open manner. She had established a trust relationship which enabled her to approach a question which has a very personal dimension. She had to consider the level at which each child was operating in order to design a successful lesson.

The plan she used was derived from her knowledge of recent attempts to reconcile the false dichotomy which has developed between the cognitive and affective dimensions of development. Programs which emphasize the affective development of children from three to eight years of age are emerging.[1] Many of these materials rely heavily upon the work of Sigmund Freud and Abraham Maslow. Each of these psychologists has attempted to answer the question, "Why do we behave as we do?"

Maslow connected behavior to the satisfaction of human needs.[2] He established a hierarchy of needs beginning with physiological needs and then moving upward through safety, love, esteem, to the final stage of development—self-actualization. Children up to age seven or eight act primarily to satisfy needs for physiological survival, safety, love, and esteem.

A person may satisfy these needs at various levels. For example, the physiological need for food may be met by hamburger or haute cuisine. The important point to consider is that the need must be satisfied. And further, lower level needs must be satisfied before a person attempts to satisfy higher level needs. It is difficult to imagine a starving person considering the question of love of country.

While emphasizing the affective, our friend in Bay City did not neglect the cognitive. Her lessons were influenced by recent publications which draw heavily from the writings of Jean Piaget and Jerome Bruner. Piaget and Bruner are most directly identified with developmental psychology.[3] Developmental psychology is based on the concept that every individual passes through several identifiable stages as he matures. At each step, his thinking skills are more highly developed. Piaget and Bruner agree that there are four stages and that a person passes through these stages at his own rate of speed between birth and age sixteen.

One might assume that as an individual's cognitive ability develops, he might alter the level of need satisfaction. A two or three year old child asks, "Why?" and "Why?" and "Why?" An eight year old places the answer in context with all he has learned to that point. He has the power to decide whether he is satisfied knowing that "the clock runs on electricity" or whether he needs to have additional information.

Efforts to unite some of the theoretical elements from both cognitive and affective based programs have been slow to emerge. The classroom incident described earlier was the attempt of one teacher to accomplish this unification.

Her efforts were supported by the use of an approach which

attempts to identify instructional stages by incorporating both cognitive and affective dimensions of learning. Figure 1 shows how these stages are interwoven.

Figure 1

Interacting Stages of Psycho-Social Development (3 to 8 years old)

Stage	Cognitive Functioning	Affective Functioning
Initial-Exploratory	Awareness ↔	Egoizing
↕ ↕	↓ ↓	↓ ↑
Structured-Dependent	Consequence ↔	Governing

Most children can function intellectually when asked to perceive (assuming some motor and language development) certain physical objects in their environment. This "awareness" and the ability to communicate it is an initial cognitive function. Most children, by the age of three, are able to record and predict "consequence" of personal actions. However, disjunctive reasoning is usually absent, so the child is prevented from dealing effectively with multiple causation. He is largely incapable of early problem-solving behavior.

Affectively a child's need for psychological safety, security, recognition, and love dominates his actions and reactions. The authors have labeled this behavior as "egoizing." Socialization processes interacting with the child's nature and increased intellectual functioning lead most children (in pursuit of ego development) to seek knowledge of power relationships, i.e., the "governing" relationship. The child seeks to control personal behavior, become self-reliant, as well as to begin to comprehend power relationships outside himself. Inner conflicts (anxiety-frustration) build up in children as they discover that the real world was not built exclusively for them.

Hence, this teaching paradigm must include the following criteria:

1. Some recognition of the cognitive limits of young children,
2. Natural or innate needs of children, and
3. Conceptions of the external world in which the child is or will be socialized.

The writers have labeled the first interacting stage of development as initial-exploratory. This stage is characterized by the innate drives which move the young child to explore and comprehend his immediate physical environment. Movements initially are restricted by the physical limits of his crib and by his lack of control over his body. Random behavior is gradually replaced through physical maturation as the child gains control of his arms and legs. Behavior is also shaped through external stimuli provided by adults, to greater physical, personal, and social "discoveries."

This drive for fulfillment of basic needs for physical and psychological survival are eventually countered by the forces of socialization. Here, behavior is characterized not only by innate drive but also by increased intellectual functioning—consequence. Rules and expectations, all carrying a set of positive and negative sanctions, are encountered. Most children become aware of this controlling power of significant adults prior to formal school experiences. We have labeled this instructional state as "structured-dependent."

It seems then, that if these two forces are interacting within the child, educational institutions ought to provide him with experiences constructed from this realization.

An initial-exploratory situation is difficult to briefly describe and isolate. It is built with adult regard for the physical safety of the child and some judgment of what is educationally worthwhile. The British Infant School Model of education with an environment of many stimulating alternatives is one example.

A semi-unstructured experience offering alternatives to kids to check perceptions would also qualify. Teachers interested in having their children become more aware of their feelings might ask five year olds to tell, act out, or draw a picture describing how one of a series of pictures makes them feel. (Child picks picture.) Pictures might include such things as:

1. a baby crying,
2. a child playing alone (and/or in group),
3. a rainy day,
4. birds in flight,
5. dog chasing a child, or
6. a mother cooking.

In such a lesson awareness is emphasized and choice is only partially restricted. The content is concrete experience and was selected because of the perceived psychological needs and interests of the children.

The kitten lesson is an attempt to illustrate instruction in the structured-dependent stage. Both awareness and consequence are emphasized.

In this lesson the teacher made a decision on a personal value and then structured her lessons with reference to the emotional needs and intellectual development limits of her young children. Consequence is a mediating force in this structured-dependent lesson. She opens the procedure at the conclusion to allow those children capable of more sophisticated thinking to do so.

A brief overview of a paradigm of instruction has been presented, with teaching illustrations. The intent is to encourage critical analysis by the reader to determine its merits. It hopefully represents one of numerous efforts to reflect instructionally the profound psychological contributions of men like Freud, Maslow, Piaget, and Bruner.

THE SCHOOL ASSEMBLY AS CREATIVE PACE-SETTER FOR MORAL DEVELOPMENT

Lisa Kuhmerker, *Professor of Curriculum and Teaching, Hunter College, Bronx, New York.*

Assemblies can be deadly. They can hold the audience captive so that the individual child becomes convinced that the teacher's only duty in life is to fix her/him with an eagle eye and say: "Whatever you're doing, stop it." They can make the individual child feel bored, rebellious, manipulated and unimportant. Assemblies can be not merely a chore, but a source of anxiety to teachers and children responsible for developing such programs.

The trend to omit or reduce the frequency and length of assemblies, especially for very young children, has seemed like a blessing to many teachers. They find that the benefits of assemblies can be achieved by other, smaller group encounters. They heave a sigh of relief and dismiss the problem.

Educators in Great Britain do not have such an option. The Education Act of 1944 mandates a daily school assembly. British assemblies may have been or may continue to be as deadly as some of their American counterparts, but for the moment the British are stuck with them. In the midst of educational evolution toward the open classroom, however, assemblies have come up for critical evaluation and renovation. On a recent trip to study moral education and the learning of values in school settings. I found myself attending selected assemblies in Infant and Junior Schools in Inner London—and loving them.

At the end of World War II the Church of England surrendered control of parochial schools to the State with the understanding embodied in the religious provisions of the Education Act that there would be regular religious instruction based upon a locally agreed-upon syllabus. The school day was to begin with a corporate act of worship, with safeguard for teachers or children who did not want to participate in non-denominational Christian worship.

At the time of the Education Act, the provision for a religious assembly seemed relatively uncontroversial. It soon became obvious, however, that the population of many county schools was by no means homogeneous. There were sizeable groups of Hindus, Sikhs, Moslems, Roman Catholics, Jews, and Humanists without a common Christian denominator. When the authorities took a closer look at the religious affiliations of the parents of their school population, they found not only religious diversity, but that only ten percent of the population were church-goers of any sort. This raised the real question of whether or not a religious assembly was reflecting the values of the community. The law mandated a common assembly, but did it have to be a religious one? Could the school hold secular assemblies? Of what might these consist? Moral education in the broadest possible sense could be part of the solution. What could be substituted for the preaching that was an obviously ineffective teaching technique? How could children "learn to do morals"?

Interest in such questions was a very practical concern for the Heads of Infant and Junior schools. First of all, these administrators have a great deal of influence in shaping school policy, much more influence over all parts of the school life than American administrators generally have. In addition, since schools tend to be small units, frequently with less than 300 pupils, Heads have some teaching and supervisory responsibilities, in addition to their administrative roles, that bring them into daily contact with their children. The Head who makes an educational decision gets immediate feedback on the effectiveness of his policy. Generally it is the Head of the school who plans and carries out the daily assembly.

At its best, the school assembly sets the tone for the school and the school day. It is more than a time for the dissemination of messages and the giving of cheers for the local sports team. What to do, every day, five days a week? The problem has led to considerable dialogue in the educational literature and to a series of study groups and working parties.

About five years ago the British Humanist Association initiated an organization called the Campaign for Moral Education. It has two to three hundred members and it was through the hospitality of some of its members that I had an opportunity to visit a series of schools in some of the poorest sections of Inner London, where educators were developing open classrooms and secular assemblies.

A common denominator in the schools I visited was spirited group singing. The songs carried a message part of the time. For example, one popular song posed the question: "When I needed a neighbor, were you there?" and had a chorus that repeated: "And the creed and the color and the name won't matter. Were you there. . . .etc." But it was just as likely that the Head of a school might reach for his guitar and introduce his song with no more ado than to say: "I haven't sung for ages." In every school I visted, the Head also served as the music instructor. He knew his children as a result of many individual and small group contacts; he taught them the songs and knew who could play or "fake" an accompaniment to each song. In this way children had an immediate chance to put their new skills to use, without having to be solo performers.

The "theme" for the day was likely to take no more than 10 minutes. In an Infant School the children had an opportunity to smell a variety of foods and plants. "We are grateful for good things to smell" was the unobtrusive message. A Junior School listened to Aesop's fable about the argument between the sun and the wind about which one was the stronger. In this case, the message was developed through role playing. Were there different ways in which one could get one's mother to do something one wanted? What was likely to happen if one tried to use force? If one used gentle persuasion?

The novel or unfamiliar was introduced to children in small doses. Perhaps some of the children were primarily used to rock and roll music. Still, they would not become restless during a two-minute segment of classical music while they were filing in and out of the assembly hall. Such a small bit of time also easily served as a first introduction to African or Indian music.

A series of assembly programs might focus on a broad theme. At the William Tyndale Junior School in Islington, Mr. Alan Head (the Head) devoted two weeks to the theme of moods and feelings. Music was the vehicle through which the topic was first introduced: "How does this music make you feel?" "What other kinds of feelings do people have?"

It was obviously accepted in a matter-of-fact way that children might react to such stimuli through creative writing at any time of the day. That morning's question released a veritable flood in ten-year-old Tony, and five poems poured out. I am sure he invested no energy in any other part of his school day, with the possible exception of lunch and gym, but no one would argue that his day was not well spent. Such a spurt of creative effort does not emerge out of the blue. It presupposes many occasions when teachers shared good literature with children. It presupposes that briefer and more primitive efforts on Tony's part received attention and approbation. It could not have happened in a casual way anywhere except in an open classroom; the product is dependent on the process.

In the traditional classroom both the quality and quantity of Tony's output would be unusual, so all four of his poems are presented, with no alteration except the addition of punctuation on my part:

WORRY

I'm worried,
I'm so worried I'm frightened.
What's going to happen?
Who knows?
Got to be brave.
Who's worried?
Not me.
I'm brave,
Brave as a bear.
Oh no! It's time to go to the dentist.

FRIGHT

I've just had a terrrible fright
It came fast,
It went fast,
Before you could say
Jack Robinson.
What was it?
My Day saying "boo."

LONELINESS

Shut off from the world
On my own
Nowhere to go
Nothing to do
No one to talk to
Lots of people
But do I know them?
No.
I'm new around here.

BOREDOM

What shall I do?
Nothing.
You say nothing.
I've been doing that
 for the last half hour.
I shall die of boredom,
I know.
I'll sit down.
What shall I do?
No, I've done that already.

Tony Medlicott, age 10

Lest the reader think that Tony is unusually motivated or creative, here are samples of other contributions on the same themes that children brought to the principal's office during the next few days. A ten-year-old from Biafra also knew the feeling of boredom:

BOREDOM

Sitting on a chair
All by myself
Writing, scribbling
I'm bored
 Bored to death.
I get up on a chair
I walk to the mirror
And I think: what horrible hair!
I ask myself
What can I do:
Nobody's bored
They are happy
I - I'm bored to death.

I go back to my chair
And I rest my head on my
    hands and I think.
I think so hard that I lay my head
    on the table and fall asleep.
I am bored to death.

I hear a bang
I wake up
I look around me
I'm still bored.
I stand up
And I sit down again.
I'm so bored
I go to sleep.
I'm bored,
Bored to death.

Grace Oji, age 10

A nine-year-old and an eleven-year old both wrote poems about anger:

FURIOUS

I am bubbling with rage
I am struggling to try not to argue
I know I am furious
But it is cooling, cooler, cooler.
Then I realize what had happened.
I had been argry.
Oh no, it's starting again!
I am steaming and bubbling like a kettle.
I am on fire
But I have sat in some water.
Oh, what a relief!

Sally Denby, age 9

ANGER

My blood boils
My eyes are red
My stomach turns
ANGer! ANGer! ANGer!
    (ang printed in red)
My heart beats
faster
faster

faster
My blood boils
My eyes turn red
My stomach turns
ANGer! ANGer! ANGer!
My face turns red with
ANGER

        Russell Beach, age 11

The dreams of little children are not in pastel colors, it has been well said. Here are two poems about fear; the second was written by one of the few middle-class children in the school:

FEAR

Bang!
   Crack!
Noises all around me.
I'm frightened
For there are shadows above my head.
   oooh!
      oooh!
I must get out of this tunnel
Before it gets dark.

        Catherine Burger, age 10

FEAR

A door opens, it creaks.
There are weird shadows all around
I cannot make a sound -
I hear footsteps, a door slamming.
Suddenly there is a bloodcurdling scream.

It is past midnight
I feel a knife point to my back
I am alone -
Suddenly I hear a clinking chain
It is night when the ghosts reign
   Clanking
      Squeaking
         Creaking
There are spirits flitting around the room
Then I fall asleep.

        Mary Mitchison, age 10

Loneliness was the theme of a girl who had to cope with the reality of family neglect:

LONELINESS

I'm all one!
MUM! DAD! Where are you?
JOHN! JIM! JENNY!
Where are you?

Where are they all?
JOHN! JIM! JENNY!
I hear the echoes as I call
MUM! DAD! Where can they be?

NO BREAKFAST!
NO TEA!
MUM! DAD!
Are you in?

Nothing clean.
JIM! JOHN! JENNY!
JIM! JOHN! JENNY!
JIM! JOHN! JENNY!

As I call
The echoes ripply by!
And by and by!
          Sharon Fordham, age 11

An effort to express a sense of wonder about life shows through this simple recital of daily routine:

BEDTIME

I climb up the stairs.
Bedtime.
I wonder why?
I wonder why?
But I like my nice warm bed.
Cozy bed.
Cozy bed.
I switch on the light.
Read a book.
Sit on the bed.
I wonder why?
I wonder why?

> Morning is best.
> Morning is best.
> I come down wide awake.
> Eat my breakfast.
> I wonder why?
> I wonder why?
> Bedtime.
> Bedtime.
> Morning.
> Morning.
> Breakfast.
> Breakfast.
> I wonder why?
>
> Lance Walsh, age 11

And one more example, a little poetic fantasy from a small immigrant boy:

> **SADNESS**
>
> I am a sad world
> Which goes around the moon
> It's all dark here
> I don't know what to do
> The stars shine here
> But don't know who
> The stars shine here
> And don't know what to do
> Just don't know what to do
> I am a sad world
> Which goes around the moon.
>
> Milay Mustafa, age 10

Meanwhile, Mr. Head was priming the pump for further thinking and creative effort related to the theme of moods and feelings. "I have a surprise for you. I brought you a visitor," he announced at assembly. He disappeared through the exit and reappeared a moment later with a papier-mache figure about two-and-a-half feet tall. "This is Fred," he announced as the group began to snicker. "Why did you laugh?... You expected a visitor who would be walking?...What mood did this put you in?...You were surprised?...You think Fred looks funny?"

Then Mr. Head led into the consideration of the subtle way in which feelings can change: "Say, one morning you walked out into the road and you saw Fred but he was nine feet tall. How would you feel?...Supposing everything were just the same, but there were 50 Freds moving along the road...Why did you feel amused at Fred first, and then frightened?...If you saw big Fred, what would you do?...Would you shake his hand?"

This is how one eight-year-old responded to the fantasy about Fred:

STRANGE THING

> My body bubbles
> My teeth rattle
> I think I am afraid.
> I run, no, I'll stay and talk.
> Yes, I'll stay and talk.
>
> Adrian Turner, age 8

A group of our nine-year-olds announced to their teacher after assembly that they wanted to make up a play about moonmen. In an obvious take-off on "Fred," the story was built around a set of characters with long noses whose mysterious power depended on these removable appendages. The effort engendered great hilarity but did not get coherent enough to be shared with anyone.

In another classroom there must have been a follow-up discussion about the way people treat those who are unfamiliar or "different." Apparently all the children knew the same retarded boy who inspired these poems:

THE BOY WHO WAS DIFFERENT

> There is a boy in our flats
> Who does nothing but laugh.
> We call him Snuggly Jo.
> He is a very nice boy
> But only myself and my gang like him.
> He is fifteen this year
> And is not a very playful boy
> But just likes walking with my gang
>   and I.
> Sometimes on a winter's night
> He sits in the park
> And watches the birds eat the crumbs
> Which he is throwing from his cold blue
>   hands.
> The crumbs which the boy is throwing

Are not stale, but fresh bread,
For he does not know the amount of
   money he eats.
When it is sunny
He just sits out on the same old bench
Still feeding the birds
and glaring up at the sun at the same
   time.
What a poor boy he is.

                Wendy G.

THE BOY WHO WAS DIFFERENT

I lie on my bed
I look out the window.
I see a boy
He is about fifteen.
He looks about twelve.
He is a Mongol.
Children look at him.
And laugh and whisper.
He is not shy.
He walks down the road.
He holds his mother's hand.
I pity that boy,
I do.

THE HAPPY MONGOL

The poor boy walks around all day.
Then he gets tired. He sit down against
   a wall.
Little does he know he's only got half
   a brain.
As women walk by he stares at them,
They just turn their heads and walk away.
He enjoys life very much.
He thinks the world's just like him;
It's not really.
A family drives by in a car,
The fathers sees the boy,
He reverses, they look at him,
They all start to laugh.
The poor young boy.

                Martin Taylor

THE BOY WHO WAS DIFFERENT

You're born
You get older and old.
When you have a boy that is handicapped
You cannot get a lot.
When you have heard that your child will
    die at the age of twenty
You would have a shock.
All you do is just feed him, wash him,
    bathe him and dress him.
He is thirty although his Mum expected
    him to die at the age of twenty.
But soon he died.
And that's how it all
Became a disgrace.

The range of feelings of the children in this and other London schools as well as the capacity to express themselves made my visit a pleasure. There was a freedom to move and to think; an assumption that school was a place where you could legitimately express strong feelings. There was vigor and comparatively little tension and quarreling; there was purpose amidst the superficially "blooming confusion." With abysmally low teacher salaries causing a teacher-turnover of close to one-third per year in some Inner London schools, the influence of the Heads was very significant, indeed. But it was good to see Heads function both as administrators and teacher-trainers, to see them initiate and join in the creative life of the school.

My original purpose in visiting schools had been to look at moral education; at principles and practices that affected the self-image, personality development, capacity for empathy, social skills, and decision-making skills of children in Infant and Junior Schools. I found that the open classroom was ideally suited to this purpose and that the structure of the daily school assembly complemented the self-pacing and self-selection that characterized the major portion of the day. After sensing the community feeling and seeing the degree to which an assembly can incorporate the work and feelings of individuals, I shall no longer automatically groan when I hear that "It is time for assembly."

NONSEXIST TEACHING: STRATEGIES AND PRACTICAL APPLICATIONS

David Sadker, *Associate Professor and Director, Undergraduate Studies and Teacher Education, The American University, Washington, D.C.*

Myra Sadker, *Associate Professor and Chairperson, Elementary Education, The American University, Washington, D.C.*

As we work in elementary and secondary schools to create objectives and learning opportunities that will help break down the debilitating confines of sex-role stereotyping, we have developed a practical strategy for confronting sexism. In this chapter we shall briefly review the three levels of this strategy with particular emphasis on teacher behaviors and on practical classroom lessons which teachers can adopt and adapt to confront and reduce sexism in their own classrooms.

The first level of the taxonomy is that of *Awareness*. Lessons on this level are designed to make students more cognizant of the nature of sex-role stereotyping. These lessons will help students to become aware of both overt and subtle forms of sexism.

The second level of the taxonomy is that of *Clarification*. Instruction on this level is concerned with helping students examine and clarify their feelings and values concerning sexism. Clarification naturally follows awareness. Once clarification is accomplished, then students are ready to approach the final level of the strategy.

The third level of the taxonomy is that of *Action*. After students have become more aware of the nature of sexism and have clarified their feelings and values concerning this issue, they may find that they want to take action to change either some aspect of their own behavior or some aspect of the status quo in general. The instruction on this level provides students with an opportunity and direction for change.

A second area of the action level concerns the behavior of the teacher developing what we have termed the "intentional teacher." In this section, we have suggested nonsexist directions that teachers might want to consider in relation to their own teaching patterns. But first, we shall begin on the first level of the taxonomy, the Awareness level.

Raising Awareness

Recently one of our student teachers gave an elementary school class a list of occupations and asked the class whether the various jobs could be done by males or by females or by both. Although some of the jobs caused debate and controversy, every elementary school class was in agreement on one job. Both girls and boys said that only a man could do the job of President of the United States. The student teacher then asked the class to break down the job of President, and soon a list was on the board detailing the various activities in which the President is involved. The students said the President would have to know how to

1. Travel
2. Go to parties
3. Go to meetings
4. Make decisions
5. Sign bills
6. Campaign

The student teacher then asked the class to consider each of the activities a President does and to decide whether it could be done by a male or female or by both. The class was quite unanimous as the students went down the list and wrote "both" by every item. The teacher then pointed out the discrepancy in what had occurred and asked for someone to explain why, if a woman could do all the things a President does, she still couldn't handle the job of President. The class was puzzled until one girl commented, "I never thought about it before, but I guess a woman could handle the job of being President. But because of all the prejudice, it will probably be a long time before she can get the job." There was still controversy among some students in the class, but this lesson was a beginning step in terms of helping students become aware of the sex-stereotyped nature of many occupations.

Awareness lessons can help students become cognizant of the ways sex stereotyping pervades not only occupations but every facet of society. For example, students can analyze various aspects of the media such as television and newspapers.

The enormous amount of time spent by children and adults watching television accords that medium a powerful influence on on our lives. Yet, many media messages have a negative impact on our society. One such negative impact is the treatment afforded women, particularly minority group women. Viewing television without sensitivity to the stereotypes transmitted reinforces them. A simple way to alert students to such bias is to ask them to view and analyze some television programs and commercials. The students could do counts to determine the frequency with which women appear on various shows. They could analyze the kinds of shows in which women appear, what they talk about, and how they are portrayed on commercials. When possible, students should note direct quotes to document their findings. The class should share their findings and suggest some conclusions or generalizations as to how television portrays girls and women.

As with television, the newspapers and magazines in our society accept and perpetuate stereotypes. Close examination of newspapers and magazines can help students become aware of commonly accepted biases. Again, simple frequency counts, supported with actual examples shared in a classroom discussion, can increase student awareness of sex-role stereotyping in the media. Some suggested areas for analysis of newspapers are:

- Whom are the various articles written about? Note names and count the frequency for each individual or group.
- Which groups are generally omitted or de-emphasized? Whose names are given on by-lines of articles? Can you identify certain sections of the paper or journal which are directed at certain groups?
- About whom are the obituaries?
- What are the comics about and what groups are portrayed in comic strips? How are they portrayed?
- To what audiences are advertisements directed?
- Are want ads segregated by sex? Are there "equal employment opportunity" statement in ads?
- Are there special feature sections? At which groups are they directed?

Once students become aware of stereotyping in the media, they should be able to transfer this awareness and become more sensitive to the biases and omissions that too often pervade their own textbooks.[1] It has also been found that in the twelve most popular secondary school history books there is more space devoted to the six-shooter than to the lives of frontier women, and the typical coverage given to the women suffragist movement is two lines.[2] Teachers and students can work together analyzing the bias in textbooks, and until the texts change, teachers must be knowledgeable of scholarly sources that will help redress current textbook deficiencies. Teacher awareness of the fine nonsexist children's literature which is available in most libraries can also enrich inadequate curricular materials.

Many student teachers at American University have incorporated nonsexist children's literature into the social studies curriculum in a variety of ways to effectively increase awareness of sex-role stereotyping. One student teacher, for example, built a fourth-grade social studies lesson around a picture book, *William's Doll*. She opened the lesson by asking the students to respond to a letter supposedly written to Ann Landers.

> Dear Ann Landers:
>
> My four-year-old son wants me to buy him a doll. I am troubled over his request. Do you think I should get him the doll? Please answer!
>
> Concerned

Here is one response that is representative of the answers of many of the other fourth graders.

> Dear Concerned:
>
> Boy, are you in trouble! Your son's request is sick. A boy shouldn't play with dolls. You should not get him a doll—but some better toys instead like bats and balls and guns.

The student teacher then read Charlotte Zolotow's *William's Doll*, a picture book about a boy whose request for a doll is met with derision and hostility until his grandmother comes for a visit. She immediately buys her grandson a doll so that he can cuddle it, and care for it, and learn how to be a father one day.[3] The class, particularly the boys, were not at all shy in expressing their disapproval of this book. They frequently hissed and booed, and several times the student teacher had to stop reading to get their attention. When she played the musical version of *William's Doll* on the record *Free To Be You and Me*, the class was somewhat more accepting. She then told the students that they could alter their responses to the letter to "Concerned" if they so wished, or they could leave their answers unchanged. Several students did modify their letters. "Oh, alright, get him a doll" was a typical concession. "But make sure it's a G.I. Joe." Obviously, reading *William's Doll* did not break this class's stereotype of the *machismo* male, but it did appear to increase student awareness and put a few cracks in the armor.

Another student teacher used the nonsexist book *Exactly Like Me* to stimulate an intriguing discussion among some kindergarten students about the stereotyped characteristics we commonly atrribute to males and females.

In this book a young girl makes it very clear that stereotyped feminine characteristics and occupations do not apply to her:

> They say, "Girls are sweet."
> They say, "Girls are neat."
> They say, "Girls just don't like
> to get mud on their feet."
> They say, "Girls are soft,"
> But I'm tough as a wall.
> They say, "Girls are dainty."
> But I'm not at all![4]

At this point one kindergarten girl interrupted the story and insisted that the student teacher stop reading. "I don't want to hear about that girl because I'm sweet, not tough," she said. The teacher asked the youngster to name some people who were sweet. She mentioned her mother, several aunts, and a catalogue of female friends. When asked to name people who were tough, she mentioned only males. The teacher asked if it would be possible for a girl to be sweet and tough. "No, only sweet," she responded emphatically. Her answers sparked some lively debate among the young children; the little girl left with her pigeonholed definitions of male and female not quite so firmly entrenched.

Instruction on the awareness level helps raise student consciousness concerning sexism and its effects on both females and males. Once this initial awareness has been created, the teacher may wish to move from instruction that is primarily cognitive to that which is more affective and includes student examination of attitudes and values concerning sexism.

Clarification and Analysis

Values clarification as initially developed by Raths, Harmin, and Simon in *Values and Teaching* has provided some effective strategies for helping students analyze and clarify their value perspectives.[5] We have adapted many of these strategies to help students examine their values as they pertain to the issue of sex-role stereotyping. Following are selected exercises we have developed to stimulate discussion and analysis. Some of these have appeared in the *Instructor* and in *Social Education*.[6] A more comprehensive set of nonsexist values clarification exercises is available in a multimedia kit on responding to textbook bias.[7] Some of these exercises are appropriate at the elementary level, others at the secondary level, and yet others can be used for in-service workshops with teachers and principals. It is important to remember that the goal of values clarification is not one of inculcation of values but rather of their examination and analysis.

Values Voting

In this exercise, the teacher reads aloud a question that begins, "How many of you . . . ?" Those who wish to respond affirmatively raise their hands; those who wish to respond negatively point their thumbs down; and those who are undecided or wish to pass fold their arms. This strategy gives students the opportunity to take a position on an issue and also to take note of the spectrum of opinion on that issue.

How Many of You . . .
1. Think it should be acceptable for a man to stay home as a househusband, and for the wife to be the only breadwinner?
2. Would feel somewhat uncomfortable if a female student stated that she was determined to become a heart specialist? A senator? President of the United States?
3. Have ever wished that you had been born a member of the opposite sex?
4. Think that men dislike highly intelligent women?
5. Believe a woman should be a virgin when she marries?
6. Believe a man should be a virgin when he marries?
7. Think that boys shouldn't play with dolls?
8. Think that contraceptive information should be provided in high school?
9. Think a pregnant unmarried woman should be dismissed from an elementary school teaching position?
10. Sometimes play dumb when you are with a crowd of friends?

11. Sometimes play dumb in your classroom?
12. Think that boys should help with washing dishes, making beds, and other housekeeping tasks?
13. Have read a book during the past three months in which a female from a minority group is the main character?
14. Think that it is appropriate for girls to ask boys for dates?
15. Would like to be whistled at when you walk down the street?
16. Think a woman should marry a man who is smarter than she is?
17. Think a man should marry a woman who is smarter than he is?
18. Think it is appropriate for a woman to work when she has preschool children?
19. Would not like to work for a woman boss?
20. Have ever taken some time to wonder why there is so little information about women in your textbooks?

Rank Orders

The teacher asks the class a question and suggests three or four potential answers to that question. The students then rank order their choices as to their first preference, second preference, and so on. The students can discuss their preferences in small groups or as a total class. This strategy provides students with the opportunity to make their choices from several competing alternatives.

Rank Orders
1. Which chore would you least like to do
   ___ wash the dishes
   ___ repair a broken door knob
   ___ mow the lawn.
2. Would you rather be
   ___ a model
   ___ a secretary
   ___ a forest ranger.
3. When you graduate from school, would you rather be
   ___ a doctor
   ___ an engineer
   ___ a nurse.
4. What do you feel most concerned about
   ___ sex discrimination
   ___ ecology
   ___ drugs.

5. When a man and woman marry, the best arrangement would be
   ____ the woman takes her husband's name
   ____ the man takes his wife's name
   ____ both husband and wife keep their own names.
6. Men: What kind of wife would bother you the most
   ____ one who tries to be head of the household
   ____ one who spends too much money
   ____ one who keeps a messy house.
7. Women: What kind of husband would bother you the most
   ____ one who tries to be the head of the household
   ____ one who spends too much money
   ____ one who keeps a messy house.
8. If you were forming a high school cheerleading team, would you select
   ____ an all-female team
   ____ an all-male team
   ____ a team composed of both male and female members.
9. How do you earn/or would you like to earn part-time money
   ____ babysitting
   ____ paper route
   ____ mowing grass.
10. What would be the best baseball team to represent your high school
    ____ a team made up of the best male players
    ____ a team made up of the best female players
    ____ a team made up of both the best male and female players.
11. Would you most like to take a course on
    ____ peace education
    ____ sex education
    ____ women's studies.

Unfinished Sentences

The strategy, unfinished sentences, helps students become more fully aware of emotions, attitudes, or values concerning sex roles. The students are given a list of unfinished sentences and asked to complete them either independently or to share their answers in small group discussions.

1. When I see a three-year-old boy playing with a doll, I ....
2. When I see a three-year-old girl playing with a doll, I ....

3. When I see a famous football player doing needlepoint, I ....
4. To me, women's liberation ....
5. When writing a letter to a woman, I would/would not address her as Ms. because ....
6. I would/would not vote for a well-qualified woman to be President because ....
7. Aggressive women ....
8. Aggressive men ....
9. If I had to have an operation, and the doctor scheduled to operate on me was female, I .....
10. To me, the phrase "the head of the house" means ....
11. If I could eliminate one aspect of sexism in our society, I would choose ....
12. The best way to reduce sexism in my school is to ....
13. I would/would not vote for a girl to be president of my class because ....
14. The treatment given to sex discrimination in the newspapers and television is ....
15. To me, a nonsexist book is ....
16. I think the women's movement and the movement for equality of other minority groups ....
17. My favorite nonsexist book is ....

Diaries

Diaries can be a powerful values clarification strategy, for they directly analyze the way a student spends time in his or her own life. For a week or longer, students are asked to keep a diary in which they record all thoughts, conversations, or actions having to do with sex-role stereotyping.

After the diaries have been kept for a designated period of time, the students bring them into class for analysis. This can be done privately or through small group discussion as the teacher asks the class a series of value-clarifying questions related to sex-role stereotyping in their daily lives. Following are some sample clarifying questions that might be asked. These would vary with student age level and interest.

1. How did your behavior conform to that considered appropriate for your sex role? How did your behavior not conform to that considered appropriate for your sex role?
2. What sex-stereotyped patterns did you find yourself following in your classrooms; in extracurricular activities; in athletic activities; at home; in social situations; with your friends; on dates?

3. What patterns of sex-stereotyped behavior would you like to keep? Are there any patterns of sex-stereotyped behavior that you would like to change? How will you go about doing this?

Values Continuum

The teacher places a continuum on the blackboard. Polar positions are written on either end of the continuum, and the student goes to the blackboard and places a mark on the continuum to indicate his or her position on a specific issue. The student can then explain some of the reasons behind the position taken.

Values Continuum
How do you feel about male and female sex roles?

| He-Man Harry Femme Fatale Felicia | : : : : : : : : : : : : | Androgynous Al and Alice |

How do you think women should be treated in American society?

| Put them on a pedestal | : : : : : : : : : : : : : | Draft them into the army first |

Where do you stand on abortion?

| Abortion on demand | : : : : : : : : : : : : : | Abortion under no circumstances |

Autobiographical Questionnaire

The teacher constructs questions that will help students examine their behavior in terms of various issues, in this case sex-role stereotyping. These answers can be private or shared in small groups.

Autobiographical Questionnaire: Have you ever—
- Felt angry because of sexism?
- Written a letter to the editor of a newspaper or magazine concerning sexism?
- Given time or money to an organization concerned with sexism?
- Felt that sexism was too pervasive and ubiquitous a problem to tackle?
- Were angry with a friend because of his or her sexist attitudes?
- Were angry at a parent because of his or her sexist attitudes?
- Were upset with yourself for sexist attitudes and behaviors?

Conflict Story

Read the following story and then list the names of the characters you liked the most and those you liked the least. In small groups, talk the lists over and discuss why you have rank ordered the characters as you have.

> Ms. Jones, Ms. Smith, and Ms. Dean want to institute a course on women's studies for their schools' 4th-grade classes. They do a great deal of research and they present to the principal a well-developed curriculum complete with objectives, learning opportunities, book lists, and evaluation activities. They feel there is both a need and an interest on the part of students for such a course. The principal greets their proposed course with scorn, noting, "With all we're trying to cram into the curriculum today, there's absolutely no room for this kind of foolishness." The three teachers meet with a guidance counselor and they try to enlist his support in gaining acceptance of the course. When the initially sympathetic guidance counselor, who has his eye on the assistant principalship, learns that the principal has already rejected instituting the course, he withdraws from further involvement saying, "It surely would be a nice addition to have such a course, but it's not worth upsetting the school over it." Ms. Smith is very upset by the experience, but she decides to salvage some of the course by inserting it piecemeal into her class work so the principal will not know about it. Ms. Jones is determined to keep working to get the course recognized, and she continues talking to the students, teachers, and parents to win their support. Ms. Dean considers the situation to be symbolically frustrating, and she leaves teaching to become more directly involved with the women's movement.

After student awareness has been raised and after students have had the opportunity to examine their values concerning sexism, some students may wish to move to the action level and attempt to change some aspect of society or of their own behavior that they consider to be sexist.

Action for Change

Instruction on the action level presumes a certain level of student awareness of sexism and commitment to its eradication. The following action-oriented learning opportunities allow students to take a public stand on the issue of sexism and also to modify and change sexist elements of their immediate environment.

Social Protest Literature

The American experience is one in which concerns and frustrations of various groups have often emerged in the form of social protest songs. One avenue through which students can become aware of bias against women and minority groups is through listening to recordings of social protest songs and studying them and other related literature. Then students could take the action avenue of writing their own social protest literature—songs, poetry, personal statements, essays, etc. This literature could be displayed on bulletin boards, performed in class, in assemblies, and in the community to give students pride in their work and also to heighten the awareness of others. This exercise would provide students with a mode of creative expression in writing and performing and an opportunity to take a stand on issues of inequity.

Public Position Materials

When we see people who put bumper stickers on their cars, who put posters on their walls, or who wear buttons declaring their position on a certain issue, it usually means they feel strongly about that issue. Students who feel strongly about biased treatment of women and minorities might want to express these feelings by creating their own public position materials. Creation of these public position materials such as posters, buttons, and bumper stickers provides students with practice in designing and creative writing and gives them the opportunity to express their position on sexism. Collages can be made for display.

Multimedia Presentations

One extremely effective way for students to express their concerns regarding bias is through multimedia presentations demonstrating the stereotypes that occur in textbooks and in trade books. Students can make slides of textbook pictures that show males and females, particularly women from minority groups, in stereotyped and unrealistic portrayals. Students can also make tapes of music or dialogue that would clarify and add to the impact of the slides. These slide-tape shows or other multimedia presentations could be shown to heighten the awareness of others—in class, in school assemblies, and in meetings of various groups in the community.

Student-Made Books

After teachers and students have worked together analyzing the content of their texts, they may find that the texts used in their classes include varying degrees of bias. There are a number of ways that this bias can be addressed directly to the classroom. Classroom projects can be generated in which students work individually or in groups to fill in the gaps in textbook information.

For example, history texts have been studied extensively, and it has been found that even the more recent editions still omit or neglect contributions by women, particularly women from minority groups. Students can correct these omissions and inaccurate portrayals by doing research of their own—by turning to original sources, diaries, letters, other correspondence—and by interviewing women, particularly women of minority groups who have lived through various recent historical episodes. Through such research, students can begin to write the stories of those missing from their history books. Emphasis would be on accuracy, and the supplementary work could be passed on to students in other classes. Such an exercise not only improves the version of history that students usually receive, but also helps students develop research and writing skills.

The Intentional Teacher

The scene takes place in Ms. Jones' third-grade class. It is Friday afternoon just before dismissal, and the class is straightening the room before the students leave for the weekend. Ms. Jones is attempting to direct the scattered activity.

> Bill, can you carry that pile of books to this corner? Tom, would you unwind the film from the projector and put it away? Sally and Doris, please wash the boards, and Ellen, would you water the plants? Mike, see to it, please, that the science interest center is in order. OK, things are getting too noisy. Will the boys in the right-hand corner stop making all that racket? If you boys could only be polite and well-behaved like the girls, we could get this room together much more quickly. Whew! I guess that does it. Everything looks OK, so I think we can line up. Would the girls please line up on the right side of the room and boys on the left? Girls are to leave first. School is out. See you Monday.

The teacher in this brief skit is, quite accidentally and unintentionally, creating an environment that reinforces sex-role stereotyping. Even her few-minute monologue has established some sexist patterns. By assuming that boys will do the heavier work and tasks associated with science and machinery while girls are involved in chores of a housekeeping nature, she reinforces the notion of stereotyped occupations. By emphasizing how quiet and polite the girls are as compared with the boys, she again emphasizes common sex-role stereotypes. And by separating the class on the basis of sex as the students line up to leave the room, she makes the point that the sexes are so different as to indeed be considered "opposite." Even if this teacher were to provide direct instruction concerning sexism, her own actions would belie her lesson plans. Her behavior contradicts her instruction, and children, sensitive to the incongruous and the phony, learn the unintentionally sexist message.

For effective nonsexist teaching, not only is the content of lessons important, but so, too, is the manner in which the lessons are taught. From teacher attitudes and their incidental expression in behavior, lessons in sexism can be taught. Stop for a moment and consider the following questions which reflect common sexist teaching patterns:[8]

- When you meet a new class of students, do you expect girls to do well in spelling, reading, and language arts and boys to do well in math, science, and mechanical skills?
- Do you ever use sex as a basis for separating students for classroom activity (asking students to line up by directing boys to one side of the room and girls to the other; organizing girls against boys in academic competition)?
- When you ask students to help you with school chores, do you usually expect boys to run film projectors and move books from room to room, and girls to keep attendance and banking records?
- When report cards are given out, do girls usually receive the A and B grades? (Do these grades truly reflect academic achievement, or are they a reward for more submissive and controllable behavior?)
- Do you expect girls to become teachers, nurses, and secretaries, whereas for boys, is the range of occupations that comes to mind much greater?
- Do you give more of your classroom attention to boys, both disciplining them more and talking with them more about the subject matter?
- Do you stop one sex from making demeaning comments about the other such as, "I don't want to read any dumb girl's book"?

Intentionally incorporating nonsexist attitudes and behaviors into one's teaching pattern—not only during a lesson on women and sex-role stereotyping, but during lessons in all content areas—can be difficult. There is almost need of a built-in alarm system which warns of sexist comments and behavior and helps combat years of socialization. If the rapport between student and teacher is warm and cooperative, the teacher could make a contract with students asking them to provide feedback on sexist teaching patterns.

The difficulties of establishing nonsexist teaching patterns are great, but so are the rewards. It is heartening to observe, for example, the reactions of a suburban Maryland first-grade class in which a talented teacher has been working to loosen the stereotypes that confine young minds. When the six-year-olds in this class were shown *I'm Glad I'm a Boy! I'm Glad I'm a Girl!*, the picture book that announces that boys are doctors, pilots, policemen, and Presidents while girls are nurses, stewardesses, metermaids, and First Ladies,[9] the effects of nonsexist teaching were apparent in the youngsters' reactions. Most of the students were appalled at a book they clearly saw as inaccurate.

- Not true. Girls can be Presidents too. And other stuff.
- It's too dumb and telling boys and girls what they can and can't do is wrong.
- This book doesn't tell the truth about what people can do.
- I don't like this book. It gets male chauvinist ideas into kids' heads.

Nonsexist teaching can make a difference. As Florence Howe says,

> ... the teacher is the single most powerful influence on children's school lives—more important, I believe than textbooks or other curricular materials. When teachers change, so does everything in their classrooms. When teachers begin to intervene in the rigid sex-typing of children in classrooms, when they begin to question the four-year-olds who are convinced that only boys can be sent into space, the eight-year-old girls who have already given up on math and science—only then will we have begun to create an atmosphere of equality and opportunity for our daughters and sons in schools.[10]

MULTICULTURALISM IN MORAL AND VALUES EDUCATION

Gwendolyn C. Baker, *Associate Professor of Education,*
The University of Michigan, Ann Arbor.

    An important aspect of multiculturalism is that individuals in our society be given the freedom to determine which ethnic/cultural beliefs, values, and life-styles they choose to support. Although encouraging freedom of choice, multiculturalism does impose a responsibility on each person for maintaining the beliefs and values of a common culture. This means that some people may support one or more cultural systems. The degree to which an individual can support differing cultural systems depends on how well one can maintain and manage them without conflict.
    For some of us in the United States, freedom to choose has not always been permitted. Many people whose ethnic/cultural experiences differ from the mainstream have experienced confusion and conflict. Conflicts arise when one is trying to function in the common culture, while at the same time needing and wanting to identify with another group. This situation is true for members of ethnic/cultural minority groups as well as for women. The conflict becomes even more acute with ethnic/cultural minority women. On the other hand, people having beliefs, values, and life-styles of the common, mainstream culture have had relatively little difficulty in being free "to be."
    In multicultural education individuals are socialized, taught, and encouraged to support the concept of freedom of choice. It

involves exploring one's own culture or cultures as well as others. Children come to school at a very young age and at a time when their experiences at home and with family have had great impact. Upon entrance to public schools, ethnic/racial minority children soon learn they must abandon their own values in favor of values that are being imposed from without. Gradually they learn to value what they are taught to value, even if these values conflict with their own experiences, feelings, and needs. Children gradually cease to trust what knowledge they had previously gained from their own experiences and become suspicious of their own desires and values. They cease to support and create their own cultural meanings, for they have learned that they are not worthwhile.

> Culturally different children must abandon, not only personal meanings and values, but the meanings and values of their culture also. They learn that their speech, their dress, their customs, their values are not worthwhile. They learn, therefore, that *they* are not worthwhile.[1]

For hundreds of years, schools have prepared students by transmitting those values necessary for the maintenance of a national culture. Children learn very early about patriotism and what it means to be a citizen of the United States. They are taught what determines success and what values are important to the larger society. For many youngsters who are also part of another culture, identification with national expectations and values have created a difficult conflict. It appears when one must surrender the cultural beliefs and values learned early for those preferred and perpetuated by the schools. Schools have traditionally reinforced a monocultural value system and in so doing have neglected the pluralistic fiber of our schools and country. Schools must recognize and address the reality of our culturally diverse society. Education in the United States will need to affirm cultural, ethnic, and linguistic differences as worthy of preserving and enhancing.[2]

Multicultural education is aimed at reducing personal and interpersonal conflict. Having to select new and different values from those already learned is, by definition, a source of conflict. During the early development of the United States, new values replaced old values. This value-substitution was the situation for many immigrants who came to the United States, wanting to be "American." For Blacks, First Americans, Chicanos, and Asian-Americans the opportunity to replace values with the hope of "becoming" was not offered.

The question of trading old values for new ones is very much a part of the educational process today. Values are taught to children in a variety of ways in the classroom. Many are instilled as the result of teacher behavior and expectations; others are taught more specifically through moral and values education.

Educators are often unaware of the impact they have on children's values despite the fact that teachers are usually a "significant other"—someone whose approval children seek. Constantly bombarded with value-laden stimuli, young people are under continuous pressure to conform to certain of the teacher's solid values and roles. Teachers (and other adults), thinking that theirs are desirable values and roles, too often inflexibly impose their own standards on children and are unaware of the pressure they are placing on children to conform. This kind of social influence or socialization process is often so subtle as not to be noticed.[3] While teachers should be aware of their own values in working with children, it is also important for them to realize that children from diverse cultural backgrounds and experiences may not share the values of the teacher. There is a possibility that some values will be similar or the same and that these similarities can be reinforced in the classroom. But to encourage the substitution of new values for old is not consistent with the goals of multicultural education. Barbara Blitz feels that the open classroom is more suitable than other kinds of classrooms for working on values. For her values such as respect for others and sharing are essential to the operation of this kind of classroom; opportunities for developing common values occur daily in all types of educational settings.[4]

In a discussion on moral education, David Purpel and Kevin Ryan state that "Moral education is direct and indirect intervention of the school, which affects both moral behavior and the capacity to think about issues of right and wrong."[5] They acknowledge the necessity of the school to respond to its pluralistic character, because "Many religious, racial, ethnic, and even regional groups are distinguished by their values, the philosophical and theological bases for their morality, and their different standards of behavior."[6] If moral education programs respect the rights of individuals to have and maintain different sets of values, then moral education will have incorporated some of the basic tenets of multicultural education.

In the January 1975 issue of *Social Education*, Ronald Galbraith and Thomas Jones explore the application of Kohlberg's theory of moral development to specific classroom situations. Kohlberg's theory revolves around a cognitive approach to moral development and indicates that an individual's thinking about moral situations matures according to specific sequences. These sequences are presented as three levels, each consisting of two stages. Kohlberg's approach to moral development focuses on the structural aspect of the development of thought, rather than on content. Content is usually the focus in values education or, more specifically, in the values clarification process.

According to Galbraith and Jones, the Kohlberg studies give adequate support to the idea that the structual process of moral development is the same in all individuals, regardless of culture.

> Despite divergent cultural, social, and religious backgrounds, the subjects moved through the same stages of moral development in the same sequence. While the rate of movement varied between cultures, the basic concept of universal stages of moral development emerged clearly.[7]

Moral education can be viewed as education that is either situational (that which presents itself without planning) or systematic (that which is planned into the curriculum). And moral development can be considered as "the process of individual experiences and growth by which the capacity to distinguish between standards of right and wrong is gradually achieved and becomes progressively influential in the individual's social behavior."[8]

The key to the appropriateness of moral development in schools lies in its structural approach. To indoctrinate is to impose, and to impose one's moral values upon others is not consistent with multicultural philosophy. Richard Jantz and Trudi Fulda state, "Kohlberg believes that teachers need not be concerned with indoctrination or forcing value systems upon their pupils as long as primary concern is given to promoting values which in themselves prohibit the imposition of beliefs of one group upon another."[9]

Values education appears to be similar to moral education in that it too can be situational or systematic. Values education is not only situational or systematic, but also inherent—inherent because of the teacher's role in the classroom.

Values clarification is a recognized approach to values education. Louis Raths, Merrill Harmin, and Sidney Simon believes that peoples' experiences give direction to the development of their values. Experiences are varied; children of ethnic/cultural and religious minority groups have experiences different from each other and certainly different from those experiences of the majority culture. Out of experiences may come guides to behavior, and these guides give direction to life and may be called values.

> Since we see values as growing from a person's experiences, we would expect that different experiences would give rise to different values and that any one person's values would be modified as his experiences accumulate and change.[10]

In a critique on values clarification, John S. Stewart reinforces the notion that values clarification deals primarily with the content of values and somewhat with the process but overlooks the most important aspect of the issue—the structure of values and valuing, especially in structural development.[11] In discussing content, Stewart agrees with Raths, Harmin, and Simon that people living in different countries and geographic locations would not have the same values. However, if we are dealing with the structural aspects, which are universal to all people and cultures, then diverse people have the same logic and principles of justice available to them. According to this theory, all people throughout the world pass through the same developmental stages.

The philosophy behind the values clarification approach acknowledges the existence of ethnic/cultural and religious differences but favors a more cultural approach in the actual process of values clarification. For a value to have consequence, does it need to go through all seven stages as suggested by Raths, Harmin, and Simon?[12] Caution must be taken whenever verbal or written examples are used in the process as the material might be culturally biased.[13]

Moral education and values education can be relevant to the objectives and goals of multicultural education. The need that they be relevant is great, and multicultural concepts, contents, strategies, and techniques should be integrated into all aspects of a school's curriculum. Moral education makes a contribution by providing a basis for a structural approach to the process of valuing. Values education can make a contribution if attention is placed also upon the process and structure of values, rather than on the content of values. Educators should examine values education and moral education as two ways to help bring about multiculturalism in the schools.

MULTICULTURALISM—SHOULD WE CLARIFY OR SEEK VALUES?

Claire B. Halverson, *Associate Director, Center for Program Development in Equal Educational Opportunity, National College of Education, Chicago.*

Some of the hottest items currently in the educational marketplace are paraphernalia associated with Values Clarification—books for teachers and students, as well as games and kits for students, filmstrips, workshops, and conferences. Another approach to moral/values development which is increasingly receiving attention is the Cognitive Developmental. As happens all too frequently with educational innovations, the implications of these two approaches for multicultural education have not been analyzed sufficiently.

Multicultural education must be more encompassing than Black Studies or Minority History. Essentially the job of multicultural education is to help the student grow in awareness from racism to cultural pluralism. For this to happen students need to be equipped with the knowledge, skills, values, and attitudes which will encourage them to help in redistributing power equitably among racial/ethnic groups and in developing pluralistic standards (norms, laws, rules) that make jobs, education, housing, and

---

The author wishes to acknowledge Kenneth Addison, Center for Program Development in Equal Educational Opportunity, National College of Education, and Coni Batlle, Educational Consultant, for their criticisms and suggestions for the application of moral/values education to Black Americans and Latinos respectively.

health services more available to more people. Multicultural education, therefore, has profound implications for all students of all racial/ethnic groups, although its emphasis and direction differ somewhat according to each racial/ethnic group. Those concerned with multicultural education should analyze the area of moral/values development. The following student outcomes in the field of multicultural education are relevant to moral/values development:

Knowledge
- Identify values implicit in racism and justice
- Clarify one's own values in relation to the values of justice
- Identify the nature of culture and cultures (including values) of Third World groups
- Identify value conflicts between the American creed and its actuality and between whites and Third World groups.

Values and Attitudes
- Value justice (equality, shared power, diversity)
- Value cooperation.

Skills
- Develop group cohesion and ability to work collaboratively
- Develop ability to work with and support other racial/ethnic groups
- Refine one's personal life-style to be consistent with values of justice.

Multicultural education cannot be value-free since it is opposed to racism. Its content in the area of knowledge, skills, values, and attitudes needs to be suitable for Third World students as well as for whites. And the instructional process of multicultural education needs to be likewise suitable for white and Third World students. This has implications for the process to be used in moral/values development.

Essentially, there are four approaches to moral/values development: Do Nothing, Character Education, Values Clarification, and Cognitive Developmental. A Do-Nothing approach to moral/values development is not satisfactory since it becomes an ostrich-in-the-sand approach: the hidden curriculum implies values to students. Frequently the values of racism are transmitted in this covert way. The Character Education approach, which attempts to inculcate a set of given virtues, e.g., the Boy Scout Code, also has negative implications for multicultural education. This approach has often been used by people advocating a stringent adherence to white middle class values—as they themselves choose to interpret those values. For example, a superintendent wanting to teach values if it meant wrapping the American flag around students was not concerned with exposing students to the gap between the dream of liberty and justice for all and the realities of racism. The Values Clarification and Cognitive Developmental approaches hold more promise for multicultural education, yet they, too, should be criticized and modified.

The implications of Values Clarification for multicultural education are many:

1. Values Clarification focuses on individuals and not groups. It may facilitate positive intergroup relations in a desegregated school by giving students the opportunity to know personal aspects of peers and to find thereby similar interests and concerns across racial lines. However, as with many human relations programs, the focus is apt to be on individual differences and will ignore group differences. This is based on the assumption that we ought to emphasize similarities of individuals across racial lines and minimize group differences. If these activities are structured so that racially homogeneous data cannot surface, group differences are lost. In one activity, "What's My Bag?", participants were asked to make a collage on one side of a bag depicting themselves as either a white, Native, Asian, Black, or Latino American.[1] When data from white and Third World participants were reported separately, Third World participants tended to value group identity and collective concerns while white participants tended to value materialistic and individual concerns. When data are mixed, participants do not have the opportunity to see the racial/ethnic group differences and see only similarities.

2. Values Clarification advocates openness which may not valued in all racial/ethnic groups. Values Clarification used in the desegregated classroom with the purpose of furthering intergroup relations is often based on the assumption that openness will increase intimacy. Historically, Third World peoples have had a need to conceal information from whites. George H. Wolkon, Sharon Moriwaki, and Karen J. Williams document a racial difference in openness:

> Socialization of the Black man has recognized self expression through 'playing it cool', resulting in his

> hesitation to reveal himself psychologically. Jourad and Lasakow found lower self-disclosure among Blacks as compared to Whites of the same class and educational level, White females disclosing most, followed by White males, Black females and Black males disclosing least... Blacks feel their minority status so deeply that they are unwilling to bare their feelings, even to each other.[2]

The implications for the classroom, then, are that the teacher needs to be particularly sensitive to the possible need of Third World students to protect themselves by avoiding, at times, openness with whites. This need—or at least its attendant behaviors—is not likely to change overnight.

3. *Values Clarification supports the freedom of individuals to hold whatever values they choose.* It does not involve an evident struggle to identify with universal standards of justice but emphasizes the clarification of one's own values. This ethical relativity has been frequently criticized.[3] Since one of the goals of multicultural education is to value justice and seek ethical clarity, an approach which could foster relativism is of questionable merit. Multicultural education must not be value-free in this area of justice!

4. *Values Clarification in the social-political area needs to be concerned with two major issues* if it is to be relevant to multicultural education: (1) Is there conflict between the values in the American creed and its actual policies and practices? (2) Are there differences between Third World peoples and dominant white America?

"With liberty and justice for all." "Freedom and equality." Students need to seek clarification of the meaning of these slogans, identify inherent conflicts, and identify the distinction between the American creed and the actual behavior of Americans. Justice can be interpreted as being equality of resources, diverse standards, and a shared power model of decision-making. However, each of these needs clarification. Chart 1 (at the end of this chapter) is a model suggesting issues which need further explanation. It would seem that experts in the field of personality development, such as T. W. Adorno, Abraham H. Maslow, Gordon W. Allport, and Erik H. Erikson need to be related.[4] At the end of this chapter there are two examples of activities which focus on this issue, "Equality: Caught Smoking" and "The Black and White Statue."

A second issue in the social-political area of Values Clarification is the question of value differences between Third World peoples and dominant white America. Third World social scientists have documented certain value orientations for Third World peoples which are distinct from those of the dominant culture in the United States.[5] As activities are developed for students to analyze value differences between Third World peoples and dominant White America, the sources for analyzing value differences need to be from the specific ethnic/cultural groups. In the past white social scientists have viewed value differences of Third World groups as being negative deviations, have locked value patterns into stereotypes, have obliterated value differences under the myth of a "culture of poverty," and have selectively cited only some behavior to identify a value pattern.

Chart 2 is a suggested model which includes issues significant to the identification and comparison of values of racial/ethnic groups in this country.[6] This model may be seen as a general framework and any specific activity may include some of these questions. At the end of this chapter is an activity which focuses on this issue—"Touch the Earth."

This Cognitive Developmental approach to moral/values development is based on the work of Lawrence Kohlberg and identifies six sequential stages of moral reasoning.[7] The aim of the approach is to stimulate change in an individual from the stage at which he/she currently reasons to the next higher stage. The expected outcome of the approach, stimulation of growth toward universal principles of justice, is an essential concern for multicultural education. This struggle toward identifying universal principles of justice is dramatically different from the ethical relativism of the Values Clarification approach.

The Cognitive Developmental approach holds important implications as well as concerns for multicultural education:

1. The Cognitive Developmental approach offers little guidance for defining justice. Kohlberg has given little guidance except that justice embodies liberty (compatible with liberty of others), equality (equality in terms of goods and respect which are to the benefit of all), and reciprocity. Justice defined in these terms is ambiguous as a guideline. There is an inherent conflict between liberty and equality, two principles advocated by Kohlberg. In this country equality of Third World peoples has been in direct conflict with the freedom of the individual. The freedom of the (white) individual has been supreme in such cases as the freedom of a white to use the neighborhood school vs. the equality of educational opportunity. Equality, as such, may not be equitable or just. Some teachers in an attempt to treat all students equally sometimes will take the color-blind approach and say, "I don't see my students as Black or white. To me they're all humans." This type of thinking may not allow Third World students the opportunity of expressing themselves within the context of their cultural groups and frequently places a value on conformity over diversity.

2. *The Cognitive Developmental approach emphasizes rational discussion.* John Wilson, Norman Williams, and Barry Sugarman[8] have cited some of the following aspects of moral reasoning which are affective:

> *emp:* The awareness or insight into one's own and other people's feelings. This involves knowing feelings of oneself and others and being able to describe them.
>
> *phil:* The ability to identify or relate emotionally to others so that others' feelings and interests become as significant as one's own. This would include persons outside of one's own group. Phil is a matter of acceptance, not necessarily love. It encompasses treating others as equals.

Emp might be more crucial to develop among whites as, by and large, they have been less aware of the feelings of Third World groups. Because the media has generally presented the feelings and points of view of whites, Third World groups have been exposed to the feelings of members of the dominant group. It is less likely that whites have had a similar exposure to Third World cultures.

The development of awareness into the feelings of others is more easily done in a racially and economically mixed classroom, although the classroom climate is crucial in ensuring that this awareness develops. All students need to appreciate that one's feelings are legitimate, that they exist as feelings and cannot be debated. Frequently, interracial communications are characterized by the dominance of whites. Essential to the development of *emp* would be the need for whites to listen. Sometimes in a desegregated classroom students may benefit from discussing in racially homogeneous groups, so that racial/ethnic minorities are not subject to white dominance. This would allow data on racial/ethnic viewpoints to become more clear.

The following activities were developed by the Center for Program Development in Equal Educational Opportunity and by New Perspectives on Race.[9] Some of them allow for the development of insight into the feelings of other racial groups as well as into one's own feelings:

- 'As a _____ (Black, Native, white, Latino, Asian) American' Collage[10] participants develop their own collage and, in a small group, hear the perception of others about their collage before they respond.

- Racial Autobiography—participants discuss incidents which increased awareness of race and racial prejudice, feelings about their own race and about other racial groups.

- Racism Boxes[11]—participants view objects of cultural racism such as cowboy and Indian game, taco box with Mexican taking siesta, sex-exploitation Black films, and discuss their feelings about these objects.

- Simulation and gestalt may be other methods which enable people to transcend their own experiences and gain insight into the feelings of others.

- "Star Power,"[12] a simulation of decision-making and allocation of resources in a three-tiered society, enables participants to feel powerlessness or being in power.

- George Isaac Brown[13] has developed gestalt as a confluent experience to gain affective as well as cognitive understanding into the experience and feelings of others and oneself.

3. The Cognitive Developmental approach should entail the mastery of factual knowledge and consequences. Wilson, Williams, and Sugarman call this factor in moral reasoning, "gig."[14] Whites have less knowledge, for example, of the existence of racial discrimination. An effective moral development model for multicultural education would provide ways for whites to gain knowledge of the existence and consequences of racial discrimination.

4. The Cognitive Developmental approach needs to be related to personality and cultural development theories. Kohlberg has related Piaget's work in cognitive development to moral reasoning, and it would seem that experts in the field of personality development, such as Adorno, Maslow, Allport, and Erikson need to be related also.[15] The correlation of psychological developmental theories with Kohlberg's moral reasoning has been linked by Charles Hamden-Turner[16] and by Brian P. Hall.[17]

A theory of moral reasoning and behavior ought to relate to specific developmental theories of Third World peoples, as well as to general psychological developmental theories. William E. Cross, Jr., has developed a theory of Black liberation.[18] He speaks of a five-stage theory which moves from (1) pre-encounter or prediscovery of one's Blackness, to (2) encounter or discovery of Blackness, to (3) immersion-emersion, to (4) internalization, and finally, to (5) commitment. At the "pre-encounter" stage, one accepts white perceptions and Euro-American history to the exclusion of Black experiences and even justifies exploiting other Blacks as necessary for survival. During the "encounter" stage, a Black moves from this self-hate state to questioning his/her former perceptions, which is usually precipitated by a significant event. This leads to the next stage, "immersion-emersion," during which the person immerses his/her self in Blackness, and is energized by rage at whites and guilt for having previously degraded Blackness. Although one may remain at this stage and "internalize" these feelings at stage 4, others may progress ("emerge") to stage 5 which is characterized by commitment to change in the Black community. This is the sort of developmental theory with which multicultural educators should become acquainted.

A model for moral/values development which is relevant to the goals of multicultural education needs to combine elements of both the Values Clarification and Cognitive Developmental approaches. Values Clarification offers an emphasis on affective methods and communication. The Cognitive Developmental approach offers a concern for developing universal principles of justice and the analysis of social-political issues. Educators need to examine these two approaches in their efforts to achieve educational reform that benefits the moral and values development of all students, whatever their background or heritage.

CHART 1: Value Differences Between the American Creed and Its Actuality

Equality

What are the resources?
What groups have access to the resources?
Is the same always fair?
How have freedom and equality been in conflict?
To which do you give higher priority—freedom or equality?
If a group has been denied access to resources in the past, should it be given positive discriminatory treatment?

Some Cases Around Which to Develop Activities: Equality

A school system with no Black principals and a 40% Black school population has a policy of hiring Blacks over whites, given equal qualifications.
A landlord does not have the freedom to rent to whom he/she chooses.
A principal of a formerly all-white school tells both a Black and a white student, "This is our school. We don't have to have you here."
A home owner has an offensive statue or sign on his/her front lawn, such as a slave boy or a Mexican taking a siesta.

Diversity

What are the standards which determine who gets the resources?
Are the standards relevant?
Do they discriminate against any groups?
How have standards affected Third World groups?
How diverse can standards be in this country?
On what must there be agreement?
How do unity and diversity conflict?
Should there be room for more diversity or unity in this country?
Are there times you have conformed to group standards in which you really didn't believe?
How does it affect you to conform to group standards in which you really don't believe?
What standards do you hold which you would not give up?

Some Cases Around Which to Develop Activities: Diversity

IQ tests and previous school grades are used to determine who gets into college.
Recruitment for jobs is based on referral of friends by employees.
Latino students must learn English to progress in any subject in school.

CHART 2: Value Differences of White and Third World Peoples

A. Identify a specific value conflict between a white and Third World group and the effects of this conflict.

   1. Identify the values of the dominant group expressed in this situation.
   2. Identify the values of the racial/ethnic groups expressed in this situation.
   3. Describe any conflict which results.
   4. Identify the action taken when the conflict appears.
   5. Identify how the conflict affects both groups:
      Has the Third World group had to assimilate or become alienated by being cut off from resources?
      What have been economic, political and psychological effects?

B. Identify your own values and how they affect your behavior.

   6. Identify alternative solutions.
   7. Identify which alternative you think is best.
   8. Identify what values your alternative represents.
   9. Identify anything you have ever done about this type of situation.
   10. Identify any ways you have been affected by this type of situation and how you felt.

C. Compare to similar situations and general patterns in the United States to determine value patterns.

   11. Compare values represented here by the dominant white group to values expressed in the American creed and its values concerned with justice.
   12. Identify ways this situation is or is not representative of values of the Third World group:
      Are there other situations which represent a pattern?
      Are there exceptions to the pattern?

Some Cases Around Which to Develop Activities

   White government official addresses Native American representative in an attempt to have representative surrender land. Native American speaks about land in terms of spiritual and ancestral values.

   Multi-racial group attempts to decide which holidays should be celebrated.

   A group of Black students have refused to pledge allegiance to the flag because they feel that America is racist.

Shared Power

Who makes decisions?
How do statements about who makes decisions differ from reality?

Are some groups consistently not a part of decision-making?
What effect does majority rule and at-large voting have on the minority?
What are the criteria for choosing representatives? Are they fair?
What kinds of decision-making structures would be more fair?
Who should be involved in decision-making?

Some Cases Around Which to Develop Activities: Shared Power

School Board is elected by at-large voting in a city with minority and Latino population.
Parents are chosen by the principal to be on advisory committees.
Whites decide who shall be designated as chief when negotiating treaties with Native Americans.

EQUALITY: CAUGHT SMOKING[19]

East is located in a white middle class residential section of a middle sized mid-western city. The previous fall the school district began a program of integrating its school through a busing program. Mr. Thomas, the principal at East, was committed to a philosophy of treating all of his students equally. He was fond of saying, "This administration and staff are color-blind. All of our students will be treated alike."

A problem developed for Mr. Thomas when two girls were found smoking in the restroom during the noon lunch break. One of the girls, Judy Smith, was a Black student; the other, Mary Rogers, was white.

As Judy entered Mr. Thomas' office, he asked her to sit down.

Judy (angrily) I don't want to sit down.
Mr. Thomas: O.K., stand if you wish. Now, do you know why you were asked to come to see me?
Judy: I wasn't asked, I was told.
Mr. Thomas: Then do you know why you were told to come in here?
Judy: No! You tell me.
Mr. Thomas: You know very well why you are here. You were caught smoking in the washroom.
Judy: I didn't see any signs saying no smoking.
Mr. Thomas: You know we have a no smoking rule here at East. You do admit you were smoking?
Judy: I don't admit nothing. (She turns away and stares out the window)
Mr. Thomas: (His voice rising) Look at me when I talk to you, Judy.
Judy: I don't have to look at your stupid, ugly white face. I'm leaving. (She begins to rise)
Mr. Thomas: O.K. This is our school. We don't have to have you here. If your attitude causes us to suspend or expel you, where would you go? You'll just have to shape up, because it will be much worse for you someplace else.

Judy falls back in her chair and begins to sob. She is unable to speak.

Mr. Thomas: You were caught smoking and will be suspended from school for three days. I hope this will be a lesson to you.

After Judy leaves, Mr. Thomas calls Mary Rogers.

Mr. Thomas: Sit down Mary. (Mary sits down) Do you know why you were asked to come to see me?
Mary: Yeh, I was caught smoking.
Mr. Thomas: You know smoking in school is against the rules, don't you?
Mary: Yeh, I know, but I needed a smoke. Besides, everyone does it.
Mr. Thomas: We aren't talking about everybody. We are talking about Mary Rogers.
Mary: That seems to be the case all the time. (Her voice rises). Everybody around here is talking about Mary Rogers.

Mary: (cont'd.)	You and the teachers are always picking on me. I've had it. I'm leaving. (She rises from her chair).
Mr. Thomas:	O.K. This is our school. We don't have to have you here. If your attitude causes us to suspend or expel you where would you go? You'll just have to shape up, because it will be much worse for you somewhere else.
Mary:	(Sitting back down again). I guess I really don't mean that. I don't want to quit. I'll stay.
Mr. Thomas:	O.K. You were caught smoking and know what the penalty is. You are suspended for three days.

You have heard that Judy is gathering signatures to a statement, "Thomas is a racist. He doesn't want Black kids here. East is a white school."

Discussion Questions

1. Mr. Thomas told both Judy and Mary, "This is our school. We don't have to have you here. If your attitude causes us to suspend or expel you where would you go? You'll just have to shape up, because it will be much worse for you somewhere else."
2. How did Mary and Judy respond to their meeting with Mr. Thomas?
3. Was the same treatment in this case fair?
4. Can you think of any other situations in which the same treatment is not fair?

THE BLACK AND WHITE STATUE[20]

There is a statue of a little boy standing by the driveway which leads to the Grant's house. It is one of those statues you may have often seen; the statue is supposed to represent a young Negro boy—a slave boy as a matter of fact. He holds a lantern in one hand as though he were welcoming guests. The Grants thought the statue recreated some of the hospitality of life during the plantation era.

One morning, Mr. Grant saw that his statue had been vandalized. The face, which had been jet black, was now half white and half black. A bucket of white paint was on its head, like a hat. Someone had dumped white paint over the statue. Now why would someone want to do that? It took Mr. Grant hours to clean up the mess. He worked with turpentine and soap and finally went to the store to buy materials to repaint the statue.

Several days later, Grant woke up to find the entire statue painted white. Grant wondered: "Who could be so inconsiderate?" Again he changed the white statue to a Negro boy. The next day, Grant found the following note in his mailbox: "Why don't you integrate your slave?"

Discussion Questions

1. What does Grant's behavior show is really important to him?
2. Does Grant show more of a concern for equality of all peoples or freedom of each person to do what he/she wants?
3. What does the painter show is important to him/her?
4. What is the conflict expressed in this situation?
5. What effect do you suppose the appearance of the slave boy has on Blacks? On whites?
6. How does the painting of the statue affect Grant?
7. What alternative resolutions for Grant and for the painter are possible? Arrange the list in a continuum from one positive polar idea to the opposite.
8. Decide which alternative step you would take and tell why.
9. What effect would this have on Grant? On the painter? On Blacks? On whites?
10. Have you ever come in contact with something which is a symbol of racism, such as a joke, a Civil War Flag, and advertisement? Have you ever done anything about it?
11. How are the following situations similar and/or different from "The Black and White Statue?"

    Protest of civil rights workers that Blacks should be served in restaurants vs. restaurant owners' statements that they should be free to decide who to serve.

    Taco Company which uses advertisement of Mexican taking a siesta.

12. Is the situation of "The Black and White Statue" representative of other similar situations?
13. In similar situations how has the conflict affected Whites? Third World peoples?

TOUCH THE EARTH[21]

Addressing the government commissioners at Warner's Hot Springs at the turn of the century, Cecilio Blacktooth speaks about why her people would not surrender their land:

"We thank you for coming here to talk to us in a way we can understand. It is the first time anyone has done so. You ask us to think what place we like next best to this place, where we always lived. You see the graveyard out there? There are our fathers and our grandfathers. You see that Eaglenest mountain and that Rabbithole mountain? When God made them, he gave us this place. We have always been here. We do not care for any other place.... We have always lived here. We would rather die here. Our fathers did. We cannot leave them. Our children were born here—How can we go away? If you give us the best place in the world, it is not so good for us as this... This is our home... We cannot live anywhere else. We were born here and our fathers are buried here.... We want this place and not any other....

There is no other place for us. We do not want you to buy any other place. If you will not buy this place, we will go into the mountains like quail. and die there, the old people, and the women and children. Let the Government be glad and proud. It can kill us. We do not fight. We do what it says. If we cannot live here, we want to go into the mountains and die. We do not want any other home."

Discussion Questions

1. What is the problem in this case?
2. What does Cecilio Blacktooth's behavior show was really important to her?
3. What do you think was important to the government officials?
4. What is the conflict expressed in this situation?
5. Identify alternative solutions.
6. Identify the solution which you think is best.
7. What values do you think your alternative choice represents?
8. Identify anything you have ever done about this type of situation involving land conflict between Native Americans and whites.
9. Is this situation of conflict over land typical or not?
10. What has usually happened in situations involving conflict over land between Native Americans and whites?
11. How has this affected both Native Americans and whites?

Role Play Approach

1. What does Cecilio Blacktooth's speech indicate is really important to her and her people?
2. Compare the values expressed by Blacktooth with values indicated by actions of Native Americans in the last 10 years such as the Menominee Indians at the Alexian Novitiate and at Wounded Knee.
3. Complete the stem question, "If I had to move out of my neighborhood_____."
4. Participants role play various people in a forced move caused by urban renewal. Some participants role play various members of family groups.

Each family group could have a different type of structure. Each family meets to discuss their reactions to the government forced move. Next, in a family fishbowl council, one member of each family meets to discuss his or her strategy in dealing with the government.

5. Simultaneously, federal, state, local government representatives together with a few of the affected community group meet to plan government strategy related to the forced move.
6. Following steps 4 and 5 the family fishbowl council and the government team meet and confront one another. After 5 minutes of this confrontation the role play ceases. Here is how the role play looks up to now:

Stage 1	Family meets	Government and community representatives meet
Stage 2	Family fishbowl council meets	Government team meets
Stage 3	Confrontation meeting between family fishbowl and council and government team.	

7. On large sheets of paper groups 1, 2, 3, 4 list values which were developed or implicit in their discussion. Each member of each group then ranks each value for him or herself on a scale of 1 (low) to 10 (high). Within each group a new list of the highs is developed. Groups then share and discuss their results and the reasons for their thinking. This includes how ideas changed from stages 1-2 and why, and how their thought was affected by becoming a representative.
8. Compare the values of Cecilio Blacktooth with those indicated in the role play above.
9. What usually happened in situations involving conflict over land between Native Americans and whites?

VOCATIONAL EDUCATION AND THE CHANGING AMERICAN WORK ETHIC

Charles W. Curry, *Instructor (Ed.D.), Program of Agricultural Education, Division of Vocational and Technical Education, College of Education, Virginia Polytechnic Institute and State University, Blacksburg.*

The American work ethic is presently in the midst of an evolution. A team of more than 100 life insurance executives working for the Institute of Life Insurance in New York researched the changing American work ethic recently and concluded that, ". . . the traditional American work ethic is eroding. More and more Americans are goofing off, are looking to the government for support and financial security, no longer find meaning in their work, no longer find that their work provides them with satisfaction, pleasure or achicvement."[1]

On the other hand, Kenneth Hoyt, a career education specialist in guidance, counseling, and educational psychology has stated, "The nature of work and the work ethic is changing. Much of what was once done by hand is now done by machine. It is true that many additional things now done by human labor could be automated, were it not that people are willing to do these tasks cheaper . . . . Individual incomes and national strength still rest upon productivity."[2]

Today as we look at the institution of work in our modern society, the following facts may be observed:
 1. Average workers, better educated than their parents, often find themselves working beneath the level of their ability and aspirations.

2. Less than half of the white-collar workers and only one-fourth of the blue-collar workers would choose to enter the same field of work if they were able to start again.
3. Foreign products are becoming more competitive on the American market.
4. Management complains of high rates of sabotage, negligence, absenteeism, alcoholism, and drug addiction, which are eroding efficiency and production.
5. Unemployment is at an unprecedented high rate of over seven percent.

The evolution of a new work ethic is certainly a just cause for the concern of all Americans. In our interdependent society, citizens are dependent upon a host of other workers in every aspect of the labor force for the products and services necessary to maintain or improve their standards of living. The new work ethic could be highly constructive or very detrimental to American society because it is presently at a crossroads and receiving very little direction from the institutions within society. We can become a society of freeloaders, or we can become a nation where hard work is again considered noble and necessary and all honest work is dignified.[3]

What, then, are the agents that bring about change in our society regarding the work ethic? The federal and state governments, educational institutions, limited natural resources, technology, acts of nature, and the world political balance are a few of the factors that may affect societal change.

Educational institutions have the wherewithal and the obligation to assert some positive leadership in directing the evolution of our new work ethic. Until the recent career education movement, this change was delegated solely to a system of vocational education. Melvin Barlow, historian for the American Vocational Association, stated, "Vocational education's ideal was to perpetuate the American work ethic under the best of conditions for the individual and the society in which he lives."[4] In view of the fact that more than half of the total number of secondary students never enroll in a vocational course, this goal was perhaps an unrealistic one. Vocational education, however, is in as good a position as any of our institutions to bring about constructive change in our eroding work ethic.

Max Weber developed a persuasive argument that the Protestant work ethic was instrumental in the rise of modern capitalism. According to Weber, the central satisfaction in life was the sense of having done a job well.[5] Money was not important for what it could buy but rather as the visible evidence of a job well done. It was this attitude of intrinsic motivation that inspired the self-made person, the capitalist entrepreneur, and the conscientious hard-working employee.

Most of the American colonies were settled by Protestants seeking religious and economic freedom. The settlers brought their attitudes toward hard work with them. These attitudes reflected the beliefs of the Protestant reformer, Martin Luther, who described work as one's calling and advanced the theory that the best way to serve God was to do as perfectly as possible the work of one's calling.[6]

Calvinism adopted the theme that people were obligated to God to extract the maximum amount of wealth for their work and that no one should be exempt from work. The Puritans advanced the Protestant work ethic one step further by theorizing that diligence in work was regarded by God with greater profits, while individuals who were less profit motivated were most certainly adamant sinners being punished for their lack of initiative.[7]

In America, upward social mobility became more of a possibility for the colonists than it had been in their native countries. The rich earth and available natural resources that the settlers found here almost assured success to any individual who was willing to work.[8] The quest for upward mobility brought another factor into the American work ethic which was a strong desire for achievement in education and training. Parents in America wanted the educational advantages for their children that they themselves had been unable to have. Education became a prerequisite for upward mobility and a unique part of the American work ethic.

The American work ethic, then, centered around one or all of the following themes:
1. Hard work is the key to success.
2. Whatever the task you find yourself doing, do it well.
3. Individual dignity and fulfillment in our society can only be given in and through work.

These seem like admirable goals for any individual and society. Why then do we find ourselves in an era which has questioned the future of work? Why is the meaning and value of work changing for many Americans?

The era of increased efficiency in the production of goods resulted from the advent of power, the division of labor, the innovation of interchangeable parts, and the assembly line. For the first time America was producing great surpluses and this increased a trade potential in the world market. At the same time, the individual worker moved further and further from participating in the final product.[9] Hoyt reflected upon these changes when he wrote, "Ironically, those very changes that have increased our potential for work productivity—mass production, automation, cybernation and occupational technology—have resulted in making the work ethic, in its classic form, less meaningful and seemingly less appropriate for the individual worker."[10] The traditional American work ethic has become a victim of progress.

It is inevitable that some changes in the present American work ethic will take place. Responsible educators should take this opportunity to insure that changes benefit both the individual worker and society as a whole. The following eight changes with respect to the evolving new work ethic should have implications for all vocational programs:

1. The definition and meaning of work will be redefined and broadened.
2. There will be a shift in emphasis from a goal of maximum output to utilization of maximum human potential.
3. The jobs of the future will provide for the satisfaction of higher order needs (self-esteem, social satisfaction, and self-actualization).
4. Occupations will be chosen on the basis of a realistic self-image, an awareness of the tasks involved in the occupation, and a systematic method of narrowing down or weeding out alternatives.
5. Equal opportunity will be provided for entrance into any occupation regardless of race, sex, or age.
6. There will be revamping of values, integrity, and attitudes associated with work.
7. The labor force will move in the direction of more service-oriented occupations and away from production oriented occupations at a rapid rate.
8. The association of leisure time or avocational activities with the meaning of work will need to be classified.

Is the purpose of work to earn money so the worker can enjoy life or is the purpose of work to enjoy life and obtain satisfaction? C. Wright Mills explains our present work attitude by saying that everyday we sell little pieces of ourselves and at night we try to buy them back with coins.[11] The challenge for educators, then, is to broaden our students' concept of work to include as much as possible of our whole selves.

As the new work ethic evolves, increased emphasis will be placed on the maximum utilization of our human resources and less emphasis will be placed on maximizing production output efficiency. A major thrust of the 1980's will be reducing the unemployment percentage. Businesses and industries will implement more job enrichment programs, and Uncle Sam will probably sponsor additional public benefit work programs.

An all-out effort to reach maximum use of human potential should begin in early childhood and continue throughout life. Vocational educators must accept their students on the levels which they find them and move them forward from there. Exploration of potential careers and also an exploration of the self and the development of a realistic self-image will become an increasingly important function of the educational institution. This is a continual process and should not start or end during the school years.

In our society today, the lower order needs of people are usually met. Very few of us go hungry or without shelter or clothing. The government, civic groups, and churches help to meet these lower order needs of our citizenry. Maslow's hierarchy of human needs has been substantiated by numerous other research studies and is now generally accepted.[12] If human needs do arrange themselves in hierarchies of prepotency, and the appearance of one need rests on the prior satisfaction of another more prepotent need, then the majority of the working force in our country is now ready for self-esteem and self-actualization. Most workers have already satisfied their physiological, safety, and affection needs and have thereby developed a need for self-esteem. Most workers have a need for a stable, firmly based, high evaluation of themselves. They want self-respect, appreciation by others, achievement, recognition, attention, and prestige. Our new work ethic should find more and more workers reaching the top rung in the needs hierarchy—self-actualization. As Maslow puts it, " . . . an artist must paint, a poet must write, if he is to be ultimately happy. What a man can be, he must be."[13]

There is a discriminating process that restricts peoples' access to occupations; the result is that only a small number of occupations are available to each person. Grade point averages, costs of training, initiations, sex, age, physical attributes or limitations, enrollment limitations, and kinships are only a few of these control mechanisms. The control becomes evident when we find individuals switching into careers for which they have had no training, working in jobs below their educational attainment, or taking a job in which they have little or no interest simply because there is no available employment suitable for them.

Although our working force is rapidly moving toward equality in employment, it will be quite a while before our society reaches an equilibrium on this matter. Providing an equal opportunity for males and females to enroll in vocational courses is certainly an incomplete solution to the immense problem of sex role stereotyping. Providing equal opportunity for inner city minority-dominated populations or the culturally disadvantaged youth of extreme rural America also continues to present a mammoth problem. Equal opportunity must also be provided for the gifted, the handicapped, and the mentally retarded to help them reach their human potential and achieve occupational success. Equal opportunities for all persons is a challenge for society. To study our work force with a possible eye on change, we must examine all our attitudes and values toward work—the destructive as well as the constructive ones.

Employee crime is one of the major areas of crime in America which is not reflected in FBI statistics. Ripping off the company by its own employees costs businesses between $15 billion and $50 billion annually.[14] Employee crime ranges from the pilfering of pens, pencils, and envelopes for home use to the manipulating of accounts and stealing hundreds of thousands of dollars at a time.

Although an estimated 87 percent of employee crime is theft related, a company may also be the victim of sabotage. This means not only literally throwing a wrench into a machine but also such activities as disrupting schedules so employees rack up much overtime.[15] Since practically all businesses stay in business to make a profit, losses are passed along to the consumer in the form of higher priced products. Society pays the price for its failure to impart high moral values, integrity, and positive work attitudes within its citizenry.

One of the biggest challenges for educators is identifying the negative attitudes of students toward work and providing the appropriate attitudinal adjustment instruction. Aiding individual students to come to grips with their own attitudes by helping them take positive steps toward improving their attitudes could be one of the most valuable contributions of the career education movement. Students need to develop pride in a job well done, ethical conduct, integrity, and honesty. Some teaching techniques are more valuable for making positive attitudinal adjustment than others.

Almost three-fourths of the total increase in civilian employment is expected to be concentrated in the service industries group. In 1980, two out of three jobs are expected to be service- rather than production-oriented. This trend indicates the importance that human relations skills will play in the characteristics of the worker in the future. Research studies indicate that from 60 to 80 percent of workers today lose their jobs, not because they are unskilled but because they fail to get along with people. The development of communication skills, human relations skills, and the ability to tolerate and appreciate others will be even more important to workers of tomorrow.

The relationship between leisure time activities and work will need to be developed in the near future. Basically, most Americans work a 40-hour week. Two separate schools of thought may be expressed concerning the relationship between leisure and work. Carl McDaniels has stated that one's vocation is work plus leisure activity.[16] He based this concept on the fact that one of the Seven Cardinal Principles of Education adopted in 1917 was, "worthy use of leisure time." Kenneth Hoyt, on the other hand, stated, "Distinctions between work and play are becoming fuzzier, but they must not be allowed to disappear altogether." He goes on to say, "We cannot make the world a better place simply by wishing, dreaming, or hoping. Instead, we must strive through productive efforts to make it better—and that is work."[17] To relate the concept of leisure activities to vocational education is risky business; however, vocational programs should not be limited to instructional areas where employment is probable but should include many avocational areas as well.

Vocational education has, since its inception, utilized several unique educational concepts in an attempt to direct the evolving American work ethic. Vocational student organizations, supervised occupational experience programs, the four-pronged approach ("learning by doing"), and an occupationally-oriented curriculum design all provide a stimulus for developing intrinsic motivation and therefore positive work attitudes.

The United States Office of Education has stated that "Vocational education is concerned with total student development."[18] As instructional programs are planned, consideration must be given to meeting all human innate needs. The development of knowledge and skills alone will not meet all of the needs of students. In a study by the Carnegie Foundation, it was found that, " . . . technical training counts for only 15 percent in the success of an individual, while personal qualities count for 85 percent."[19] Individuals before achieving success must develop intrinsic motivation. One school of psychology has classified the factors involved in self-motivation as follows: self-advancement, curiosity, competition, ownership, creativeness, desire for approval, gregariousness, and altruism.[20] Vocational education has concentrated on these motivation factors in an effort to develop self-actualization within the individual.

Competitive events, degrees of membership, recognition of achievement, code of ethics, and all other activities and purposes of the vocational student organizations can be related directly to those factors needed for intrinsic motivation. Vocational student organizations are unique teaching tools designed to develop the student's intrinsic motivation and its attendant affective qualities of leadership, cooperation, citizenship, patriotism, pride, character, scholarship, and thrift. They are based upon innate human needs and are designed to develop the total student for a successful role in society.

Although there are other effective methods of teaching work attitudes, none are more successful than actual on-the-job experience. Several types of supervised experience programs are utilized by vocational educators to provide the occupational experience essential for obtaining job entry level (or higher) skills.

One type of supervised experience program is the cooperative educational experience. Cooperative education may be defined as occupational experience away from the home or family business, with a signed agreement for wages or other reimbursement. The cooperative experience must—

1. Be related to the student's occupational objective.
2. Be supervised by the vocational teacher and employer.
3. Be related to the instructional program.

According to N. H. Hunsicker, cooperative experience programs may vary in their length of duration from weeks to years, but they must have a planned set of competencies that the student is to acquire while employed.[21] Cooperative programs may or may not involve released schooltime during the academic year. If students are involved in cooperative programs during the school day, then coordination time during the school day would be absolutely necessary in order that proper supervision of the student's occupational experience is assured. Other work experience programs may involve full or part ownership. Students participating in these types of supervised experience programs are involved as entrepreneurs. Record keeping, human relations, and decision-making skills are essential in making management level decisions when the student receives occupational experience in an ownership situation.

The vocational curriculum is developed through the utilization of a four-pronged curriculum design. Classroom experiences provide teaching techniques, ranging from small group discussions to brainstorming. Debates, contests, games, panel discussions, supervised study, self-analysis, and transactional-analysis are only a few of the many teaching techniques which are student oriented and provide an excellent basis for attitude adjustment. Laboratory experiences provide an opportunity to apply the knowledge gained in the classroom, gain additional knowledge, and develop skills which have occupational as well as vocational utility. Experiments, demonstrations, projects, models, and product production are a few of the many techniques which provide self-motivation and contribute towards the building of a positive work attitude.

Vocational student organizations add the dimensions of character, cooperation, leadership, citizenship, and ethics to the total development of the individual. Through student organization activities, each individual has an opportunity to develop socially

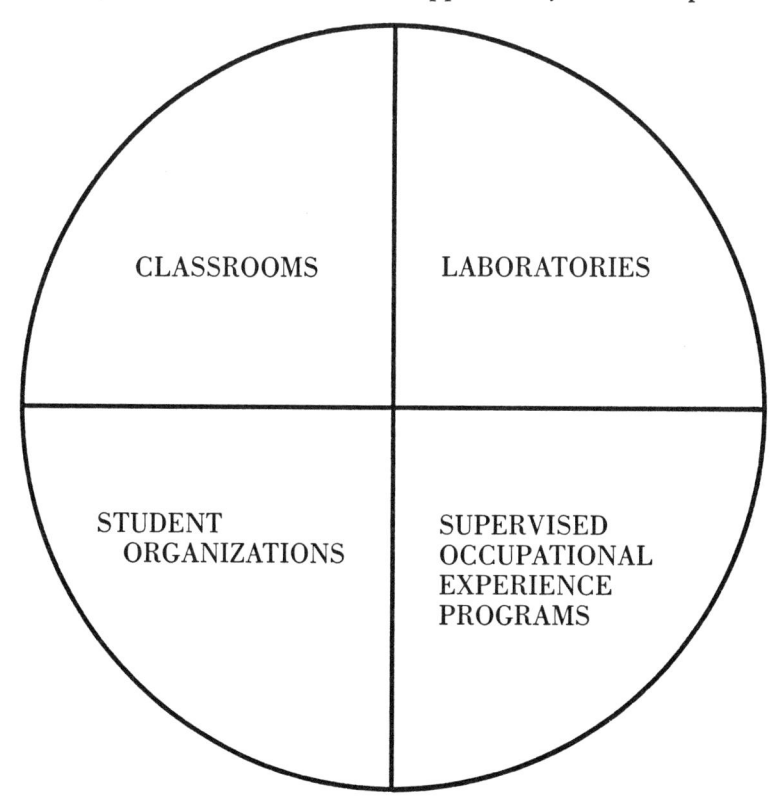

CLASSROOMS	LABORATORIES
STUDENT ORGANIZATIONS	SUPERVISED OCCUPATIONAL EXPERIENCE PROGRAMS

THE FOUR-PRONGED APPROACH – LEARNING BY DOING

with an emphasis on actual social service. Supervised experience programs provide the important link between being a student and being a member of the working force. Every worker must pass through this transition period. Planned supervision by both educators and employers makes the change easier and provides positive work attitude reinforcement.

All teachers should consider the work attitudes of their students in relation to the subjects they teach. The following eight general topics of instruction can be incorporated into any educational situation, whether a vocational setting or not:

1. Learning about work
2. Developing personally
3. Conducting oneself ethically
4. Developing human relations skills
5. Getting a job
6. Performing on the job
7. Managing money
8. Appreciating work.

The evolving American work ethic concerns all Americans. Positive work attitudes are important for individual satisfaction as well as for the preservation of society. The development, therefore, of positive work attitudes is important for everyone. Vocational education, based on concepts that can provide positive work attitudinal adjustment, is the proper concern of all educators.

A FRAMEWORK AND STRATEGY FOR EXAMINING ENVIRONMENTAL VALUES

Elmer U. Clawson, *Assistant Professor, Department of Curriculum and Instruction, University of the Pacific, Stockton, California*

Buckley R. Barnes, *Associate Professor, Department of Curriculum and Instruction, Georgia State University, Atlanta, Georgia*

Marion J. Rice, *Professor, Department of Social Science Education, University of Georgia, Athens, Georgia*

James R. Richburg, *Academic Dean, Valencia Community College, Orlando, Florida*

Roberta Rivner, *Elementary Teacher, D. H. Stanton Elementary School, Atlanta, Georgia.*

A crisis theme in education today focuses on peoples' relationship to their environment, specifically their impact on the ecosystem, a system on which human existence ultimately depends. Unlike other animals, human beings do not merely adjust to their environment but, through learned behavior (culture), interact to change and create new ecological balances. Technology is the means by which humans alter their environment and is not the cause of this change. It is human preferences or values that determine the uses to which people direct technology. Humans not only change the external appearance of the natural environ-

---

This chapter is based in large part on the following two publications: Barnes, Buckley R., and Richburg, James, R. "Anthropology and Environmental Education." *The Journal of Environmental Education*, Vol. 5, No. 2, Winter 1973; and Rice, Marion J., and Clawson, Elmer U., "Understanding Our Environment: The Ethnological-Ecological Tradition of Anthropology." *Social Studies Review*, Vol. 14, No. 2, Winter 1975. Used with permission.

ment, the landscape, but they also create new environments with new ecological balances.

In the industrial, urban phase of human development, environmentalists have become increasingly concerned about the extent to which industrial societies can destroy the ecological balances on which planetary existence depends. Since industrial people utilize the resources from the seas and lands of all the world, a world ecological view should replace an attitude of regional ecology. But current, popular thinking that the industrial human is exclusively responsible for new ecological systems conflicts with an anthropological approach to history and the environment. For example, the cultural preferences of hunters and foragers for meat and plants profoundly affected the ecological balance of the territory they inhabited. Furthermore, the most dramatic ecological changes were initiated when plants and animals were domesticated, as systematic control of food production drastically altered the animal-plant balance.

Anthropology focuses on human beings and culture; ecology focuses on the relationship between organisms and their environment. Since human beings are organisms and are related to two kinds of environment—natural and cultural, it is useful to consider the overlapping traditions in anthropology and ecology which help us better understand the problems of the environment.

The current emphasis in environmental education is on the destructive and baneful influence of a technological, industrial society. Virtually all human economic activity produces both "goods" and "bads." The increased production of "goods" has almost inevitably produced an increase of "bads" or "negative goods."[1] To overfocus on the "bads" or damaging aspects of technology does have the usefulness of attracting attention and increasing students' awareness of environmental problems, but it does not, however, help to bring technology into perspective. The problem is not to stop the increase of technology but to direct research and development activity toward the discovery of those technologies which produce more "goods" and fewer "bads."[2]

One contribution of anthropology to current environmental concerns is that it provides a time and space perspective. The perspective does not minimize the dimensions of the impact of modern technology, but it suggests that we today have two advantages over our preliterate forebearers—consciousness of the phenomenon, and more knowledge (and greater political organization) to make wiser ecological decisions.

Anthropology provides examples of how preliterate people abused the environment. At one time it was popular to ascribe the extinction of the large mammals of the Upper Pleistocene era to climatic change. There is now some evidence that the Paleo-Indian of the Western Hemisphere hunted the big game to extinction.[3] Likewise, the aborigines of Australia killed the big kangaroo, and the Maori of New Zealand in historic times exterminated the moa, an ostrich-like bird.[4]

People have been such successful predators that they have killed off many species. The anthropological perspective suggests that early technology, such as the digging stick or spear, may have been just as dangerous to a way of life as is modern technology to present-day culture. If today, because of greater numbers and technology, the environment can be abused in a shorter time, the converse is also true. People do have a constructive technology as an alternative to destructiveness.[5] The school curriculum should provide a balanced view of technology, one that helps students develop an understanding of the relationship between the wise use of technology and the improvement in the quality of life.

A second contribution of anthropology to the current environmental concern is the emphasis that, after all, human beings are a part of nature. Too much of the crisis approach to the environment tends to relegate humans to the sidelines as intruders. People, like other animals, are dependent upon and part of the physical environment, with one significant difference. Through culture, people make modifications of the environment so that it is difficult to find any environment that has not been affected by humans.

Like other animals, humans have the need for food, shelter, habitat, and reproduction. As a generalized rather than a specialized animal, humans are not restricted to a particular ecological niche but adapt to and utilize a wide variety of environments. No species other than human beings are found in such diverse natural environments (biomes) as arid deserts, tiagas, tropical rainforests, subpolar regions—although humans live in greater numbers in the temperate grass and woodland regions which support a more abundant food supply. By studying human beings in a variety of biomes, the relationship between people and nature can be made explicit.

A third contribution of anthropology to the development of a better understanding of the use of technology is understanding culture (at any level of technology) as human adjustment to an environment. If the cultural inventory is relatively sparse—a low level of technology—the environmental influence is more pronounced, as with the Kung Bushmen of southern Africa or the Australian aborigines. Modern societies, with higher levels of technology, have been able to reduce but not eliminate the environmental influence. An anthropological-ecological view of culture is one which does not regard culture as an abstraction of social behavior but rather as an adjustment pattern of a group of people living in a particular place with continuous food and water requirements. This view considers the interaction of both society (a group of socially organized individuals) and its culture (the behavioral adjustments necessary for social organization and biological sustenance) with the real environment. This point of view is not unique to anthropology; it is shared by human geography and human ecology as well.

Anthropologists have concluded, as a result of cross-cultural studies, that three types of relationships exist between societies and their natural environments. The first type is based on the belief that people are at the mercy of the natural environment. The second is that people should live in harmony with the natural environment. And the third is that people should control the natural environment.[6]

The three types of relationships involve level of technology, geographical environment, and values. One might hypothesize that as technology increases and climatic factors become more favorable, a society moves from being at the mercy of its environment. At the option level, cultural determinants (values) operationalize to influence the society's choice. Specific examples of the three types of relationships between humans and their natural environment follow.

First, the culture of middle-class America. Middle-class Americans, by and large, behave as if nature is to be controlled or modified to suit their convenience. Young children in the elementary grades may not have discovered this. Older children may realize it but accept it as the universal way to behave toward the environment. Or they may have a vague awareness that various societies relate in different ways to the natural environment, but probably have not given it much thought.

These relationships can be brought to the students' attention by means of expository, deductive, or inductive teaching strategies. The inductive method, which begins with raw data and concludes with generalizations developed by the students, will be described here.

First, present the students with specific information regarding human relationships to the natural environment in the United States. Pictures of fields being plowed, freeways and dams being built, and factories discharging waste into rivers are useful materials to use with young children. Books, resource speakers, field trips, and media presentations can be used with all age levels.
    Once adequate evidence of the American society's behavior toward the environment has been presented, ask the students to describe what they saw, read, or heard. Their responses may be listed on the chalkboard or on chart paper. Next, ask them what the descriptions have in common in terms of the effect on the natural environment. Finally, ask them to write or state a sentence or two—a generalization—that describes what the American attitude toward the environment seems to be.
    Repeat this procedure using a society that has a different value orientation toward the natural environment. One of the Polynesian societies would be appropriate. To the Polynesians of the past, the earth, the sky, the water, even the volcanos were Gods to be feared, worshipped, and pleased. When a volcano erupted or a tidal wave flooded a village, the Gods were considered to be angry and sacrifices were often made to appease them. Polynesians dared not attempt to modify their environments to any great extent for fear of offending the Gods.
    After the students have examined information about one or more Polynesian societies, ask them what they saw, heard, or read, what the descriptions had in common in terms of the effect on the environment, and finally, what the Polynesian attitude toward the natural environment seemed to be.
    The same inductive teaching procedure can be followed as students investigate another society, one that sees itself as living in harmony with its natural environment. The Navajos of the American Southwest could serve as an excellent case study of a society that modified its environment through agriculture. The land sustained life and was revered rather than feared. Further, the land was not abused. First, have the students examine evidence of the group's relationship to its natural environment. Second, ask what the descriptions have in common in terms of the effect on the environment, and third, ask what the Navajo attitude toward the environment seems to be.
    After examining three different societies, students can contrast the three different types of relationships illustrated by these case studies. Further case studies may be examined and labeled according to the type of relationships that are predominantly exhibited.

Students may want to learn how anthropologists study other cultures to determine people-environment value orientations. High school and college anthropology texts are available from a variety of publishers. Elementary school materials that can be used for the study of anthropological methods can be ordered, for example, at minimal cost from The Anthropology Curriculum Project at the University of Georgia. Some of the methods described in these materials include participant observation, interviewing, the use of informants, and the keeping of accurate field diaries.

Through the anthropological case study approach described in this chapter, students can come to realize that the way Americans relate to the natural environment is not the only way. They will learn that other societies relate in different ways—ways that may be more beneficial to people in the long run.

This goal can be accomplished by asking students to predict the future of societies such as those decribed here. The teacher might ask, "What will America be like if we continue to relate toward the natural environment as we have in the past?" After students make some predictions about the future of the United States and the other societies they have studied, they are at a point where they should be encouraged to make a value judgment. They can be asked, "Is this the future you want for your country? If not, what future do you want? What are the alternatives and the consequences of each? Which of the three types of people-environment relationships do you prefer?"

The next question to ask students is, "How can we change our society in order to establish the type of relationship we want?" A change model, which has been adapted from rural sociology, may be useful as students consider how to implement change in our society.

The first step in the change model is to make people aware of the need for and the desirability of a change. Television and other popular media are useful at this awareness stage. Second, additional information must be made available for those who reach the interest stage. Third, people reach the evaluation stage when they examine the information and decide whether or not they want to take any action. If they continue to be interested, they move into the fourth stage, which consists of small scale trials. If the trials are successful, the change may be adopted on a more widespread basis. It should be noted that most people don't reach the adoption stage as a result of research, statistical evidence, or the mass media. They are influenced more by friends, neighbors, salespersons, and change agents.

Unfortunately, change doesn't take place as smoothly or as quickly as the model may imply. The concept of resistance to change has been explored by anthropologists who have postulated the following reasons why people resist change:

1. Habit, a liking for familiar ways
2. Conservatism, a wish to keep things as much as possible the way they are
3. Reverence for the past, an imaginary goodness given to old things or to the "good old days"
4. Vested interest, a threat to a person's financial status, prestige, or position
5. Difficulty in finding a new way to replace the old
6. Hostility to an innovation, because of bad results of a first trial
7. A general outlook which is afraid of new things
8. Cost in time and energy
9. Fear of linked change, i.e., one change will cause another
10. Conflict with early learning.

Let us turn now to what the teacher can do to provide the student with a cross-cultural perspective about people and their relationships with the natural environment. Teachers belong to one of the largest groups of change agents in the country—and people are greatly influenced by change agents. Because of their influence, teachers should—

- Become familiar with the anthropological point of view and methodology.
- Increase their knowledge of and their ability to use expository, deductive, and inductive teaching strategies.
- Learn about values clarification models and techniques.
- Start locating and organizing potential teaching materials to use in this anthropological approach. Pictures from magazines, study prints, case studies, newspaper and magazine articles, resource speakers, and field trips can all make significant contributions to a teaching program. Some of the newer elementary social studies textbook series emphasize the relationship of people to their environments, and there are many informative and beautifully written children's tradebooks.[7]
- Try this approach for just a short period of time. Having tried it successfully on a small scale, teachers probably will adopt this approach as part of an environmental education program.

Looking out may, in effect, be the best way of looking in. The anthropological perspective—one that makes the economic-environmental-cultural relationship explicit—may provide the best vehicle for helping students understand the value-laden problems and alternatives that confront people in their technological, industrial society.

POP MUSIC AND VALUES CLARIFICATION

Richard Simms, *Associate Professor of Education, North Texas State University, Denton, Texas.*

Motivating today's students in school is a problem of crisis proportions. They have grown up in an audiovisual world dominated by television and have been exposed at an early age to educational programs, such as "Sesame Street" and "Electric Company." Through contact with the various types of news media, these youngsters become aware of events as they occur half way around the world. The result is that many children come to school more sophisticated, more cosmopolitan, better informed, and with greater verbal facility than their parents had at the same age. This modern early-childhood environment, rich in audiovisual sensory stimuli, has "spoiled" students in terms of what they expect of school.

Teachers are expected to compete with a multi-media world for the students' attention and interest—no mean task to be sure. Teachers are immediately out of the running if they try to rely on the tired, worn-out approaches of the past which center on lecture, answering questions at the end of the chapter, and test taking. Teachers must make some value judgments about what is worth teaching in their fields. In so doing, one would hope that the social studies teacher would be concerned with equipping students with the tools to make basic decisions about their own lives. Since such decisions should be based on the students' values, students need to be given the opportunity to develop their own value systems. Sidney Simon, Louis Raths, and others have called much attention to the process known as "values clarification" in which the emphasis is on individuals evolving their own personal value systems rather than their simply adopting the values of their parents or teachers.

One successful technique for developing values clarification has been the use of popular music. This approach has the obvious advantage of utilizing a medium (music) which is very important to most young people. In so doing, the teacher is breathing new life into the social studies curriculum. Lyrics to current hit songs are also an excellent point of departure for class discussion of burning social issues.

In order to make the best use of this approach, teachers should solicit from their students the names of songs currently popular with young people. The students can also provide a copy of song lyrics to be duplicated and distributed to the class. Next, each teacher and students should prepare a list of questions (both recall and open-ended types) for each song. Each record is played in class and then the teacher or one of the students leads a discussion of the various interpretations of the lyrics and their social implications. To make this technique work, it is crucial that the students' favorite songs, and not those of the teacher, are used. In order to further illustrate how songs can be used in the social studies classroom, lyrics and appropriate questions from three songs follow.

"Lean On Me"*

Lean on me when you're not strong and
I'll be your friend, I'll help you carry on,
for it won't be long till I'm gonna need
somebody to lean on.

Please swallow your pride if I have things you
need to borrow,
for no one can fill those of your needs that
you won't let show.

You just call on me, brother, when you need a hand.
We all need somebody to lean on.
I just might have a problem that you'll understand.
We all need somebody to lean on.

If there is a load you have to bear,
that you can't carry, I'm right up the road.
I'll share your load if you just
call me . . . call me . . .

Discussion Questions

1. What is the theme of "Lean on Me"?
2. Do we all need someone to lean on from time to time?
3. How do you feel about admitting to others that you have problems?
4. What is the value of sharing your problems with a friend?
5. Can you identify with "Lean On Me"? Explain why or why not.
6. Do you have friends like the one described in the song? Are you that kind of friend to someone?
7. Does the kind of relationship referred to in "Lean On Me" also exist between countries? Give examples.
8. What do the words ". . .for no one can fill those of your needs that you won't let show" mean to you?
9. Write a brief story using the theme of "Lean On Me."

---

*"Lean On Me" by Bill Withers. Copyright © 1972 by Interior Music Corp. (BMI) Administered by Irving Music, Inc. (BMI) All Rights Reserved. Used by Permission.

"Black and White"*

The ink is black, the page is white,
Together we learn to read and write.
A child is black, a child is white.
The whole world looks upon the sight, the beautiful sight.
And now a child can understand
That this is the law of all the land, all the land.

The world is black, the world is white.
It turns by day and then by night.
A child is black, a child is white.
Together they grow to see the light, to see the light.
And now at last, they plainly see
They will have a chance at liberty, liberty.

The world is black, the world is white.
It turns by day and then by night.
A child is black, a child is white.
The whole world looks upon the sight, a beautiful sight.

The world is black, the world is white.
It turns by day and then by night.
A child is black, a child is white.
Together they grow to see the light, to see the light.

The world is black, the world is white.
It turns by day and then by night.
A child is black, a child is white.
The whole world looks upon the sight, a beautiful sight.

The world is black, the world is white.
It turns by day and then by night.
A child is black, a child is white.
Together they grow to see the light, to see the light.

Discussion Questions

1. What is the song's message?
2. What is referred to with the words "And now a child can understand/That this is the law of all the land"? Do you think it is significant that the song was written in 1956, although not recorded until 1972 by "Three Dog Night"? Explain.

---

*"Black and White," words by David Arkin, music by Earl Robinson. Copyright © 1956, 1972 by Templeton Pub. Co., Inc. Sole selling agent: Shawnee Press, Inc., Delaware Water Gap, PA 18327. Used by permission. Recorded in 1972 by "Three Dog Night" on their *Seven Separate Fools* album.

3. What are some of the landmark court cases dealing with desegregation?
4. What are several possible interpretations of the lyrics "The world is black, the world is white"?
5. What do you think is meant by the lyrics: "The ink is black, the page is white, together we learn to read and write"?
6. Does the song "Black and White" convey an optimistic or pessimistic view of integration?
7. In your opinion, does this song give a realistic picture of the current status of integration?
8. Give several examples which indicate that integration is working. Give examples which indicate that integration is not working.
9. Do you think that most people consider the sight of a black child and a white child playing together beautiful?
10. In one page, give your views on integration.

"The World Is A Ghetto"*

Walking down the street, smoggy eyed.
Looking at the sky, starry eyed.
Searching for a place, weary eyed.
Crying in the night, teary eyed.
Don't you know that it's true that for me and for you,
The world is a ghetto.
Don't you know that it's true that for me and for you,
The world is a ghetto.

Wonder when I'll find paradise.
Somewhere there is a home, sweet and nice.
Wonder if I'll find happiness.
Better give it up now, I guess.
Don't you know that it's true that for me and for you
The world is a ghetto.
Don't you know that it's true that for me and for you,
The world is a ghetto.

There's no need to search anywhere.
Happiness is here, have your share.
If you know your love, be secure.
Paradise is love, to be sure.
Don't you know that it's true that for me and for you,
The world is a ghetto.
Don't you know that it's true that for me and for you,
The world is a ghetto.

Don't you know that it's true that for me and for you,
The world is a ghetto. The world is a ghetto...

Discussion Questions

1. What is a ghetto? Have you ever visited a ghetto? How would you feel about living in a ghetto?

2. What evidence can you give to show that "The world is a ghetto"? What evidence would indicate that the world is not a ghetto?

3. In addition to a ghetto being a physical place, can it also be a state of mind?

4. What measures can be taken to eliminate ghettos?

5. On the whole, do you consider the world to be a ghetto? Why or why not? How do you think most other people would respond to that question?

---

*"The World Is A Ghetto." Recorded by "War" on their album *The World Is A Ghetto.* Copyright © 1972 by Far Out Productions, Inc. Used with permission.

VALUES AND HEALTH EDUCATION

Robert D. Russell, *Professor of Health Education, Southern Illinois University, Carbondale.*

Values underlie an individual's attitudes and motives, which combine to predispose her/him to act in certain reasonably predictable ways. Each person shares certain values with others, yet rare would be the occurrence of even two people with completely identical values . . . and even rarer an individual with an absolutely unique value shared with no other human. Sociologists, who study various groups of people in a culture, devised the concept of social class, asserting that certain social and economic values and behaviors would be shared by segments of the population, which would cut across other lines—like race, religion, sex, geographic origin.

Today, a new understanding of society has revealed that the old social class stereotypes do not hold, making it difficult to generalize. For example, there may be as many differences among individuals labeled "middle class" as there are similarities.

Professional health educators are not all alike. As groups within the culture develop and exhibit more diversity from one another, the need for even greater health education variation may increase. A general observation would be that health educators vary across a continuum. The two poles of this continuum are shown at the top of the next page.

| Almost Any Behavior as Long as It Helps a Person Function | Particular Specified Behaviors and Non-Behaviors for Health |

I have seen no evidence presented or guesses hazarded as to where a central tendency for present practitioners would be. Health textbooks would seem to be definitely toward the right side—toward fairly specific behaviors. But this is all very abstract and theoretical. How does this show what people feel and do?

What and how to eat should be a good first example. The prevailing values for health education are most likely to be: (1) daily meals should provide a balance of the essential nutrients, provided by a balance of foods from the Four Food Groups; (2) protein is essential, and meat, being the best source of high quality protein (all the amino acids needed) should be eaten; and (3) eating in patterns that produce obesity (weight ten percent or more over recommended poundage) should be avoided. These dominant values reflect the specific behaviors on the right of the continuum.

How could a health educator respond to the following variations—reflecting somewhat different values represented by the left side of the continuum?

Variant	Possible Response
"We have very little money to spend on food. . . . By the time we buy those things we always have eaten and like to eat, there's usually not enough money for foods that would make a better balance."	"Let's explore all the foods you've always eaten and like and see what possible new combinations could achieve a better balance. How about an initial goal of one balanced meal a week and working toward one a day. . . ?"
"I'm fat and I know it, but I see no point in punishing myself by dieting. I like to eat, and I'm going to eat what I like for as long as I live."	"The health risks from obesity are less when you don't smoke and do exercise. There are healthier ways to be fat . . . and if you keep your mental outlook positive and happy, that, too, can be in your favor."
"People have no right to take the lives of animals for their own selfish purposes. Eating meat is barbarian. Being a strict vegetarian like I am keeps your mind clear and open to vibrations that meat eaters just can't experience."	"I'd bet your best vibrations would result from a good balance of plant foods—plenty of nuts and peanut butter and soy bean dishes plus fruits and vegetables . . . and, remember, milk and eggs don't diminish the life of a cow or chicken. . . ."

Of course, there are other variations, but these three represent groups that are poor, have personal preferences, are satisfied with obesity, and might be referred to by health personnel on the right of the continuum as "kooky food faddists." Can the health education messages be geared to their values? Should they be?

Drinking of alcoholic beverages is another arena for potential value variation. Health education's dominant values are more apt to be: (1) do not drink; (2) if you drink, do not get drunk; and (3) do not drive after drinking. Variants from the right of the continuum follow:

Variant	Possible Response
"No drinking at all should be tolerated. Alcohol is a liquid narcotic that kills brain cells with every drink and turns men and women into barbarous animals. People who drink deserve all the harm that comes to them . . . and more."	"No drinking at all is certainly the safest behavior . . . but a fair, objective look at those who drink probably does not show most drinkers as barbarous animals. When dislike of a behavior turns to vindictiveness, one must question if that is healthy behavior."
"I like to drink and I like to get drunk. I work hard most of the time. . . . I'm a responsible . . . even compulsively proper person. But then I like to 'tie one on'. . . and get really drunk. I say, and my friends agree, that I never get sloppy or nasty . . . just witty, loose . . . even occasionally brave and foolhardy."	"There are safe ways and dumb ways to drink to drunkenness. One important thing is to be with friends, particularly some who don't get drunk. After a certain 'feel good' point, drinking more will make you feel worse . . . learn from your bad nights as well as your good ones."

In these instances, one variant was toward an ultra-safe behavior, which resulted in some loss of best functioning in other dimensions of living. Admitting that there are safer ways to do unsafe things is a possibility and a challenge for health education.

Secular health education is tempted to put down spiritual approaches to regaining health. Working from some common grounds is another possible and potentially healthy educational strategy. The dominant values can be stated as: (1) diagnosis and decisions about appropriate treatment should be made by a licensed physician or dentist; (2) treatment is based on scientific understanding of cause and effect—physical ailments typically require physical remedies, and mental problems require mental therapy. The religious point of view is listed as the variant below. A possible common ground response is in the right hand column.

Variant	Possible Response
"Disease and illness are real. They are caused either by evil forces or by God Himself in order to test a person. God is the only Healer, but He often uses certain 'special servants' to whom He gives the gift of healing. Healing comes through faith and prayer . . . but only if God wills it."	"There are various ways one can define evil. Physicians and dentists simply have other terms. God can use all kinds of healers. He certainly uses trained doctors to bring about many cures. He works in normal as well as spectacular ways."
"Departures from health are not real, but outward manifestations of a lack of proper relationships with God. Restore that relationship through prayer and reading, and health returns. We Christian Scientists may, under severe conditions, obtain medical care, but what is done does not bring about healing . . . this comes only from restoring the right relationship."	"You Christian Scientists are very willing to read and learn about life. If Christ were a scientist he certainly would take the scientific position of being willing to try something that has worked in other similar situations. If it is the relationship that is important . . . fine. Having medical or dental care too should not harm the restoration of relationships."

In the realm of sexuality the dominant values would seem to be (1) premarital sexual intercourse, because it can result in a number of problems, is not recommended; (2) if intercourse does occur, pregnancy and venereal disease should be prevented; (3) if an unwanted pregnancy occurs, a safe legal abortion is preferable to an illegal one and perhaps to an unwanted child; (4) if venereal disease is contracted it should be treated early and medically. The variations on these values are many—in the direction of more control and the punishment of sex acts, in the direction of real female-male equality, and in the direction of values that accept the inevitability of sexual acts, many of which will be exploitative. Since this is not a chapter on sexuality, some readers may feel that sexual examples are already in abundance. . . perhaps redundance. Those who do not feel so are invited to mentally construct some variants, with appropriate healthy messages.

There also are some variant values when it comes to the actual teaching-learning process, particularly in the classroom setting. One value that dominates for most teachers would be a perspective on present and future from their own learning experiences—you have to have some background . . . to know and understand certain things before good health decisions can be made. In the extreme, this value translates to memorizing bones and muscles before considering exercise, learning all the parts and functions of the digestive tract before considering anything about food selection and eating patterns, and, of course, being able to accurately tag the epididymis and the vas deferens before dealing with any aspects of sexual behavior. Without a teacher's perspective, some learners, in effect, say, "I see no point in that tedious task" and may be completely "turned off" when the time comes to make the application to the behavior of people. By the time the alveoli can be accurately differentiated from the esophagus, there may be no time for a decision-making discussion on smoking. If the teacher, on the other hand, is concerned that students be motivated to learn about their health, she/he may employ the value that, in considering the merits of psychotherapy vs. drug therapy for mental illness, learners come to realize they need to know some things about the nervous and endocrine system. This is the more appropriate way to get background information.

Some teachers still reflect a bit of Puritan heritage, where learning was supposed to be hard and dreary and learners had to be forced to learn. Some students still reflect this heritage—a course is not a good one unless it is difficult. If the culture and its youngsters hold this value, the system works with a fairly high failure rate. However, those advocating and carrying on the system are the relative successes. But if other values prevail, as in American culture at this time, this approach will not result in learning for some youngsters. If learning is the desired product for as many as possible, then other values need to be tried. For students who have to have some personally valid reason for learning something, an approach that starts from "where they are". . . with their own experiences . . . is more likely to produce learning.

Another dominant teacher value, embodied in most curricula, is symbolized by the announcement, "Today we are beginning a two-week unit on oral health." The value: it is good to develop a sequence of lessons that build a concept, each class section based on previous ones and leading to subsequent activities. Maximum learning thus comes, most typically, to students who attend the class regularly, have an attention span that encompasses the total class session, and possess the ability, natural and developed, to tie each day's activities with the other day's instructions—i.e., to think like the teacher does. For learners who do not value regular attendance or disciplined attention or who see no need to develop concepts based on relationships, the two-week unit can be a real loser.

Two possible alternatives seem feasible. One would design each day's learning activity to be complete and have integrity in and of itself. It could relate to ones before and after, but this is not necessary. It allows regular, attentive students to build larger concepts, but it can also involve and help the youngster who happens to be there . . . or awake . . . on any day. Another alternative would have one large focal concept for a whole semester or year, with all learning relating to it, though not necessarily on a day-to-day basis.

Finally, a fundamental value behind health education is the belief that taking action can make a difference in what happens in the future. Probably the most difficult variant value to confront, then, is one on inaction, stemming from the belief that doing something rarely makes any difference . . . that the individual really cannot affect his/her future in positive, predictable ways.

Is there any legitimate way to carry on health education without trying to change this value? Most would say NO . . . that the raison d'etre of health education is to urge people to realize they have or may have problems, and that there are ways to solve and prevent such departures from full functioning. Nevertheless, given the presumption of this chapter . . . it may be important to devise health education for human beings other than those with the culture's dominant values.

We have only really dealt with particular groups in the population who hold variations of some of the culture's dominant values, mostly because the total situation is almost too complex to write about. Some Black Americans affirm with conviction that there are some clearly Black values that white people cannot share. Other Black people deny this . . . or find it hard to clearly state such values. Some Black people live with one pattern of values and then work, with whites, employing a pattern somewhat different. Are a Black woman's values more predominantly Black . . . or female . . . if these are not consistent? Some young people espouse values other than those of their parents. A few seem to try to live these out in adult life, but many eventually follow patterns more like their upbringing.

Perhaps it is important to pose two very general categories of people who do not hold what are considered to be dominant values. There are two dangers in such a hypothesis, however: (1) Americans today are unlikely to be consistent . . . a group may uphold some dominant values and reject others . . . and each individual in the group is likely to have some different pattern of allegiance and belief than each other member; and (2) any particular value is not held on an all-or-none basis . . . two people may value flossing the teeth in addition to brushing, but one does it regularly and the other very sporadically. And the variations are endless. So this seemingly dichotomous categorization may be futile . . . even infuriating. But you won't know till I offer it . . . so. . . .

. . . People, mostly youth and young adults, have grown up with many of the dominant cultural values, but have rejected some of them for a counter culture. These folk tend to be relatively homogeneous with an amalgam of values, some of which are clearly counter to the dominant pattern and some of which are purifications (e.g., settling differences, internationally even, by negotiation rather than by force, or war).

. . . There are people, of all ages, who have never lived by the dominant values, mainly because of low and erratic economic functioning and/or other ethnic preferences. These folk are a very heterogenous lot, groups often being as unlike one another as they are unlike the dominant culture (i.e., Blacks in Harlem, Chicanos in East Los Angeles, whites in the Appalachians, and Blackfeet Indians in Idaho).

The major difference would be that people who have grown up with certain values and then have rejected some of them have less difficulty falling back to conformity with such than those who have grown up without them. For example:

- Willard was raised to learn and practice self-control, putting up with frustration and working out problems. He learned through life at home that alcohol use was moderate and drug use only for special, medically-prescribed purposes. As a late teenager, he chucked all these values and made the "whole drug scene" for about four years. After a close call with an overdose, he took stock of life, left the "scene," and entered college. He is now preparing for a career in pharmacy, having reaccepted most of the values of his early home life without much difficulty.

- Ben grew up in a different family setting with early remembrances of older people taking pills and drinking to excess. He grew up trying all kinds of dope, because life wasn't very shiny and promising when you were straight or sober. He is a bright boy and he has a chance to get some further education and move out of this environment. However, when things get frustrating, he finds it almost impossible not to get away from it all with a pill or a drink.

Different racial, economic, and ethnic groups have particular variations on health issues, depending on how they see the issues relating to themselves. Though American culture is awash with variations on values, there are certain discernible dominant values, some of which are expressed fairly vividly in health textbooks. Yet there are some health educators who feel that if their profession is to communicate with and motivate all persons to better health—not just those with dominant values, we must consider the merit of a position allowing almost any behavior as long as it helps a person function. But how does health education come across when one accepts the variants in values? Rather strange. . .perhaps threatening. But it may be important to try to meet the needs we have neglected.

FUTURE VALUES FOR TODAY'S CURRICULUM

Richard D. Van Scotter, *Assistant Professor of Education, Grinnell College, Grinnell, Iowa*

Jon Cauley, *Assistant Professor of Economics, Arizona State University, Tempe.*

...*A retired crane operator rocks back and forth on a mild summer evening telling his great-great-great-grandchildren what it was like to grow up in the city when he was a young boy. He has been retired for 70 years, over one half of his life. He now is 130 years old, thanks to medical advances which have arrested aging, and he can expect to live another 50 years.*

...*A college president besieged with student requests for control over the curriculum, elimination of grades, and a voice in hiring teachers sends a memorandum to the food services director. The memorandum states that henceforth all students will be served food containing a harmless, undetectable drug that will make them docile, obedient, and uncritical.*

...*A physician enters an impressive laboratory containing 500 artificial wombs. Emerging from the wombs are 500 male babies, genetically alike. Nine months earlier their "father," a prominent engineer, IQ 160, donated some skin which had been scraped from his leg by a physician.*

Today these events are fiction. Continued advancement in already rapidly developing areas of biological research will make them a reality someday. The value, or moral, questions prompted by such developments will be staggering for society.

Values education has had a place in the general curriculum for some time. Though this article focuses on the social studies, its subject matter and exercises are applicable to a variety of curriculum areas, particularly the natural sciences.

In the past, social studies has been an instrument of values enculturation in the schools. Enculturation has been brought about by teaching an acceptable body of knowledge—acceptable to the academic disciplines, society, and the community—largely through textbooks.

Contemporary social studies demonstrates a shift in emphasis toward values clarification and analysis. Though by no means has this shift been complete. As Alan Tom explains in *An Approach to Selecting Among Social Studies Curricula* (published by Central Midwestern Regional Education Laboratory in 1970), social studies classrooms still embrace two incompatible positions. One he distinguishes as "developing student commitment to particular value judgments," the other as "developing the student's ability to make rational value judgments." Nevertheless, there is a shift away from teaching values to teaching *about* values.

The movement toward values clarification and analysis is not likely to decrease in the years ahead. The treatment of values in this fashion has been emphasized, we suspect, for several reasons. Clarifying values provides a means of resolving conflicts in values. The Harvard Social Studies Project is a prime example of this position. It starts from the premise that the "American dilemma" is based on the existence of incompatible or conflicting values in society. Analyzing values provides a process of arriving at a rational, data-based position when valid judgments are necessary. The study of values also serves to foster open, flexible, and tolerant student behavior. Citizens need these qualities to cope intelligently and justly with the social problems in our society.

Generally, values or value judgments have been studied in the context of present time. If past values enter the curriculum, they do so coincidentally, through the transmission of tradition, beliefs, and knowledge related to the enculturation process.

Future values have been neglected also in social studies education, even though their study would be consistent with values clarification and analysis. Presumably the study of future values has not been included in the curriculum for at least two reasons. First, it is argued, teaching the young to openly approach today's values issues and make rational judgments will enable them to make thoughtful decisions at any time in the future. Second, future values cannot be anticipated. There is no reliable way of knowing what the issues of tomorrow will be; therefore, they must be dealt with as they arise.

The future, however, is not as mysterious and unpredictable as one would believe from looking at a school curriculum today. As the opening sketches suggest, the advent of numerous physical, biological, and technological breakthroughs is within the predictable future. Chemical control of aging in man can be expected sometime shortly after the turn of the 21st century, some 30 years from now. The use of drugs to alter specific aspects of human personality is predicted by futurists for as early as the 1980's. Human cloning, a process in which the nucleus of an ovum is removed and replaced by a somatic cell, allowing the development in a host mother of an identical twin of the person supplying the cell, may be operational by the year 2010, if research continues at the present pace.

These scientific advances and many others could have profound effects on the nature and value structure of society in the future. The profundity of these breakthroughs is intensified by the quantity and rate at which they are occurrring. As Alvin Toffler has illustrated so dramatically in his best-seller, *Future Shock,* the advent of these changes begets many additional changes. Change is taking place at a continually accelerating rate. We are supporting these advances by both research dollars and public approval. Their effects, however, will be realized not by us, but by future generations. The ramifications of today's values and the research patterns they reflect deserve study by the students of this generation who will be making decisions both now and in the future. John McHale writes, in *The Future of the Future* (Ballantine Books, 1969):

> Present scientific and technical knowledge makes it possible for modern man to create his own future, both in collective and individual terms. The future will increasingly become what man desires it to be Consequently, one of his greatest challenges is to decide how he wishes to shape the years to come.

Values are the spectacles through which a society interprets the world around it. For better or worse, they provide the basis for human beings' social interactions within the institutional framework they have built. The study of values in the social studies curriculum has been aimed at building a more free and open society. The inclusion of future values in the curriculum adds a crucial dimension to this quest.

Future values can be built on at least two distinct themes: students can identify and examine current social trends that have implications for society in the future; students can analyze the impact on society of current and future technological changes.

Social trends affect the future. Ronald Lippitt[1] has identified several trends that represent relevant images of the future for educators. One of these he describes as a trend toward "less and less tolerance for depersonalization, for being lost in the mass; less tolerance of pressures for conformity; and more expression of anti-establishment feelings." Symptoms of this trend, Lippitt points out, are evidenced in the music of pop culture, in the marked increase in attendance at religious classes on campuses, and in the tremendous development of personal-growth programs for adults across the country.

Other trends relevant to the general school curriculum include urbanization, pollution, economic growth, energy depletion, genetic engineering, space exploration, planned environments; the list is virtually endless.

Some lines of inquiry emanating from these trends can be posed by the following questions: What changes in our current values will be necessary for a continuation of this social trend? Will any new and different values develop as a result of this future trend? Will these changes in values tend to make a more open society in the future? If not, what changes could be made to halt this trend or channel it?

The following exercises are designed to give students practice in identifying social trends and in analyzing their effects on future values.

Predicting Future Values

This brief exercise is built on questions about the nature of people's values in the future. These traditional American values are classified into categories below. Prior to the exercise in class, students can discuss the meaning and nature of each value with their parents or a thoughtful adult friend. In class, the teacher can read aloud questions which begin, "Do you believe that people's values toward (*see value lists below*) will increase, decrease, or stay the same during the next 25 years?" Students can display a show of hands on each value.[2]

When the teacher has covered the lists, the class should come back and discuss the issues one-by-one. When possible, students should support their positions with reliable information. In many instances, however, their stands will be based on reasonable opinions and judgments. In summary, the class can compare their judgments with those of the expert futurists.

Self-Oriented Values
Health (+ + +)
Economic security and well-being (−)
Personal security (0)
Self-respect (+)
Self-reliance (− − −)
Personal liberty (0)
Self-advancement (−)
Self-fulfillment (+ +)
Intellectual virtues (+)
Physical virtues (0)
Readiness for hard work (− −)
Toughness (− −)
Perseverance and steadfastness (0)
Inventiveness and creativeness (+)
Appreciativeness (+)

Society-Oriented Values
Social welfare (+ + +)
Fair play (+ +)
Civil rights (+)
Justice (+ +)
Liberty (+)
Order (+)
Opportunity (0)
Charity (0)
Pride in "our culture" (− −)
Tolerance (+ +)

Group-Oriented Values
Respectability (0)
Reasonableness and rationality (0)
The domestic virtues (−)
The civic virtues (0)
Devotion to family and duty (−)
Devotion to principle (− − −)
Loyalty (0)
Friendliness, kindliness, etc. (0)
Feelings for others (+)
Personal tolerance (+ + +)
Patience (0)
Service (+)
Generosity (0)
Forthrightness (+)

Nation-Oriented Values
National freedom and independence (− −)
National prosperity and achievement (−)
Patriotism and national pride (− −)
Loyalty (to country) (− −)
Chauvinism (− − −)
Democracy (the American way) (− −)
"Public service" (0)

World-Oriented Values
Peace (+ + +)
Material achievement and progress (0)
Cultural and intellectual achievement and progress (+ +)
Humanitariansim (+ +)
Internationalism (+ + +)
Pride in the achievements of the "human community" (+ +)
Human dignity (+)

Environment-Oriented Values
Aesthetic Values (+ + +)

Changing Values

What society defines as social problems, current or future, and what it considers as alternative solutions to these problems are based on values. As values change, priorities are rearranged and new problems replace old with a resulting shift in national goals and policies. In view of this:

1. Write the following values on the chalkboard. Next to them make two columns labeled Past to Present and Present to Future.
   Sensitivity to the environment
   Monetary achievement
   Naturalism, i.e., appreciation of nature
   Material progress
   Good health
   Self-centeredness (or disregard of others)

2. Take as examples two social trends, economic growth and pollution. Discuss the relationship of the six values to these two social trends. For example, ask: "How does society's emphasis on economic growth affect one's sensitivity to the environment; likewise how does a sensitivity to the environment affect our economic growth policy?"

3. The students then should consider whether each of these six values currently is deemed more important than in the past (+), less important (−), or of the same importance (0) as in the past. Record the total number of pluses, minuses, and zeros in the Past to Present column beside each value. The class should sum the pluses and minuses of each value to obtain an index score; zeros can be treated as neutral responses and ignored. For example, if a class of 25 students gave monetary achievement 20 pluses and 5 minuses, the index score would be +15.

4. Next, ask the students if they expect each of these values to become more important in the future (+), less important (−), or remain the same (0). Record and total the responses in the column labeled Present to Future and obtain another index score.

5. Discuss the two scores obtained for each value. Are they different? Why are the scores different?

6. In conclusion, the teacher should pose the following questions: "What might have been the consequences, both now and in the future, if changes in these values had not occurred?" "What social policies were enacted as a result of these value changes?" "With reference to the column, Present to Future, do you anticipate future social legislation regarding pollution, economic growth?" Other trends can be analyzed in the same way.

What Would Life Be Like If . . .

In this exercise students are asked to consider what their lives would be like if certain events happened in their future. Each student should select a future event from the list below and prepare a short theme or composition on how it would affect his or her life. Papers should be organized around a few specific values, which could be chosen from the list in Exercise I. For example, if a student takes "What would life be like if I become very wealthy someday?" he or she could examine his or her own beliefs about the desire to do hard work, friendship, respecting others, welfare for the poor, intellectual virtues, self-reliance, and so on. Here is a list of other future events students could use for their compositions. What would life be like if . . .

. . . you could visit other planets as you visit other cities today?
. . . you retired at age 45, but lived to be 145 years old?
. . . you could communicate with others using E.S.P. (mental telepathy)?
. . . it was decided that 50 babies, the exact duplicate of you, would be artificially produced?
. . . you lived in a "raceless" society?
. . . cars were only available to rent or lease on long interregional trips?
. . . your job became obsolete every five years?
. . . it was necessary gradually to reduce the nation's economic growth rate?
. . . you were only allowed to fill one small garbage can per week?
. . . you lived in a domed city under the ocean?
. . . the personalities of your friends were constantly being artificially altered?
. . . you could read people's minds?
. . . you had a sophisticated computer implanted in your brain?

Technological innovations affect the future. Technological change is inevitable, but in itself such change is neither good nor evil. The implications of a particular change for future life, however, are important. Priority number one is to identify technologies already under development and to predict the likelihood of these becoming operational. The Institute for the Future (see footnote 3 for address) is one organization deeply involved in such work. Assuming we can accurately predict scientific developments, which developments or discoveries shall we apply to society?

Presumably, we cannot carry to fruition all potential scientific advances. As with most areas subject to the laws of economics, the principle of scarcity prevails, and society must cope with relatively unlimited wants and scarce resources. Therefore, since we cannot develop all possible scientific developments within a given time span, we must select those that will prove the most beneficial to society. A choice must be made in channeling government research funds into such fields as space exploration, military hardware, nonpollutant engines, ocean exploration, weather control, mass-administered contraceptives, or a host of other feasible areas. From another perspective, society must decide whether research and development funds should be spent on increasing an individual's life span in lieu of increasing the quality of the individual's present life, or in what proportion these funds should be divided between the two areas.

Predicting Future Innovations

This exercise is designed to introduce students briefly, but dramatically, to potential future innovations. The teacher is to read aloud one-by-one the questions listed below. After each question is read, those students who take an affirmative position should raise their hands. After completing the list, the class should discuss the reasons for their stance on each issue.

Preface each of these questions with, Who believes that . . .

... schools will consist almost totally of teaching machines, and students will learn by themselves at their own speed?

... the life span of human beings will be well over 100 years?

... children will be raised more strictly than they are now?

... life on other planets will be found?

... babies who are exact facsimiles of another human being will be produced artificially?

... people will be able to communicate through E.S.P.?

... people will be able to alter their personalities in specific ways by taking a drug?

... people in cities will walk around wearing pollution-protection masks?

... enclosed cities will be built in outer space?

... enclosed cities will exist at the bottom of the ocean?

The class can discuss whether or not these scientific and technological changes will occur and also whether or not they should occur. The latter question shifts the focus of discussion from predictions to future values consideration.

Evaluating Future Innovations

Reproduce on the chalkboard the 10 possible scientific discoveries below and construct five columns labeled Very Favorable, Favorable, Little or No Concern, Detrimental, and Very Detrimental. Discuss briefly each discovery to assure that students understand. Dates in parentheses are expert predictions for these breakthroughs.[3]

1. Chemical control of the aging process, permitting extension of life span by 50 years with a proportionate increase in the number of years of vigor (2015).

2. Sustaining the human body in frozen storage, thereby permitting it to be brought back to life at a later date (2025 plus).

3. Development of "raceless" societies among at least one half of the world's population through interbreeding (2025 plus).

4. Availability of cheap, non-narcotic drugs (non-alcoholic) to make specific changes in personality characteristics (1980).

5. A process in which the nucleus of an ovum is removed and replaced by a somatic cell, allowing development in a host mother of an individual genetically identical to the person supplying the somatic cell (1985).

6. Control of people's behavior by radio stimulation of the brain (1985).

7. Availability of complex robots which are programmable, self-adaptive, and capable of performing household chores, such as preparing meals and cleaning (1980).

8. Use of mental telepathy for communication (2025).

9. Discovery of information proving the existence of intelligent beings beyond the earth (2025 plus).

10. Maintenance of the human brain outside of the body for one month (2025).

Poll the students to obtain their opinions on the impact of each discovery if it were applied to society in the near future. After the votes for each discovery have been recorded in the appropriate columns on the chalkboard, the class can offer reasons for their responses. Following this discussion have the students vote on whether or not to apply the discovery to society.

Technology in an Open Society

Assuming a scientific discovery is applied to society, the class should examine the economic, social, political, ethical, and ecological consequences. Divide the class into five groups, one for each consequence. One member from each group would make up each panel. For example, assuming an increase in life expectancy, the panel could examine the consequences as follows:

1. *Economic:* An increase in life expectancy also will increase the number of years in which a person remains productive. Thus a 100-year life span implies that growing numbers of people beyond the age of 65 may wish to be employed. Leisure time would increase and expenditures for use of this time also would rise. Our social security structure will require revision. The enlarged senior citizen population will have unique consumer demands, such as low-speed automobiles, artificial organs, picture phones, and household robots. In spite of the presumed vitality of the older population, a maximum age of employment law might be enacted so that younger people can work.

2. *Social:* A shifting of the median age of the population may be accompanied by greater urbanization. Great leisure communities may be formed to resemble periods from the past. This artificial return to a more gracious age would provide retired citizens a choice, for example, of Colonial or Gay Nineties cities having modern advantages but requiring strict adherence to the mores and technology of the earlier era.

3. *Political:* The older people may form a political group of considerable power and significance. It is likely that they would have a large and therefore strong enough power base to enact special legislation.

4. *Ethical:* The sustaining of life, not unlike the begetting of life, places an increased obligation on society, especially if the people expect life to be increasingly enjoyable and stimulating. If the decision-makers are to maintain an open society that provides the individual with an increasing quality of life, they will have to be responsive to many of the economic, social, and political consequences described above.

5. *Ecological:* Other things being equal, longer lives mean that more people have to be supported at any given time. An increase in the population has far-reaching effects on the supply of natural resources needed to sustain human life. These resources can be depleted through human consumption, land development and displacement, and pollution.

Other technological innovations which can be successfully explored by the panel in light of the five consequences are human cloning, frozen storage of the human body, programmed robots, and personality change by drugs.

The study of future values today is critical for the construction and maintenance of an open society simply because individual and social decisions today have direct value consequences for future generations. If these value structures become inflexible as a result of neglecting the vast range of future possibilities of a society, that society will become more closed. A later decision may be too difficult to implement; that is, our values may be forced upon later generations as a result of current technological developments creating an irreversible social situation. For example, if a scientific breakthrough prolonging human life is made and applied to society, future generations will be forced to assume the economic, social, and ethical responsibilities even though they had no say in the decision.

Therefore, consideration must be given to the consequences to future generations of today's research and development decisions. It should be possible for them to initiate their *own* changes commensurate with their value preferences. In order to adequately provide for such future freedom of choice, it is mandatory to study future values with an eye to long-range social planning for maintenance of an open society.

INTERVIEW: ALVIN TOFFLER ON THE ROLE OF THE FUTURE AND VALUES IN EDUCATION

Alvin Toffler, *author and consultant*

June Grant Shane, *Professor of Education, Indiana University, Bloomington*

Harold G. Shane, *University Professor of Education, Indiana University, Bloomington.*

Since the late 1960's, U.S. educators have begun to read and hear more about "futures research," a new discipline designed to help policymakers choose wisely in terms of their purposes and values among alternative courses of action.

Hundreds of "futures" courses are now offered in schools and colleges; the U.S. Office of Education supports Educational Policy Research Centers at the Stanford Research Institute and at the Syracuse University Research Corporation; and Paul Dickson in his book, *Think Tanks,* estimates that government, industry, and the military spend perhaps $25 billion annually to shape future developments that are either sought or anticipated.

In 1970, with the publication of *Future Shock,* Alvin Toffler became an important commentator on the "premature arrival of the future" which has carried us from yesterday to tomorrow in so brief a time as to leave most of us bewildered. A former associate editor of *Fortune,* Mr. Toffler has been a visiting professor at Cornell University and a visiting scholar at the Russell Sage Foundation. In this interview, he discusses the role of the future in education.

Q. A good many teachers will undoubtedly be as interested in your new book, *Learning for Tomorrow,* as they were in

Future Shock. Can you tell us how the book came into being?

A. *Learning for Tomorrow* was designed as a manifesto for a new reform movement in education. It is not just a collection of random discursive essays. Every chapter supports in one way or another the thesis that, in education, we are now compelled to make a fundamental break with our ingrained "past orientation," our "past consciousness," if you will.

Although the contributors to the book come from a wide variety of disciplines, all agree that our educational system is rocketing toward disaster and that we cannot redirect it, no matter what innovations we introduce, unless we take a fresh look at the role of the future in education.

Q. The subtitle of your book is "The Role of the Future in Education." What do you see as a meaningful role for education in the future?

A. All of us in the high-technology nations are caught up in one of the great revolutions in human history. We are in the process of creating a new civilization which will demand new ways of life, attitudes, values, and institutions.

The young people in our schools today are going to live in a world radically different from the one we know—and a world that will be undergoing continual and, in all likelihood, accelerating change.

In such a society and in such a period of time, I can think of no more important role for education than to serve as one of the great adaptive mechanisms both for the social system as a whole and for the individual within it.

Q. Do you discuss the future of education in your book?

A. No, it is not a book about the future *of* education. It is about the future *in* education, about the *concept* of the future and the part this concept plays in learning.

The book brings together what will be the two major streams of change in education in the 1970's. One has to do with *action* and action learning—with moving education outside the classroom and involving learners with the real-life activities of society. The other has to do with the role of *time* in learning, with building "future consciousness" into the culture.

In combination, the movement toward action learning and the introduction of the future as a central component of the curriculum will have a profound impact on education.

Q. Let's talk about the first mainstream of change—action learning. Why do you feel this movement is so important?

A. We need to abandon the Neanderthal notion that

education takes place only in schools. We all know that education is not just something that happens in our heads. It involves our total biochemistry. Neither does it occur solely within the individual. Education springs from the interplay between the individual and a changing environment.

At present, action learning programs which permit a student to study off campus or outside the classroom are regarded as peripheral to the education process. In the future, we are going to have to regard action learning—a form of socially useful work—as the central theme of education and classroom learning as supportive rather than primary. This suggests a change, not just in the content of education, but in the structure of our institutions and their relationships with society as well.

Q. Would you give us an example of the kind of change that might be necessary?

A. We ought to encourage the organization of groups of learners that include people of all ages who set themselves the tasks of bringing about socially important changes in the community. In this way, action learning would develop what might be called "generation bridges" that would help to do away with our pernicious age segregation.

To function well in a fast-shifting environment, learners must have the chance to do more than receive and store data: They must have, and actually feel that they have, the opportunity to make change occur. This implies a profound shift in the present relationship between educational theory and practice.

Q. You also said that you felt the concept of "futures" should permeate education more thoroughly than it does now. Why do you ascribe so much importance to the study of the future in the curriculum?

A. Although nobody knows what lies ahead, I believe that the future remains open to a considerable degree. Certain trends or forces are at work which are probably going to be difficult for us to modify in any major way, but there are other openings and opportunities which the children we are now educating are going to have the chance to accept or reject. Anticipating these opportunities, speculating about alternatives, and being sensitized to the choices they may face, both personal and public, is an imperative part of their education.

Q. You have said, "All education springs from images of the future." Why do you feel this way when most people would say that education is influenced by tradition and our memories of the past?

A. In a slowly changing society, education tends to focus on the past because there is a general assumption that the past will simply repeat itself in the future. Today, however, when change is extremely rapid, we have to assume that the future will be radically different from the past. And this requires a fresh awareness of the role the future plays in education.

Q. One of your coauthors, Benjamin D. Singer, speaks of the "future-focused role image" or FFRI. What is your interpretation of the FFRI as opposed to the term *self-concept*—a familiar term in education?

A. The idea of self-concept has been very important, but it is a static concept. It centers on the present. The future-focused role image introduces the idea of time into the concept of self-image. It suggests that our thinking is influenced not only by what our self-image is at a given moment but also by our image of a future self.

Singer argues that a well-formulated, realistic future-focused role will serve as a highly motivating force in the student. Students characterized by such future-focused role images have an adaptive tool that is not available to those students who lack these role images.

Singer argues, and I agree, that in the absence of a coherent and appropriate future-focused role image, it is difficult for an individual to make consistent decisions and to achieve competence in the present.

Q. We understand you made some inquiries with regard to images of the future held by teenagers. What kinds of futures do they foresee?

A. Well, what I did was by no means either systematic or scientific. I simply went into a classroom and asked a lively group of teenagers to list some events they felt were likely to occur in the future. And in a few minutes I had collected almost 200 forecasts.

Q. What kinds of roles did the students see for themselves in the worlds of tomorrow they envisioned?

A. Nearly all the students tended to leave themselves out of the forecasts—a most significant finding. Of the 193 forecasts, only 16 used the word *I*. Of these, six dealt with death, which is, indeed, an easily forecastable event at some time in everyone's future.

For the most part, the kinds of futures they saw themselves moving into were simply extensions of the kinds of lives that their parents lead today.

They did not foresee that the rather shattering or monumental world events they themselves forecast—including revolutions, technological upheavals, and ecological catastrophes—would have any impact on their own lives. In short, they seemed to make a sharp distinction between a swiftly changing future "out there" and a more or less unchanged personal future.

This suggests the need to refocus the time horizon in education. If our young people are not encouraged to think of the future as something likely to require change in *their own* lives, then we are producing millions of candidates for future shock.

Q. In the 1960's, white America became more conscious of ethnic minorities. Can education help change the Black child's image of his or her future?

A. According to Alvin Poussaint, who is a contributor to *Learning for Tomorrow,* a major impediment to the kind of learning that our system requires is the negative self-image that has been produced in many young Black children by the pressures of a color-caste system.

In compensation for this, Dr. Poussaint says, the Black community is giving the Black child the necessary ego support by saying, "Look, you're OK. It may be those white folks who aren't OK."

I believe we are in no way finished with the problem of achieving an America in which all ethnic groups can find a useful and decent way of life. The Black community itself is searching for new directions and is no longer as clear about its goals as some of its more militant spokespersons thought in the 1960's.

Confusion in the Black community simply parallels the confusion in the surrounding white society as well. I would suggest that our problems can no longer be viewed dualistically in terms of integration *or* segregation, assimilation *or* separatism.

All of us, regardless of class or race, need a sense of self-mastery and of competence. This is extremely difficult for all students, white *or* Black, to achieve so long as they are viewed as some homogeneous, monolithic group that can be fitted into a rigid educational machine designed to produce yesterday's model of a middle-class white child.

Q. In the future that you see emerging, will there be a new egalitarianism with regard to sex-roles?

A. Just as our educational system has been implicitly racist, frequently against the best intentions of many teachers and administrators, so I think it has also been sexist.

The sharply distinctive male-female role images that the schools have assigned to students in the past have been responsible for a great deal of damage in our society. We need a movement toward what might be called "role freedom" for both men and women.

Q. As roles for women change, what provisions do you see for the caring of children?

A. Clearly, one of the things that the women's rights movement has been saying is that there must be a well-developed, day-care system to free women to take on roles outside the home if they wish to do so.

But, in addition to this, another alternative might present a great opportunity for us. That is to have men play a new role in the home. I think we are going to develop a system under which both men and women alternate in the work force during certain periods in their lives.

Under this system, during some years the wife earns a living and the man stays at home; then she comes back to the home, and he goes back into the labor force. Also, I believe we will see the development of a pattern in which a single job is shared by a husband and wife.

My own hunch is that instead of a single solution to the question of how children are going to be reared, there will be many, many experiments. Out of these will come a few reasonable solutions. Of course, millions of people will stick with the conventional system or attempt to stick with it.

Q. Many people feel that along with other minorities older citizens have been neglected and cast aside as useless. What does the future suggest for this group?

A. Earlier, I talked about building generational bridges and stated that action learning could help. It is bad for people to be segregated by age, just as it is bad for them to be segregated coercively by sex or race. In fact, I believe that the breakdown of age segregation in education is going to be one of the major goals of the 1970's.

Our communities are filled with people at different age levels who have acquired an astonishing variety of useful skills. It seems to me quite feasible for schools—perhaps elementary schools, but certainly secondary schools, universities, and colleges—to match a young learner with an older person who is already practicing the skill that the student wishes to learn.

Today society is undergoing a process of radical fragmentation. It is beginning to require not merely many thousands of new occupations that never existed in the past, but new personality types, new roles, and certainly new human skills. We will need to find new ways to transmit these skills from old to young—and in the opposite direction as well.

Q. How do you envision that education could help match young learners with mature learners?

A. No school system can offer a curriculum sufficiently diverse to provide all the skills the society needs without tapping the information now stored in the craniums of tens of thousands of nonteachers. Many of these persons actually could turn out to be superteachers if we arranged learning appropriately.

No child should ever go through his or her early educational years without having the opportunity to meet a person engaged in an occupation in which the child might be interested. To deprive the child of this is to deprive him or her of an important step in the formation of his or her future-focused role image.

We need a system of "community mentorships" with tens of thousands of "adjunct teachers and professors" woven throughout society—a system in which students are introduced to people in the community and regularly visit them in their offices and homes, to question them and learn from them. Many people in our society who are capable of teaching many things are now cut off from the educational system by what I would regard as false notions of professionalism and would welcome the chance to be useful educationally.

Q. In recent years there has been deepening concern about moral education for the future. Do you think schools have a responsibility to help alleviate the present value crises?

A. Very much so. We have ducked the question of values in education for the last generation or more. There are quite natural and understandable reasons for this. It took a tremendous struggle on the part of progressive educators to loosen ecclesiastical and political controls on our school systems. This struggle to free the schools from the imposition of traditional orthodox values by the church and state, however, occurred during the period of what might be called "naive scientism."

Q. Are you referring to the so-called scientific or educational testing movement of the 1920's?

A. No. I am saying that this struggle took place during a period when the dominant culture looked to science to solve its problems. One of the spillovers from science into education was the notion of value-free education—neutral education.

Now we are a lot wiser about this. We realize that values are inculcated and transmitted in virtually any interaction between human beings. Therefore, despite our attempts to provide "objective" curriculum or neutral cognitive materials, we find it cannot be done. This being the case, we cannot escape the issue of values.

Q. How would you suggest that we go about facing the issue?

A. I am not arguing for a return to the past—to the heavy-handed inculcation of orthodoxy or, for that matter, orthodox antiorthodoxy. We need to move the whole issue to a higher level. Rather than inculcating a simple set of well-defined values—which may or may not be acceptable in a highly diverse society and which may or may not be appropriate in our rapidly changing world—we would do better to inculcate the value of knowing one's own values.

Our society is in desperate need of institutions that will help everyone, not just youngsters, sort out their own conflicting and confused value systems. People cannot make consistent and competent decisions in pursuit of their own futures, if their personal value systems are riddled with contradictions.

It seems to me that one of the most important forms of assistance that we can give people to help them cope with rapid change is to help them clarify their own values.

It is a crime against learners to make them go through the educational process without at some point—if not at all points—encouraging them to ask themselves some serious questions, such as what life is for, why they pursue one direction instead of another, and why some things seem more valuable to them than others.

The purpose of introducing action learning and the future into education is to help produce people better able to cope with change in a highly change-filled society. Coping with change implies making decisions, and decisions cannot be made without criteria. Criteria, in turn, are based on implicit or explicit values.

As society undergoes the turmoil of a cultural and social revolution, which is, in fact, what I think is now happening, the underlying value system begins to change. As our society fragments, the value system, too, fragments; the consensus splits. We begin to move to what superficially seems like an anything-goes society.

I would urge all educators to begin personally to face value questions and then to introduce them into the classroom.

Q. You seem to feel strongly about this issue of values, Mr. Toffler. Have you had some personal experiences which strengthen this conviction?

A. Yes. Back in 1966 in my first course on the future, I asked my students to tell me how the course had affected them or whether it had affected them at all. The responses indicated to me that talking about the future raises some very sensitive value questions.

For example, if we face serious problems of overpopulation, should I have more than one child or even one child? With certain kinds of technology implying this or that threat to the environment, should I pursue my career as an engineer?

These kinds of questions became the center of preoccupation when the students wrote about how the course had affected them. Something then began to dawn on me, the need for me to help make *implicit* values in that classroom *explicit*.

For example, in a discussion of population, when an individual says that the globe should support no more than so many billion human beings, he or she is making more than a statistical statement. Any such statement is related to his or her values with respect to resource consumption and implies a value statement about what one regards as a minimum level of human subsistence.

There are opportunities in every subject to extract the value issues hidden behind what on the outside looks like an "objective" mass of information. So I would argue strongly than an emphasis on futures implies not only an emphasis on *possible* and *probable* futures but a very strong emphasis also on *preferable* futures. And at that point we are talking about values.

THE CHALLENGE OF VALUE COMMITMENT

Lawrence Senesh, *Professor of Economics, University of Colorado, Boulder.*

There are two smart clocks in the lobby of the Department of Commerce in Washington, D.C., and they are in competition with each other. As the seconds of one clock tick away, it shows the rising population of the United States. As the seconds of the other clock tick away, it shows the rising Gross National Product. Up to now, the GNP clock has run far ahead of the population clock—an indication of the steadily rising standard of living in the United States.

Today the average citizen of the United States has about 40 times more goods and services than the average Ethiopian, and 80 times more goods and services than the average Asiatic Indian. While the GNP of the United States is 1.2 trillion dollars, the GNP of the entire world is only 3.0 trillion dollars. To bring everyone up to the standard of living in the United States, the GNP of the rest of the world would have to rise to 18 trillion dollars. Such a six-fold increase is an environmental and technological impossibility.

Now comes the mystery: even though we are richer than everyone else, our high incidence of violent conflict and our numerous social tensions indicate that we are very discontented. Because of inflation, our savings shrink overnight and our financial security is threatened. Because of layoffs due to recession and technological unemployment, our seemingly secure jobs are in fact insecure. Although we go to sleep with confidence in those at the helm, we wake up to realities which cast shadows on the integrity of our political leaders—and upon whole branches of government. Some observers, like the *London Economist,* think we are on the verge of a nervous breakdown. But why?

The predictability of our institutions is being shaken, and this unpredictability weakens our social system and those values on which our social system rests. Without predictability, no society can survive.

Values are objectives and ideals which individuals and societies find good and desirable. Values reflect what individuals and societies find proper and beautiful. Values guide individuals and societies in establishing priorities. Today the values which have guided the United States and which constitute the foundations of our social system are being challenged. Let us consider these values.

The most important values underlying the economic system are:

1. *Progress.* Adam Smith thought that progress was achieved through the market system; Utopian socialists thought that progress could be achieved through the creation of an environment wherein people could be perfected; and Karl Marx derived the process of progress from a materialistic interpretation of history.

2. *Material advancement and comfort.* We have been raised to believe that hard work leads to economic success, and that economic success can be measured directly in terms of the quantity of goods produced and consumed, and in terms of accumulated capital stock. As more goods and services have been produced our appetites have now literally outgrown the resources of the earth. Our commitment to material advancement and comfort has been challenged by environmental considerations, by limitations on natural resources, and by the discontent of the developing countries. We may have to shift our value preferences to a life where the emphasis is not on quantity, but on quality. If this shift of values does not take place voluntarily, it may take place authoritatively, and this could mean the loss of a democratic society.

3. *Hard work.* Our economic system is based on the value of hard work. Individual and group survival on the American frontier demanded hard work, and the old rule was, "Who does not work, does not eat." Hard work ceased to be a reality, however, for today the exploitation of energy resources has destroyed the demand and respect for physical labor and, along with it, the work

ethic. Our value commitment to hard work has been challenged by the passing of the frontier, the exploitation of non-human energy resources, the substitution of mechanical for human means of production, and by such social programs as compulsory retirement. Abandoning our value preferences for hard work, can we find another way to satisfy our need for a sense of personal achievement?

4. *Economic freedom.* Our economic system is built on the value of economic freedom. We say we are free to become producers, but uneven distribution of economic power in the market makes it increasingly difficult to enter business. We say that economic freedom encourages competition, yet much business tends to protect itself from competition by bigness and product differentiation. We say we are free as customers, but the consumer's freedom in the market is distorted by a barrage of advertising which influences choices.

The most important values underlying the political system are:

1. *Democracy.* Our political system is based on the value commitment to democracy, and American democracy is based on two philosophical beliefs. First, that every citizen has "certain unalienable Rights." Second, that a free, just, and peaceful society, a prerequisite for democracy, is, as the Founding Fathers believed, attainable. Thomas Jefferson believed that, "Trusted with destinies of the solitary republic of the world, the only monument of human rights, and the sole depository of the sacred fire of freedom and self-government, from hence it is to be lighted up in other regions of the world." However, Daniel Moynihan's speech in the United Nations, in 1976, contrasts with Jefferson's view of 1776. Moynihan acknowledged that American democracy is not the prevailing system of the world, nor the system for which other nations are yearning.

If democracy is being challenged elsewhere in the world, it is also being challenged within the United States. Our commitment to democracy is realistic only if a political system prevails that guarantees the distribution of political power among the legislative, executive, and judicial branches of the government so that none of them can make arbitrary decisions. The recent challenge to this assumption has been vividly dramatized by Senator Sam Ervin, Jr., a figure who seemed to amble over from the Constitutional Convention to the television era to tell us that the President of the United States declared the Republic to have been in mortal danger from internal enemies. The White House felt that the

Republic had to be defended, and this led to the unprecedented centralization of political power in the White House, a situation which seriously challenges our value commitment to democracy.

2. *Freedom of speech.* Our political system is built on the value of freedom of speech, which is guaranteed to all citizens by the First Amendment to the Constitution. Freedom of speech is necessary if truth is to prevail, yet in reality, we do not like to exercise this freedom. We avoid disagreements and are told that if we want to keep our friends, we should never argue about religion or politics. Although we may keep our friends in this manner, we deny ourselves the right to express our opinions.

Silence is often the enemy of freedom, as it can give consent to tyranny and injustice. Pericles summed up the value of speaking out when he said, "In Athens, we think that silent men are useless."

3. *Political socialization.* Our political system rests on a political socialization that acts as an antidote to intolerance and anti-social behavior. Political socialization is a long and arduous process. Its purpose is to make people feel that they are a part of a political society and that their participation counts. The most powerful tool of political socialization is American history.

History shows that the United States is not a melting pot, but a kaleidoscope of different ethnic backgrounds, different attitudes, and different interpretations of our national destiny. American history offers a great variety of episodes. People of different cultural backgrounds can always identify themselves with at least some of these episodes and heroes. One group may identify with Nat Turner; another group with Abraham Lincoln; and a third group with Jefferson Davis. This diversity serves, at the same time, as a unifying force. American history, with all its variety, can keep society together by virtue of the multitude of loyalties which are possible within it.

Unfortunately, as U.S. history is usually taught, it does not reveal its multi-cultural variety and richness; consequently, many groups within the nation do not feel themselves to be a relevant part of American political society.

The most important values underlying the cultural system are:

1. *Power of reason.* We say we believe in the power of reason, we pay lip service to rational objectivity, and yet we reason one way and act another. Despite the known dangers of cigarette smoking, smoking is increasing in the United States. Despite the fact that conflict management is recognized as a condi-

tion for social evolution, violent group conflict in the United States is increasing. Despite the cataclysmic threat of future war, the balance of terror continues and armaments escalate. Despite the increasing money spent on driver safety education, it was found not to be as efficient in reducing death rates resulting from accidents as are laws which coerce the use of the safety belt. And despite counseling on the consequences of alcoholism, the fear of a test for drunken driving is a more effective deterrent than reasoning.

2. *Pragmatism.* Our cultural system is based on the notion of pragmatism, a belief that the value of an idea may be judged by its effectiveness, and on our ability to solve problems. The bent for practicality and inventiveness is a distinctive part of the American tradition, from the pioneer tinkerers who invented a type of plow and windmill to meet the demands of the American prairies, to the contestants who design their own vehicles to meet the demands of the local Soap Box Derby.

The conquest of the American West may be viewed as a grand test of American pragmatism and ingenuity. The pioneers faced up to the reality of the Great Plains and solved the problems on the spot. We are used to witnessing the immediate solution of problems, but when we are faced with such problems as widespread unemployment, our faith in pragmatism and in our ability to solve problems tends to break down. Although it is not possible to measure the effects of many of our actions immediately, we still insist on testing everything for immediate results. The lack of immediate results drives us to despair. We introduced legislation to cope with the problems of poverty, discrimination, inequality of opportunity, transportation and urban renewal. In each case, the program ended with disappointment, because results could not be measured immediately. Can you imagine what would have happened to the faith of Saint Francis of Asissi if he had measured his charity to the poor in terms of their rehabilitation?

3. *Science and technology.* Our cultural system is based on the notion that science and technology are guiding us toward Utopia. Science wields extraordinary power to predict the future course of events and has made humans most adaptive creatures, capable of responding to anticipated future events.

Scientists, though, must be guided in their research by values which will insure the beneficial use of scientific discoveries and inventions. The search for knowledge should be left free, but scientific discoveries should not be harmful to body, mind, or spirit. Rabelais said, "Science without conscience is the ruination of the soul." In 1851, Prince Albert opened the Great Exhibition in London with these words, "Nobody who has paid any attention to the peculiar features of the present era will doubt for a moment that we are living in a period of the most wonderful transition, which tends rapidly to accomplish that great end to which all history points: the realization of the unity of mankind." While no one would deprecate such an end, technology has often turned out to be a sacred cow that gives sour milk.

Technology developed on the assumption that the ecostructure can be replaced by a technostructure. Because the earth is a static system and technology is a dynamic one, the technologists' assumption of unlimited growth is being challenged by our awareness of the earth's resource limitations and by the ecologists' insistence that technology and nature must be in harmony.

Technology developed on the assumption that the outcome of tecnology can be predicted. Dr. Faustus, Dr. Jekyl, Dr. Caligari, and Dr. Strangelove were all well-intentioned, but the unforeseen consequences of their actions were dangerous to humanity. Dr. Frankenstein wanted to create a new race of superior beings. It was only when his work was done and he stepped back to view it as a whole that its true and terrifying character appeared. Modern technologists should contemplate the possibility that miracle drugs can produce miracle microbes.

Technology developed on the assumption that it was the ultimate expression of free will. Ironically, technology may be endangering free will by making the human being the potential victim of pharmaceutical manipulation and genetic engineering.

It is clear that the values which underlie the economic, political, and cultural sectors of our social system have been challenged. Our society finds itself in a value crisis which has the potential to transform the social and natural landscape into a wasteland that will offer our young people no hope for the future. Rather than permit a wasteland to occur, we should begin now to work for value commitments through which humanity's best aspirations can be realized.

The adoption of values is an emotional as well as a rational matter. The foundations of knowledge and art are made up of a system of values: truth, freedom, peace, justice, and excellence. These are the values which guide people to greater perfection in all areas of knowledge and art.

1. *The ubiquity of values.* As the framework of understanding enlarges, people move toward universalities in all their endeavors. One example is in the area of science. Scientific curi-

osity in various parts of the globe is bringing together the great variety of knowledge into an elegantly simple design. As J. Bronowski has said, "The constant urge of science...[is] to broaden the likeness for which we grope under the facts.... And it is the unity of nature... for which our thought reaches.... We seek to find nature one, a coherent unity. This gives to scientists their sense of mission...."[1]

Just as scientific knowledge is moving toward universality, so art is moving toward the universals which underlie all human experience. Every civilization strives for the expression of beauty and truth. Not only is the existence of artists universal, but the vision which artistic works contain points to the universality of all human experience.

Both scientific advancement and works of art would be unthinkable if science and the arts did not draw their strength from a set of values which includes commitment to truth, beauty, liberty, excellence, peace, and justice. Without these values the search for knowledge and artistic expression could not exist. Without knowledge and art, human beings would be relegated to the level of vegetables. These are value commitments which make the human being an humane being.

2. *Values and psychological growth.* According to Eric Fromm, "valuable" or "good" is that which contributes to the development of human potentialities and which furthers vitality. "Negative" or "bad" is everything which strangles life and paralyzes human activity.[2]

Since truth, liberty, peace, justice, and excellence make humans joyful, interested, and active, these values enhance psychological growth. According to Fromm, a person deprived of freedom becomes resigned and loses vitality, or becomes hostile and aggressive. The question is: Which set of qualities is more human—to be active or passive, curious or disinterested, creative or dull?

If the value preferences are for quantity rather than quality, where the mechanical is more valued than the human, and where growth charts ignore the human costs of the widening income gap, the result will be dehumanization and unconcern for the individual's psychological growth—which help deteriorate society.

3. *Values and planning for the future.* If the present trends continue, the future of the world is environmental deterioration, a widening income gap, increases in terrorism and authoritarianism, a static economy, and hunger. As the concentration of economic power increases, it fosters the concentration of political power and

undermines democracy. The consequences of all these trends are dehumanizing. To escape this dehumanization, people must act on their value commitments both in the present and in the future.

People can change these trends, but to do this, there will have to be a re-arranging of the hierarchy of values. To offset environmental deterioration, people may have to prefer quality of life to quantity of material goods. To lessen the violence in society, people may have to make greater commitments to the building of a peaceful society. They may have to practice day after day nonviolent ways of resolving conflicts. To keep the income gap from widening, people must value justice and equality more. To check the spread of authoritarianism, people will have to place greater value on freedom and truth.

Changing our values is neither improbable nor impossible. Value commitments are not unalterably fixed. The increase of the world's population, the exponential rate of resource depletion, and the human threat to the ecosystem may compel us to change our value preferences. Science and technology may shape our future in such ways as to necessitate a change in our value preferences if we want to live with the consequences of science and technology. As global communication increases and cultural isolation diminishes, our awareness of the values of other cultures and their effect upon us may invite us to alter our own commitments.

The set of values necessary for building a more perfect future—those of truth, freedom, peace, excellence, love, beauty, and justice—is a system of interrelated values, each of which depends on and supports the others. It is a closed system. One cannot have both racism and justice, nor armaments and peace, nor bigotry and love, nor unlimited production and environmental excellence.

Because this set of values is the basis of human psychological health and a prerequisite in planning for the future, it must be nurtured in the students of our schools. Abraham Maslow has argued that, "Education must be seen as at least partially an effort to produce the good human being.... an education which leaves untouched the entire region of transcendental thought is an education which has nothing important to say about the meaning of human life."[3] In this statement, Maslow brings to mind the comment by John Dewey that, "The aim of education is growth or development, both intellectual and moral. Ethical and psychological principles can aid the school in the greatest of all constructions—the building of a free and powerful character."[4]

An education which generates knowledge without adding the balance wheel of moral values makes possible such aberrations as Nazi physicians "experimenting" in the concentration camps and German rocket scientists who continue their work without regard for which side they are on. Using knowledge to improve human society leads to full humaneness and the full development of human potential, both individual and societal. We should realize that such improvement and development involve two factors:

First, human will is necessary. Children must be taught that values exist, and that there are hierarchies in values. Teachers must point out that values can help children's lives to flourish and help children to build a better world—otherwise children will wander in a wasteland which we have helped to create.

Second, we must realize that the process of internalizing and applying humane values is a never ending process: the horizon is always beyond us.

Furthermore, students and teachers need to realize that humane values can be drawn from many cultures:

> He has shown thee, O man, what is good; and what doth the Lord require of thee. But to do justly, and to love mercy, and to walk humbly with thy God. *(Old Testament)*
>
> Do unto others as you would have them do unto you. Blessed are the peacemakers. *(New Testament)*
>
> Justice demands that virtue and happiness should be brought into harmony. (Emannuel Kant)
>
> The superior man is satisfied and composed; the mean man is always full of distress. (Confucius)
>
> The spokes of the wheel are the rules of pure conduct: justice is the uniformity of their length; wisdom is the tire; modesty and thoughtfulness are the hub in which the immovable axle of truth is fixed. (Gautama Buddha)
>
> The perception of beauty is a moral test. (H. D. Thoreau)
>
> Anything which obscures the fundamental moral nature of the social problem is harmful. (John Dewey)
>
> The good life is one inspired by love and guided by knowledge. (Bertand Russell)

Immanuel Kant in *The Critique of Judgment, Part II,* also formulated a categorical imperative, based on justice, as a guide for moral decisions: "Always act toward the other as an end, not as a means. Always choose only what you would be willing to have everyone choose in your situation."

The world community has committed itself to the values expressed in the United Nations Universal Declaration of Human Rights: "All human beings are born free and equal. They are born with reason and conscience. They should act toward one another in a spirit of brotherhood."

The fundamental values of our society which the Declaration of Independence expresses are as inspiring now as 200 years ago: "We hold these truths to be self-evident, that all Men are created equal, that they are endowed by their Creator with certain unalienable Rights, that among these are Life, Liberty, and the Pursuit of Happiness."

Further, in the Constitution our Founding Fathers gave us the mandate, "To form a more perfect Union, establish justice, insure domestic tranquility, provide for the common defense, promote the general welfare, and secure the blessings of liberty to ourselves and our posterity."

These are the values which unite human beings and which promote harmony between the individual and the environment. These are values which do not counsel expediency nor glorify mere survival—meaningless objectives for truly human beings. These are the values which harmonize with the human ability to strive after noble aspirations. These are the values which should be taught to our children. The discussion and internalization of these values should be a part of our social science curriculum.

These sets of values could guide the behavior of our young people and our society in the following areas:

- Respect for the environment
- Differentiation between beauty and ugliness
- Respect for the welfare of others
- Respect for freedom of speech and assembly
- Striving for perfection through hard work and innovation
- Recognition of the importance of justice
- Recognition of the importance of domestic tranquility

- Recognition of the importance of setting goals
- Recognition of the importance of establishing harmony within oneself, between oneself and others, and between oneself and the environment
- Promotion of the general welfare.

Young and old must enter into a grand alliance with each other. Teachers and students must ask together day after day, "What is the good life?" "What is the good man?" "What is the good woman?" "What is the good society?" "What are my obligations to society and to my fellow human?" "What is justice?" "What is truth?" "How can I lead a joyful and meaningful life?" "What should I be loyal to?" "What is my vision of the future?" "What are the value commitments necessary to mold the present into the future?"

As we seek answers to these questions, we should also bear in mind the fourteenth verse of the thirteenth chapter of the Hebrews: "Here we have no enduring city, but seek the city which is to come."

SELECTED READINGS FOR THE REVISED EDITION

1. Archambault, Reginald D. "Criteria for Success in Moral Instruction." In *Moral Education*, edited by Barry I. Chazan and Jonas F. Soltis, pp. 159-69. New York: Teachers College Press, Teachers College, Columbia University, 1973.
2. Atkinson, R. F. "Instruction and Indoctrination." *Philosophical Analysis and Education*. London: Routledge and Kegan Paul, 1965.
3. Baier, Kurt, and Rescher, Nicholas, eds. *Values and the Future: The Impact of Technological Change on American Values*. New York: Free Press, 1969.
4. Beck, C. M., and others, eds. *Moral Education: Interdisciplinary Approaches*. Toronto: University of Toronto Press, 1971.
5. Bellanca, James A. *Values and the Search for Self*. Washington, D.C.: National Education Association, 1975.
6. Blatt, M., and Kohlberg, L. "The Effects of Classroom Moral Discussion upon Children's Level of Moral Judgment." *Merrill-Palmer Quarterly*, September 1970.
7. Brown, Nina W. "Teaching How to Be Parents: Why Not?" *Character Education Journal* 2 (Winter 1973): 12-13.
8. Burkholder, S.; Ryan, K.; and Blanke, V. E. "Values, the Key to a Community." *Phi Delta Kappan* (March 1981): 483-85.
9. Carbone, Peter F., Jr. "Reflections on Moral Education." *The Record* 71 (May 1970): 598-607.
10. Casteel, J. Doyle, and Stahl, Robert J. *Value Clarification in the Classroom: A Primer*. Pacific Palisades, Calif.: Goodyear Publishing Co., 1975.
11. Chadwick, James, and Meux, Milton. "Procedures for Value Analysis." In *Values Education: Rationale, Strategies, and Procedures*, edited by Lawrence E. Metcalf, pp. 75-119. 41st Yearbook of the National Council for the Social Studies. Washington, D.C.: The Council, 1971.
12. Chazan, Barry I., and Soltis, Jonas, F., eds. *Moral Education*. New York: Teachers College Press, Teachers College, Columbia University, 1973.
13. "Compendium of Information on Evolution and the Evolution/Creationism Controversy." National Association of Biology Teachers, 11250 Roger Baron Drive #19, Reston, VA 22090. ($5.00) (n.d.)
14. Counts, George S. "Should the Teacher Always Be Neutral?" *Phi Delta Kappan* 51 (December 1969): 188.
15. Crittenden, Brian. "A Comment on Cognitive Moral Education." *Phi Delta Kappan* 56 (June 1975): 695-96.
16. Curwin, Richard L., and Curwin, Geri. *Developing Individual Values in the Classroom*. Palo Alto, Calif.: Learning Handbooks, 1974.
17. Duffey, Robert V. "Moral Education and the Study of Current Events." *Social Education* 39 (January 1975): 33-35.
18. Dunfee, Maxine. *Teaching for Social Values in Social Studies*. Washington, D.C.: Association of Childhood Education International, 1974.
19. Ezer, Melvin. "Value Teaching in the Middle and Upper Grades: A Rationale for Teaching But Not Transmitting Values." *Social Education* 31 (January 1967): 39-40.
20. Ford, G. A., and Lippitt, G. L. *Planning Your Future: A Workbook for Personal Goal Setting*. San Diego: University Associates, 1976.
21. Fraenkel, Jack R. "Strategies for Developing Values." Washington, D.C.: National Education Association, 1975.
22. Franks, Betty B., and Howard, Mary K. *People, Law, and the Futures Perspective*. Washington, D.C.: National Education Association, 1979.
23. Friedman, Paul G. *Interpersonal Communication: Innovations in Instruction*, Washington, D.C.: National Education Association, 1978.
24. Galbraith, Ronald E., and Jones, Thomas M. *Moral Reasoning: Teaching Strategies for Adapting Kohlberg to the Classroom*. Anoka, Minn.: Greenhaven Press, 1976.
25. Goldbecker, Sheralyn S. *Values Teaching*. Washington, D.C.: National Education Association, 1976.

26. Goodman, Joel. *Turning Points: New Developments, New Directions in Values Clarification.* Vol. 1 and 2. Saratoga Springs, N.Y.: Creative Resources Press, 1978.
27. Grove, Cornelius. *Communications Across Cultures.* Washington, D.C.: National Education Association, 1976.
28. Hall, Brian P. *Values Clarification as Learning Process: A Sourcebook.* New York: Paulist Press, 1973.
29. Hall, Robert, and Davis, John. *Moral Education in Theory and Practice.* Buffalo, N.Y.: Prometheus Books, 1975.
30. Harmin, Merrill, and others. *Clarifying Values Through Subject Matter: Applications for the Classroom.* Minneapolis: Winston Press, 1973.
31. Hawley, Robert C. *Value Exploration Through Role Playing.* New York: Hart Publishing Co., 1974.
32. _____, and Hawley, Isabel L. *Human Values in the Classroom: A Handbook for Teachers.* New York: Hart Publishing Co., 1975.
33. Heath, Phillip A., and Weible, Thomas D. *Developing Social Responsibility in the Middle School.* Washington, D.C.: National Education Association, 1979.
34. Howard, Mary K., and Franks, Betty B. *The Biological Revolution: Examining Values Through the Futures Perspective.* Washington, D.C.: National Education Association, 1976.
35. Howe, Leland W. *Personalizing Education: Values Clarification and Beyond.* New York: Hart Publishing Co., 1975.
36. Jantz, Richard K., and Fulda, Trudi A. "The Role of Moral Education in the Public Elementary School." *Social Education* 39 (January 1975): 24-28.
37. Jones, Peg J., and Norman, Carol A. *The Status of the American Family: Policies, Facts, Opinions, and Issues.* Washington. D.C.: NEA Research, 1979.
38. Kauffman, D. L., Jr. *Futurism and Future Studies.* 2d ed. Washington, D.C.: National Education Association, 1980.
39. Kluckhohn, F. R. and Strodbeck, F. L. *Variations in Value Orientations.* Evanston, Ill.: Row Peterson, 1961.
40. Koberg, D., and Bagnall, J. *Values Tech.* New York: William Kaufmann, 1975.
41. Kohlberg, Lawrence. "The Child as a Moral Philosopher." *Psychology Today* 7 (1968): 25-30.
42. _____. "Moral Development and Education of Adolescents." In *Adolescents and the American High School*, edited by Richard Purnell, pp. 144-62. New York: Holt, Rinehart and Winston, 1970.
43. _____. "Moral Development and the New Social Studies." *Social Education* 5 (May 1973): 369-75.
44. _____. *Stages in the Development of Moral Thought and Action.* New York: Holt, Rinehart and Winston, 1970.
45. _____ with Whitten, P. "Understanding the Hidden Curriculum." *Learning* 1 (1972): 10-14.
46. _____, and Selman, Robert L. *Preparing School Personnel Relative to Values: A Look at Moral Education in the Schools.* Washington, D.C.: ERIC Clearinghouse on Teacher Education, 1972.
47. _____. "High School Democracy and Educating for a Just Society." In *Moral Education: A First Generation of Research*, edited by R. Mosher. New York: Praeger, 1980.
48. _____. *Essays in Moral Development: The Philosophy of Moral Development.* Vol. 1. San Francisco: Harper Row, 1981.
49. Kurtines, William, and Greif, Ester Blank. "The Development of Moral Thought: Review and Evaluation of Kohlberg's Approach." *Psychological Bulletin* 81 (1974): 453-70.
50. Lockwood, Alan. "A Critical View of Values Clarification." *Teachers College Record* (October 1975): 35-50.
51. Lockwood, Alan L. *Values Education and the Study of Other Cultures.* Washington, D.C.: National Education Association, 1976.
52. Mattox, Beverly A. *Getting It Together: Dilemmas for the Classroom.* San Diego: Pennant Press, 1975.

53. McClelland, D. C. *How Character Develops: The Development of Social Maturity* (Vol. 1); *Education for Values* (Vol. 2). New York: Irvington Press, 1982.
54. Mehlinger, Howard D., and others. *Global Studies for American Schools*. Washington, D.C.: National Education Association, 1980.
55. Metcalf, Lawrence E., ed. *Values Education: Rationale, Strategies, and Procedures*. 41st Yearbook of the National Council for the Social Studies. Washington, D.C.: The Council, 1971.
56. National Education Association. "Darwin vs. Genesis." *NEA Now*, Nov. 30, 1981.
57. _____. *Approaches to Teaching Values* (filmstrip). Washington, D.C.: The Association, 1976.
58. _____. *Looking at Values* (filmstrip). Washington, D.C.: The Association, 1976.
59. _____. *Values and Valuing—Parents and Students*. Washington, D.C.: The Association, 1976.
60. Paulson, Wayne. *Deciding for Myself: A Values Clarification Series*. Minneapolis: Winston Press, 1974.
61. Purpel, David, and Ryan, Kevin. "Moral Education: Where Sages Fear to Tread." *Phi Delta Kappan* 56 (June 1975): 659-62.
62. Raths, Louis; Harmin, Merrill; and Simon, Sidney. *Values and Teaching: Working with Values in the Classroom*. Columbus, Ohio: Charles E. Merrill, 1966.
63. Reed, Donald. *Health Education: The Search for Values*. Englewood Cliffs, N.J.: Prentice-Hall, 1977.
64. Reimer, J. "Moral Education: The Just Community Approach." *Phi Delta Kappan* (March 1981): 485-87.
65. Rienzo, B. A. "The Status of Sex Education: An Overview and Recommendations." *Phi Delta Kappan* (November 1981): 192, 193.
66. Rokeach, M. *Value Survey*. Sunnyvale, Calif.: Halgren Tests, 1967.
67. _____. *The Nature of Human Values*. New York: Free Press, 1973.
68. Scharf, P., ed. *Readings in Moral Education*. Minneapolis: Winston Press, 1978.
69. Shaftel, Fannie R., and Shaftel, George. *Role-Playing for Social Values: Decision-Making in the Social Studies*. Englewood Cliffs, N.J.: Prentice-Hall, 1967.
70. Siegel, H. "Creationism, Evolution, and Education: The California Fiasco." *Phi Delta Kappan* (October 1981): 95-101.
71. Silver, Michael. *Values Education*. Washington, D.C.: National Education Association, 1976.
72. Simon, Sidney B. *Meeting Yourself Halfway*. Niles, Ill.: Argus Communications, 1974.
73. _____, and Clark, Jay. *Beginning Values Clarification: Strategies for the Classroom*. San Diego: Pennant Educational Publications, 1974.
74. _____, and O'Rourke, Robert. *Developing Values with Exceptional Children*. Englewood Cliffs, N.J.: Prentice-Hall, 1977.
75. _____; Hawley, Robert C.; and Britton, David D. *Composition for Personal Growth: Values Clarification Through Writing*. New York: Hart Publishing Co., 1973.
76. _____; Howe, Leland W.; and Kirschenbaum, Howard. *Values Clarification: A Handbook of Practical Strategies for Teachers and Students*. New York: Hart Publishing Co., 1972.
77. Stewart, John S. "Clarifying Values Clarification: A Critique." *Phi Delta Kappan* 56 (June 1975): 684-88.
78. Thomas, M. D., and Melvin, A. I. "Community Consensus Is Available on a Moral Valuing Standard." *Phi Delta Kappan* (March 1981): 479-82.
79. Toffler, A. *Learning for Tomorrow: The Role of the Future in Education*. New York: Vintage Books, 1974.
80. Weiner, Elizabeth H. *Unfinished Stories for Facilitating Decision Making in the Elementary Classroom*. Washington, D.C.: National Education Association, 1980.

—Sheralyn S. Goldbecker
Alfred S. Alschuler

FOOTNOTES AND REFERENCES

Part One

Freedom, Intelligence, and Valuing, pp. 9-17.

[1] Whitehead, Alfred North. *The Function of Reason.* Princeton University Press, 1929. pp. 28-29.

[2] Sherrington, Sir Charles Scott. *Man on His Nature.* Cambridge: Cambridge University Press, 1938.

[3] Harris, Harold, editor. *Astride the Two Cultures: Arthur Koestler at 70.* New York: Random House, 1976.

[4] Morison, Robert S. "Toward a Common Scale of Measurement." *Daedalus,* vol. 94, No. 1; Winter 1965.

[5] *Ibid.*

[6] *Ibid.*

[7] *Ibid.*

[8] Whitehead, *loc. cit.,* p. 23.

[9] Dewey, John. *Human Nature and Conduct.* New York: Modern Library, 1950.

[10] Dewey, John. *Theory of Valuation.* Chicago: The University of Chicago Press, 1939.

[11] Dewey, John. *The Quest for Certainty.* New York: G.P. Putnam's Sons (Capricorn Books), 1960.

[12] *Ibid.,* p. 278.

[13] Whitehead, *op. cit.,* p. 43.

[14] Raths, Louis E.; Harmin, Merrill; and Simon, Sidney B. *Values and Teaching.* Columbus, Ohio: Charles E. Merrill Publishing Co., 1966.

[15] Brogan, D.W. *The Price of Revolution.* New York: Harper and Brothers, 1951.

The Cognitive-Developmental Approach to Moral Education, pp. 18-35.

[1] Dewey, John. "What Psychology Can Do for the Teacher." *John Dewey on Education: Selected Writings.* (Edited by Reginald Archambault.) New York: Random House, 1964.

[2] These levels correspond roughly to our three major levels: the preconventional, the conventional, and the principled. Similar levels were propounded by William McDougall, Leonard Hobhouse, and James Mark Baldwin.

[3] Piaget, Jean. *The Moral Judgment of the Child.* Second edition. Glencoe, Ill.: Free Press, 1948.

[4] Piaget's stages correspond to our first three stages: Stage 0 (pre-moral), Stage 1 (heteronomous), and Stage 2 (instrumental reciprocity).

[5] Kohlberg, Lawrence. "Moral Stages and Moralization: The Cognitive-Developmental Approach." *Man, Morality, and Society.* (Edited by Thomas Lickona.) New York: Holt, Rinehart, and Winston, in press.

[6] Rest, James; Turiel, Elliott; and Kohlberg, Lawrence. "Relations Between Level of Moral Judgment and Preference and Comprehension of the Moral Judgment of Others." *Journal of Personality* 37: 225-52; 1969.
Rest, James. "Comprehension, Preference, and Spontaneous Usage in Moral Judgment." *Recent Research in Moral Development.* (Edited by Lawrence Kohlberg.) New York: Holt, Rinehart, and Winston, in preparation.

[7] Many adolescents and adults only partially attain the stage of formal operations. They do consider all the actual relations of one thing to another at the same time, but they do not consider all possibilities and form abstract hypotheses. A few do not advance this far, remaining "concrete operational."

[8] Krebs, Richard, and Kohlberg, Lawrence. "Moral Judgment and Ego Controls as Determinants of Resistance to Cheating." *Recent Research in Moral Development.* (Edited by Lawrence Kohlberg.) New York: Holt, Rinehart, and Winston, in preparation.

[9] Rawls, John. *A Theory of Justice.* Harvard University Press, 1971.

[10] Not all freely chosen values or rules are principles, however. Hitler chose the "rule," "exterminate the enemies of the Aryan race," but such a rule is not a universalizable principle.

[11] Rawls, John, *loc. cit.*

[12] Kohlberg, Lawrence, and Elfenbein, Donald. "Development of Moral Reasoning and Attitudes Toward Capital Punishment." *American Journal of Orthopsychiatry,* Summer 1975.

[13] Hartshorne, Hugh, and May, Mark. *Studies in the Nature of Character: Studies in Deceit* (Vol. I), *Studies in Service and Self-Control* (Vol. II), *Studies in Organization of Character* (Vol. III). New York: Macmillan Co., 1928-30.

[14] As an example of the "hidden curriculum," we may cite a second-grade classroom. My son came home from this classroom one day saying he did not want to be "one of the bad boys." Asked "Who are the bad boys?" he replied, "The ones who don't put their books back and get yelled at."

[15] Restriction of deliberate value education to the moral may be clarified by our example of the second-grade teacher who made tidying up of books a matter of moral indoctrination. Tidiness is a value, but it is not a moral value. Cheating is a moral issue, intrinsically one of fairness. It involves issues of violation of trust and taking advantage. Failing to tidy the room may under certain conditions be an issue of fairness, when it puts an undue burden on others. If it is handled by the teacher as a matter of cooperation among the group in this sense, it is a legitimate focus of deliberate moral education. If it is not, it simply represents the arbitrary imposition of the teacher's values on the child.

[16]The differential action of the principled subjects was determined by two things. First, they were more likely to judge it right to violate authority by sitting in. But second, they were also in general more consistent in engaging in political action according to their judgment. Ninety percent of all Stage 6 subjects thought it right to sit in, and all 90% lived up to this belief. Among the Stage 4 subjects, 45% thought it right to sit in, but only 33% lived up to this belief by acting.

[17]No public or private word or deed of Nixon ever rose above Stage 4, the "law and order" stage. His last comments in the White House were of wonderment that the Republican Congress could turn on him after so many Stage 2 exchanges of favors in getting them elected.

[18]Parilch, Bindo. "A Cross-Cultural Study of Parent-Child Moral Judgment." Doctoral dissertation. Cambridge, Mass.: Harvard University, 1975. Unpublished.

[19]Blatt, Moshe, and Kohlberg, Lawrence. "Effects of Classroom Discussions upon Children's Level of Moral Judgment." *Recent Research in Moral Development.* (Edited by Lawrence Kohlberg.) New York: Holt, Rinehart, and Winston, in preparation.

[20]Kohlberg, Lawrence; Scharf, Peter; and Hickey, Joseph. "The Justice Structure of the Prison: A Theory and an Intervention." *The Prison Journal,* Autumn-Winter 1972.

[21]Kohlberg, Lawrence, and others. *The Just Community Approach to Corrections: A Manual, Part I.* Cambridge, Mass.: Education Research Foundation, 1973.

[22]An example of the need for small-group discussion comes from an alternative school community meeting called because a pair of the students had stolen the school's video-recorder. The resulting majority decision was that the school should buy back the recorder from the culprits through a fence. The teachers could not accept this decision and returned to a more authoritative approach. I believe if the moral reasoning of students urging this solution had been confronted by students at a higher stage, a different decision would have emerged.

Values Clarification: It Can Start Gently and Grow Deep, pp. 36-47.

For information about current values clarification materials and a schedule of nationwide training workshops, contact the National Humanistic Education Center, Springfield Road, Upper Jay, New York 12987.

[1]Simon, Sidney B. *Meeting Yourself Halfway.* Niles, Ill.: Argus Communications, 1974. p. 81.

[2]Reported in Kirschenbaum, Howard. *Recent Research in Values Clarification.* Mimeographed paper. Upper Jay, N.Y.: National Humanistic Education Center, 1974. pp. 5, 6.

[3]Simon, Sidney B. "Values Clarification and Shalom." *Colloquy:* July-August 1972. p. 19.

[4]Quinlan, Mary Kay. "Values Clarification—Understanding Yourself." *Rochester Democrat and Chronicle:* July 20, 1974. pp. 1B, 3B.

[5]Covault, Thomas. "The Application of Value Clarification Teaching Strategies with Fifth-Grade Students to Investigate Their Influence on Students' Self-Concept and Related Classroom Copying and Interacting Behaviors." Unpublished doctoral dissertation. Columbus: Ohio State University, 1973.

[6]Wenker-Konner, Ronnie; Hammon, Eileen; and Egner, Ann. *A Functional Analysis of Values Clarification Strategies on the Participation Rate of Ten Fifth-Graders.* Burlington: Department of Special Education, University of Vermont, 1973.

[7]Simon, Sidney B., and Hart, Lois B. "Values Clarification, Making Your New Year Better!" *Cross Talk*, December-January-February, 1973-74.

[8]It is impossible to list all the schools now using values clarification, but, as an example of its increasingly wide acceptance, all the language teachers at Kenston High School in Cleveland, Ohio, use it; it is a junior high elective at a parochial school in Woburn, Massachusetts; and it is used in drug education in the Tempe, Arizona, elementary schools. A more comprehensive list of nationwide uses of values clarification can be obtained by sending a self-addressed, stamped envelope to: Sidney B. Simon, Values Workshop, Box 846, Leverett, Mass. 01054.

[9]Harmin, Merrill. *Making Sense of Our Lives.* Multi-media kit. Niles, Ill.: Argus Communications, 1973.

[10]Curwin, Gerri and Rick, and others. *Search for Values.* Dayton, Ohio: Pflaum/Standard, 1972.

[11]Bartel, Brady. "A Bargain in Self-Development." *Momentum*, February 1973.

[12]Paulsen, Wayne. *Deciding for Myself.* Multi-media kit. Minneapolis, Minn.: Winston Press, 1974.

[13]Further information concerning values clarification can be obtained from Howard Kirschenbaum, National Humanistic Education Center, Upper Jay, N.Y. 12987, or from Sidney B. Simon, Box 846, Leverett, Mass. 01054.

Values Education in a Confluent Social Studies Curriculum, pp. 48-58.

[1] For new publications on values education, see:

Casteel, J. Doyle, and Stahl, Robert J. *Value Clarification in the Classroom: A Primer.* Pacific Palisades, Calif.: Goodyear Pub. Co., 1975.

Hall, Brian P. *The Development of Consciousness: A Confluent Theory of Values.* New York: Paulist Press, 1976.

Hawley, Robert. *Value Exploration Through Role Playing.* New York: Hart Publishing Co., 1975.

Hawley, Robert and Isabel. *Human Values in the Classroom.* New York: Hart Publishing Co., 1975.

Howe, Leland and Barbara. *Personalizing Education: Values Clarification and Beyond.* New York: Hart Publishing Co., 1975.

Mattox, Beverly. *Getting It Together: Dilemmas for the Classroom.* San Diego, Calif.: Pennart Press, 1975.

Nelson, Jack L. *Values and Society.* Rochelle Park, N.J.: Hayden Book Co., 1975.

Sullivan, Edmund V. *Moral Learning.* New York: Paulist Press, 1975.

[2]Hillman, Aaron W. "Concepts and Elements of Confluent Education." Santa Barbara, Calif.: Confluent Education Development and Research Center, 1975. pp. 3-7.

[3]Shiflett, John M. "Beyond Vibration Teaching: Research and Curriculum Development in Confluent Education." *The Live Classroom.* (Edited by George Isaac Brown.) New York: Viking Press, 1975. pp. 127-28.

[4]*Ibid.*, pp. 128-29.

[5]Hillman, Aaron W., *op. cit.,* pp. 10-11.

[6]Raths, L.; Harmin, M.; and Simon, S. *Values and Teaching: Working with Values in the Classroom.* Columbus, Ohio: Charles E. Merrill, 1966. pp. 25-37.

[7]Kohlberg, Lawrence, and Gilligan, Carol. "The Adolescent as Philosopher: The Discovery of Self in a Postconventional World." *Daedalus* 100: 1051-86; Fall 1971.

[8]Kohlberg, Lawrence. "From Is to Ought: How to Commit the Naturalistic Fallacy and Get Away With It in the Study of Moral Development." *Cognitive Development and Epistemology.* (Edited by Theodore Mischel.) New York: The Academic Press, 1971. pp. 181-85.

[9]For a detailed discussion of cognitive moral development, see:

Kohlberg, Lawrence. *Collected Papers on Moral Development and Moral Education.* Cambridge, Mass.: Harvard University Press, 1973.

[10]Kohlberg, Lawrence. "The Cognitive-Developmental Approach to Socialization." *Handbook of Socialization Theory and Research.* (Edited by David Goslin.) Chicago: Rand McNally & Co., 1969. pp. 348-52.

[11]For further discussion of Gestalt psychology and confluent education, see:

Yoemans, Thomas. "Search for a Working Model: Gestalt, Psychosynthesis, and Confluent Education." *The Live Classroom.* (Edited by George Isaac Brown.) New York: Viking Press, 1975. pp. 132-58.

Values Education Processes, pp. 59-63.

[1]Raths, Louis E.; Harmin, Merrill; and Simon, Sidney B. *Values and Teaching.* Columbus, Ohio: Charles E. Merrill Publishing Co., 1966.

[2]Fraenkel, Jack R. *Helping Students Think and Value.* Englewood Cliffs, N.J.: Prentice-Hall, Inc., 1973.

[3]_____.*How to Teach About Values.* Englewood Cliffs, N.J.: Prentice-Hall, Inc., 1976 (in press).

[4]Dalis, Gus T., and Strasser, Ben. B. *Values Education.* Los Angeles: Office of the Los Angeles County Superintendent of Schools, 1974.

[5]Mattox, Lois A. *Getting It Together.* San Diego: Pennant Press, 1975.

[6]Galbraith, Ronald E., and Jones, Thomas M. *Moral Reasoning.* Anoka, Minn.: Greenhaven Press, 1976.

School and Society: Barriers to Values Education, pp. 64-71.

[1]Galtung, Johan. "Schooling and Future Society." *School Review* 83: 543; August 1975.

[2]Hein, George E. *Open Education: An Overview.* Newton, Mass.: Education Development Center, 1975.

[3]Bryant, Bunyan I.; Chesler, Mark A.; and Crowfoot, James E. "Barometers of Conflict." *Educational Leadership* 33: 17-20; October 1975.

[4]Henry, Jules. *Culture Against Man.* New York: Random House, 1963. p. 295.

[5]Beck, Clive, and Sullivan, Edmund V. "Moral Education in a Canadian Setting." *Phi Delta Kappan* 56: 701; June 1975.

[6]Dewey, John. *Moral Principles in Education.* Boston: Houghton Mifflin Co., 1909.

[7]Dewey, John. *The School and Society.* University of Chicago Press, 1900.

[8]Dewey, John. *Moral Principles in Education,* p. 43.

[9]Dreeben, Robert. *On What Is Learned in School.* Reading, Mass.: Addison-Wesley Publishing Co., 1968.

[10]Jackson, Philip. *Life in Classrooms.* New York: Holt, Rinehart and Winston, 1968.

[11]Goffman, Erving. *Asylums.* New York: Doubleday Anchor Books, 1961.

[12]Spady, William G. "The Impact of School Resources on Students." *Review of Research in Education.* Itasca, Ill.: F. E. Peacock Publishers, 1973. pp. 135-77.

[13]Grannis, Joseph. "The School as a Model of Society." *Harvard Graduate School of Education Association Bulletin* 12: 15-27; Fall 1967.

[14]*Ibid.,* p. 18.

[15]*Ibid.,* p. 20.

[16]Beck, Clive, *op. cit.,* p. 700.

[17]*Ibid.*

[18]Sizer, Nancy F., and Sizer, Theodore R. *Moral Education: Five Lectures.* "Introduction." Cambridge, Mass.: Harvard University Press, 1970. p. 7.

[19]Stewart, John. "The School as a Just Society." *Values Education.* (Edited by John Meyer, Brian Burham, and John Cholvat.) Waterloo, Ontario: Wilfrid Laurier Press, 1975. pp. 149-64.

[20]Kohlberg, Lawrence, and Whitten, Phillip. "Understanding the Hidden Curriculum." *Annual Editions: Readings in Education, 1973, 1974.* Guilford, Conn.: The Dushkin Publishing Group, 1973. p. 212.

[21]Kohlberg, Lawrence. "The Cognitive-Developmental Approach to Moral Education." *Phi Delta Kappan* 56: 670-77; June 1975.

[22]Jencks, Christopher, and others. *Inequality: A Reassessment of the Effect of Family and Schooling in America.* New York: Basic Books, 1972. p. 9.

[23]Scriven, Michael. "Cognitive Moral Development." *Phi Delta Kappan* 56: 694; June 1975.

Part Two

Strategies for Clarifying the Teaching Self, pp. 87-94.

[1]Including Louis E. Raths, Merrill Harmin, Sidney B. Simon, and Howard Kirschenbaum.

[2]Kirschenbaum, Howard. "Beyond Values Clarification." *Readings in Values Clarification.* (Edited by Sidney B. Simon and Howard Kirschenbaum.) Minneapolis, Minn.: Winston Press, Inc., 1973. pp. 92-110.

For a complete list of materials available in values clarification, as well as information concerning workshops, resource persons, etc., write: National Humanistic Education Center, 110 Spring Street, Saratoga Springs, NY 12866.

[3]This strategy was created by Joel Goodman, Assistant Director for Program Development and Consultation Services, National Humanistic Education Center, Saratoga Springs, New York. The author encountered Dr. Goodman's strategy at a Professional Development Academy conducted by the Michigan Education Association, Professional Development Division.

[4]Much of the pioneering work in the use of the "Environmental Descriptions" was done by Dale V. Alam, Associate Professor of Curriculum and Instruction, Erickson Hall, Michigan State University, East Lansing, MI 48824.

From Inculcation to Action: A Continuum for Values Education, pp. 95-102.

[1] Numerous approaches to the study of values have been developed. See, for example: *Social Science Education Consortium Newsletter;* November 20, 1974. We've limited our framework to the more prevalent approaches—values inculcation, clarification, analysis, moral reasoning, and action learning.

[2]Many of the exercises developed by Richard Van Scotter and Jon Cauley in "Future Values for Today's Curriculum" (a chapter in this book) fit neatly into our continuum, particularly at the clarification and analysis levels.

[3] Barth, James L., and Shermis, Samuel. "Defining the Social Studies: An Explanation of Three Traditions." *Social Education* 34:745; November 1970.

[4] Simon, Sidney B.; Howe, Leland W.; and Kirschenbaum, Howard. *Values Clarification: A Handbook of Practical Strategies for Teachers and Students.* New York: Hart Publishing Co., Inc., 1972.

[5] For further discussion, see Simon, Sidney B., and deSherbinnin, Polly. "Values Clarification: It Can Start Gently and Grow Deep.." *Phi Delta Kappan* 56: 679-83; June 1975.

[6] Raths, Louis E.; Harmin, Merrill; and Simon, Sidney B., *Values and Teaching: Working with Values in the Classroom.* Columbus, Ohio: Charles E. Merrill Publishing Co., 1966. pp. 28-30.

[7] Simon, Howe, and Kirschenbaum do not include a specific activity on political or economic beliefs in "Values Continuum Strategy No. 8." *Values Clarification: A Handbook of Practical Strategies for Teachers and Students.* pp. 116-28. A social studies, history, or government teacher who is adapting values clarification for a course could easily devise a values continuum on political and economic systems.

[8] Kohlberg, Lawrence. "From Is to Ought." *The Journal of Philosophy:* pp. 164-65; October 25, 1973. Quoted by Kohlberg in "The Cognitive-Developmental Approach to Moral Education." *Phi Delta Kappan* 56: 671; June 1975.

[9] *Ibid.*

[10] Kneller, George F. *Introduction to the Philosophy of Education.* New York: John Wiley and Sons, Inc., 1964. p. 74.

[11] Dewey John. *Experience and Education.* New York: Collier Books, 1938. p.34.

[12] Silberman, Charles E. *Crisis in the Classroom.* New York: Vintage Books, 1974. p. 9.

Conducting Moral Discussions in the Classroom, pp. 103-120.

[1] Kohlberg's research findings are not without their critics. See, for example, Kurtines, William, and Greif, Esther B. "The Development of Moral Thought: Review and Evaluation of Kohlberg's Approach," *Psychological Bulletin,* August 1974, 81:8, pp. 453-470.
Simpson, Elizabeth L. "Moral Development Research: A Case Study of Scientific Cultural Bias," *Human Development,* 1974, 17, pp. 81-106.
Phillips, D. C., and Kelly, Mavis E. "Hierarchical Theories of Development in Education and Psychology," *Harvard Educational Review,* August 1975, 45:3, pp. 351-375.
Rest, James. "The Cognitive Developmental Approach to Morality: The State of the Art." *Counseling and Values,* Winter 1974, 18:2, pp. 64-78.

[2]Moshe, Blatt, and Kohlberg, Lawrence. "The Effects of Classroom Moral Discussion Upon Children's Level of Moral Judgment," *Journal of Moral Education*, 1975, 4, pp. 129-161.
Lieberman, Marcus. "Evaluation of a Social Studies Curriculum Based on an Inquiry Method and a Cognitive Developmental Approach to Moral Education." Paper presented to AERA Annual Meeting, April 1975. (16 pp.)

[3]This dilemma situation is based on a story created by Dr. Frank Alessi, a member of the staff of the Carnegie-Mellon/Harvard Values Education Project. He is now Social Studies Chairperson of the Cortland (New York) City Schools.

[4]An earlier version of this strategy has been presented in detail in Galbraith, Ronald E., and Jones, Thomas M. "Teaching Strategies for Moral Dilemmas," in *Social Education*, Vol. 39, No. 1, January 1975, pp. 16-22. Ronald Galbraith is currently Director of the Division of Teacher Education/Curriculum Development of the American Institute for Character Education in San Antonio, Texas; Thomas Jones is a member of the social studies faculty of West Irondequoit High School in Rochester, New York.

[5]For a detailed analysis of probe questions as used in this strategy see Fenton, Edwin; Colby, Anne; and Speicher-Dubin, Betsy. "Developing Moral Dilemmas for Social Studies Classes" (unpublished paper available from Moral Education and Research Foundation, Harvard University).

[6]See the annotated bibliography by Linda Rosenzweig in *Social Education*, April 1976.

[7]Galbraith, Ronald, and Jones, Thomas M. *Moral Reasoning: Teaching Strategies for Adapting Kohlberg to the Classroom* (Anoka, Minnesota, Greenhaven Press, 1976).
Fenton, Edwin, and Kohlberg, Lawrence. *Learning to Lead Moral Discussions: A Teacher Preparation Kit* (Pleasantville, New York, Guidance Associates, 1976).

The Developmentalists' Approach to Alternative Schooling, pp. 121-129.

[1]Fenton, Edwin. *Teaching the New Social Studies*. New York: Holt, Rinehart and Winston, 1966.
Oliver, Donald. *Teaching Public Issues in the High School*. Boston: Houghton-Mifflin, 1966.

[2]Cooley, Charles. *Social Organization*. New York: Charles Scribner & Sons, 1916.
Mead, George Herbert. *Mind, Self, Society*. Glencoe, Ill.: Free Press, 1933.

[3]Lewin, Kurt. *Resolving Social Conflicts*. New York: Harper & Row, 1945.

[4]Argyris, Chris, and Shoen, David. *Theory in Practice*. San Francisco: Jossey-Bass, 1974.

[5]Kohlberg, Lawrence. "Stage and Sequence." *Handbook of Socialization*. (Edited by David A. Goslin.) New York: Russell Sage, 1967.

[6]Kohlberg, Lawrence. "Cognitive Developmental Theory and the Practice of

Collective Moral Education." *Collected Papers on Moral Development and Moral Education.* Cambridge, Mass.: Moral Education Research Foundation, 1973.

[7]Silberman, Charles. *Crisis in the Classroom.* New York: Random House, 1970.

[8]Kohlberg, Lawrence, and other members of the Center for Moral Education at Harvard University. Unpublished proposal to the Ford Foundation, 1976.

[9]Scharf, Peter. *The Just Community.* Needham, Mass.: Humanitas Press, 1977. (In press.)

Humanizing Through Value Clarification, pp. 130-134.

Dunham, Joseph; Nylin, Donald; Valesano, James; and Yanker, Mary. "Value Education." Handbook. Aurora, Ill.: Value Education Project and Juvenile Protective Association, 1975. Mimeographed.

Harmin, Merrill; Kirschenbaum, Howard; and Simon, Sidney B. *Clarifying Values Through Subject Matter: Applications for the Classroom.* Minneapolis: Winston Press, 1973.

Raths, Louis E.; Harmin, Merrill; and Simon, Sidney B. *Values and Teaching.* Columbus, Ohio: Charles E. Merrill, 1966.

Rokeach, Milton. *Beliefs, Attitudes, and Values.* San Francisco: Jossey-Bass, 1968.

Simon, Sidney B.; Howe, Leland W.; and Kirschenbaum, Howard. *Values Clarification: A Handbook of Practical Strategies for Teachers and Students.* New York: Hart Publishing Co., 1972.

Toffler, Alvin. *Future Shock.* New York: Bantam Books, 1970.

Values Clarification vs. Indoctrination, pp. 135-143.

For information about current values-clarification materials and a schedule of nationwide training workshops, contact the National Humanistic Education Center, Springfield Road, Upper Jay, New York 12987.

[1]Most of these strategies are from Simon, Sidney B.; Howe, Leland W.; and Kirschenbaum, Howard. *Values Clarification: A Handbook of Practical Strategies for Teachers and Students.* New York, Hart Publishing Co., Inc., 1972.

Values Clarification: Some Thoughts on How to Get Started, pp. 144-147.

[1]A revised version of this article will appear in: Read, Donald; Simon, Sidney; and Goodman, Joel. *Exploring Our Values: Perspective, Process, and Strategies for Working with Values in Health Education.* Englewood Cliffs, N.J.: Prentice-Hall, Inc., 1977. (In press.)

[2] The following are sources of ideas for values activities, clarifying responses, third-level lessons, and ways of using values clarification:

Raths, Louis; Harmin, Merrill; and Simon, Sidney. *Values and Teaching.* Columbus, Ohio: Charles E. Merrill, 1966.

Simon, Sidney; Howe, Leland; and Kirschenbaum, Howard; *Values Clarification: A Handbook of Practical Strategies for Teachers and Students.* New York: Hart Publishing, 1972.

Harmin, Merrill; Kirschenbaum, Howard; and Simon, Sidney. *Clarifying Values Through Subject Matter.* Minneapolis: Winston Press, 1973.

Kirschenbaum, Howard, and Simon, Sidney, editors. *Readings in Values Clarification.* Minneapolis: Winston Press, 1973.

Goodman, Joel. "Sid Simon on Values Clarification." *Nation's Schools* 92: 39-42; December 1973.

_____. "Values Clarification: A Review." *1976 Annual Handbook for Group Facilitators.* (Edited by John Jones and J. William Pfeiffer.) Iowa City, Iowa: University Associates, 1976.

Simon, Sidney, and Goodman, Joel. "Values Clarification and the School Psychologist." *International Encyclopedia of Neurology, Psychiatry, Psychoanalysis and Psychology.*

[3] These articles provide some food for thought about the need for values clarification:

Simon, Sidney, and Goodman, Joel. "Values Shock." *Adult Leader* 6: 16-17; September-October-November 1973.

Goodman, Joel, and Walker, Marie Hatwell. "Values Clarification: Helping People to Feel More Value-Able." *Ohio's Health* 28: 11-15; September 1975.

[4] For ideas on ways to diagnose students' needs and interests, see:

Goodman, Joel, and Hawkins, Laurie. "Value Clarification: Meeting a Challenge in Education." *Colloquy,* 5: 18-22; May 1972.

Goodman, Joel. "Kids' Komments: Diagnosing Students' Learning Styles." *Connecting* 2: number 5; January 1975.

[5] For a listing of national workshops focusing on personal and professional growth, write to Dr. Joel Goodman, National Humanistic Education Center, 110 Spring Street, Saratoga Springs, NY 12866.

[6] Kirschenbaum, Howard; Simon, Sidney; and Napier, Rodney. *Wad-Ja-Get?* New York: Hart Publishing, 1971.

[7] If you want a taste of theory and practical "how-to's" of humanistic approaches to evaluation, see:

Goodman, Joel. *The Development, Implementation, and Evaluation of a Humanistic Process Education Program.* Unpublished doctoral dissertation. University of Massachusetts, 1975.

[8] The National Humanistic Education Center has published the *Manual for Professional Support Groups* which encourages people to form local groups

which might engage in any of the following: sharing values clarification strategies, brainstorming new strategies, discussing readings, problem-solving, developing facilitating skills, creating values units in curricula, learning about the "cousins" of values clarification (related fields in humanistic education), and focusing on personal growth.

Value Decisions and the Acceptability of Value Principles, pp. 148-158.

[1] Coombs, J., and Meux, M. "Teaching Strategies for Value Analysis." *Values Education: Rationale, Strategies, and Procedures.* 41st Yearbook. Washington, D.C.: National Council for the Social Studies, 1971. pp. 29-74.

[2] Evans, W. Keith, and Applegate, Terry P., and others. *Rational Value Decisions and Value Conflict Resolution: A Handbook for Teachers.* Salt Lake City: U.S. Office of Education, ESEA Title III, 1974. p.456.

[3] *Ibid.*, pp. 1-360.

[4] Evans, W.K., and Applegate, T.P. *Value Analysis Dissemination Project.* Final report. Salt Lake City: U.S.O.E., ESEA Title III, 1976. 59 pp.

[5] For a more complete discussion of commitment to value principles, see: Coombs, J. "Objectives of Value Analysis." *Values Education: Rationale, Strategies, and Procedures.* 41st Yearbook. Washington, D.C.: National Council of the Social Studies, 1971. pp. 1-28.

Exploring Social Issues: A Values Clarification Simulation Game, pp. 159-170.

[1] Klietsch, Ronald G., and Wiegman, Fred B. *Directory of Educational Simulations, Learning Games and Didactic Units.* St. Paul, Minn.: Instructional Simulations, Inc., 1969. p. 1.

[2] Fromm, Erich. *The Sane Society.* New York: Holt, Rinehart and Winston, 1955. p. 69.

[3] Raser, John R. *Simulation and Society: An Exploration of Scientific Gaming.* Boston: Allyn and Bacon, Inc., 1964. p. 116.

[4] Postman, Neil, and Weingartner, Charles. *Teaching as a Subversive Activity.* New York: Delacorte Press, 1969. p. 66.

[5] *Ibid.*, p. 81.

Developing Values Awareness in Young Children, pp. 171-176.

[1] See for example:
Bessel, Harold, and Palomares, Waldo, developers. *Methods in Human Develop-*

ment. San Diego, Calif.: Human Development Training Institute, 1967. Neo-Freudian materials for early childhood. Theory and teaching handbooks have been developed for 4-6 year olds.

Dinkmeyer, Donald, developer. *Developing Understanding of Self and Others (DUSO).* Kit. Circle Pines, Minn.: American Guidance Services, Inc., 1970.

Brown, George Isaac. *Human Teaching for Human Learning: An Introduction to Confluent Education.* Toronto: Viking Press, 1971.
See particularly Chapter Six ("Eight Months in the First Grade: A Day-to-Day Journal in Confluent Education") by Gloria Costillo.

[2] Maslow, A.H. *Toward a Psychology of Being.* New York: D. Van Nostrand, Co., 1962.

[3] Two particularly provocative books concerned with increasing cognitive functioning in young children are:

Pines, Maya. *Revolution in Learning: The Years from Birth to Six.* New York: Harper & Row Publishers, 1967

Sharp, Evelyn. *Thinking Is Child's Play.* New York: Avon Books, 1969.

Nonsexist Teaching: Strategies and Practical Applications, pp. 189-203.

[1] *Dick and Jane as Victims.* Princeton, N.J.: Women on Words and Images, 1972.

[2] Trecker, Janice Law. "Women in U.S. History High School Textbooks." *Social Education* 35: 248-60; March 1971.

[3] Zolotow, Charlotte. *William's Doll.* (Illustrated by William Pene DuBois.) New York: Harper & Row, 1972.

[4] Phillips, Lynn. *Exactly Like Me.* Chapel Hill, N.C.: Lollipop Power, 1972.

[5] Raths, Louis; Harmin, Merrill; and Simon, Sidney. *Values and Teaching: Working with Values in the Classroom.* Columbus, Ohio: Charles E. Merrill, 1966.

[6] Simon, Sidney; Sadker, Myra; and Sadker, David. "Where Do You Stand?" *Instructor,* September 1974.
Sadker, Myra, and Sadker, David. "Clarifying Sexist Values." *Social Education,* December 1973.

[7] Resource Center on Sex Roles in Education. *Kit on Textbook Bias.* Washington, D.C.: The National Foundation for the Improvement of Education and the National Education Association, n.d.

[8] Sadker, Myra. "Sex Bias Questionnaire." *Sexism in School and Society.* (Edited by Nancy Frazier and Myra Sadker.) New York: Harper & Row, 1973. pp. 213-14.

[9] Darrow, Whitney. *I'm Glad I'm a Boy! I'm Glad I'm a Girl!* New York: Simon & Schuster (Windmill), 1970.

[10] Howe, Florence. "The Teacher and the Women's Movement." (Introduction to *Sexism in School and Society.)* New York: Harper & Row, 1973. p. XIV.

Multiculturalism in Moral and Values Education, pp. 204-208.

[1] Goldmark, Bernice. "Inquiry into Values." *Teaching Social Studies to Culturally Different Children.* (Edited by James A. Banks and William W. Joyce.) Reading, Mass.: Addison-Wesley, 1971. p. 198.

[2] Arciniega, Tomas A. "The Thrust Towards Pluralism: What Progress?" *Educational Leadership:* 1031; December 1975.

[3] Collier, Calhoun C., and others. *Modern Elementary Education: Teaching and Learning.* New York: Macmillan Publishing Co., 1976. p. 33.

[4] Blitz, Barbara. *The Open Classroom.* Boston: Allyn & Bacon, 1973. p. 231.

[5] Purpel, David, and Ryan, Kevin. "Moral Education: Where Sages Fear to Tread." *Phi Delta Kappan* 56: 659; June 1975.

[6] *Ibid.,* p. 660.

[7] Galbraith, Ronald, and Jones, Thomas. "Teaching Strategies for Moral Dilemmas: An Application of Kohlberg's Theory of Moral Development to the Social Studies Classroom." *Social Education* 39: 17; January 1975.

[8] Good, Carter V., editor. *Dictionary of Education.* 2nd edition. New York: McGraw-Hill Co., 1959. p. 167.

[9] Jantz, Richard, and Fulda, Trudi. "The Role of Moral Education in the Public Elementary School." *Social Education* 39: 24; January 1975.

[10] Raths, Louis; Harmin, Merrill; and Simon, Sidney. *Values and Teaching: Working with Values in the Classroom.* Columbus, Ohio: Charles E. Merrill Publishing Co., 1966. p. 27.

[11] Stewart, John S. "Clarifying Values Clarification: A Critique." *Phi Delta Kappan* 56: 684; June 1975.

[12] See: Raths, Louis; Harmin, Merrill; and Simon, Sidney. *Values and Teaching: Working with Values in the Classroom.*

[13] See, for example: Metcalf, Lawrence F., editor. *Values Education: Rationale Strategies and Procedures.* Forty-first yearbook of the National Council for the Social Studies. Washington, D.C.: NCSS, 1971. pp. 75-119.

Multiculturalism—Should We Clarify or Seek Values? pp. 209-224.

Condensation of a chapter prepared for a book in preparation by H. P. Baptiste, Jr., Carlos Cortes, and Judith Palmer.

[1] Developed by the Center for Program Development in Equal Educational Opportunity, National College of Education, Chicago.

[2] Wolkon, George H.; Moriwaki, Sharon, and Williams, Karen J. "Race and Social Class as Factors in Orientation Towards Psychotheraphy." *Counseling Psychology* 19 (no. 3): 312; 1972.

[3]For other criticism, see:

Lockwood, Alan L. "A Critical View of Values Clarification." *Teachers' College Record* 77 (no. 1): 35-50; September 1975.

Steward, John S. "Clarifying Values Clarification: A Critique." *Phi Delta Kappan* 56 (no. 10): 684-88; June 1975.

[4]Adorno, T. W. *Authoritarian Personality.* New York: Doubleday & Co., Inc., 1971.

Maslow, Abraham H. *Motivation and Personality.* New York: Harper & Row, 1970.

Allport, Gordon W. *The Nature of Prejudice.* Garden City, N.Y.: Doubleday & Co., Inc., 1954.

Erikson, Erik. *Childhood and Society.* New York: W. W. Norton & Co., Inc., 1950.

[5]Foster, Badi G. "Toward a Definition of Black Referents." *Beyond Black or White.* (Edited by Vernon J. Dixon and Badi G. Foster.) Boston: Little, Brown & Co., 1971.

Forbes, Jack D. "Teaching Native American Values and Cultures." *Teaching Ethnic Studies Concepts and Strategies.* (Edited by James A. Banks.) Washington, D.C.: National Council for the Social Studies, 1973.

Herold, Leslie P.; Ramierz III, Manuel; and Castenada, Alfredo. *Mexican-American Values and Culturally Democratic Educational Environments.* Austin, Texas: The Dissemination Center for Bilingual Bicultural Education, 1974.

[6]This model was developed by Claire B. Halverson, in collaboration with Kenneth Addison of the University of Wisconsin at Madison.

[7]See another chapter in this anthology: "The Cognitive-Developmental Approach to Moral Education" by Lawrence Kohlberg.

[8]Wilson, John; Williams, Norman; and Sugarman, Barry. *Introduction to Moral Education.* Baltimore: Penguin Books, 1967.

[9]Center for Program Development in Equal Educational Opportunity, National College of Education, Chicago.

"Developing New Perspectives on Race." New Perspectives on Race, Detroit.

[10]Developed by Pat A. Bidol, New Perspectives on Race, Detroit.

[11]Developed by Claire B. Halverson and Bettye Latimer.

[12]Simile II. "Star Power." La Jolla (Calif. 92037, P.O. Box 1023): Simile II, n.d.

[13]Brown, George Issac. *Human Teaching for Human Learning: An Introduction to Confluent Education.* New York: Viking Compass Books, 1971.

[14]Wilson, John, *loc. cit.*

[15]Adorno, T. W.; Maslow, Abraham H.; Allport, Gordon H.; and Erickson, Erik, *loc. cit.*

[16]Hampden-Turner, Charles. *Radical Man: The Process of Psycho-Social Development.* New York: Doubleday & Co., Inc., 1971.

[17] Hall, Brian P. "A Confluent Theory of Value Development." Unpublished paper.

[18] Cross, William E. "Discovering the Black Referent: The Psychology of Black Liberation." *Beyond Black or White.* (Edited by Vernon J. Dixon and Badi G. Foster.) Boston: Little, Brown & Co., 1971.

[19] Developed by Douglas Risberg, St. Cloud College, St. Cloud, Minn. Unpublished paper.

[20] The first three paragraphs are adapted from: *Black and White Statue.* Sound filmstrip. Tarrytown, N.Y.: Prentice-Hall Media, Inc., n.d.

[21] The first three paragraphs are taken from: McLuhan, T. C., compiler. *Touch the Earth: A Self Portrait of Indian Existance.* New York: Pocket Books, 1972. p. 28.

The Discussion Questions were developed by Clarie Halverson.

The Role Play Approach was developed jointly by Eliezer Krumblein, University of Illinois, Chicago, and by Claire B. Halverson.

Vocational Education and the Changing American Work Ethic, pp. 225-234.

[1] Shearer, Lloyd. "The Next 20 Years." *The Roanoke Times Parade* (Roanoke, Virginia). February 15, 1976. p. 5.

[2] Hoyt, Kenneth, and others. *Career Education: What It Is and How to Do It.* 2nd edition. Salt Lake City, Utah: Olympus Publishing Co., 1974. pp. 37-44.

[3] Lee, Mildred K. *The Changing Work Ethic—Discussion Guide.* Pleasantville, N.Y.: Guidance Associates, 1973.

[4] Barlow, Melvin L. "Vocational Education and the American Work Ethic." *American Vocational Journal* 48: 27; (No. 1) 1973.

[5] Weber, Max. *The Protestant Ethic and the Spirit of Capitalism.* (Translated by Talcott Parsons.) New York: Charles Scribner's Sons, 1930.

[6] Tilgher, Adriano. *Homo Faber: Work Through the Ages.* (Translated by Dorothy C. Fisher.) Chicago: Henry Regnery Co., 1958.

[7] Ibid.

[8] Barlow, Melvin L. *History of Industrial Education in the United States.* Peoria, Ill.: Charles A. Bennett Co., Inc., 1967.

[9] Venn, Grant. *Man, Education and Work.* Washington, D.C.: American Council on Education, 1964.

[10] Hoyt, *op. cit.*, p. 67.

[11] Mills, C. Wright. *White Collar: The American Middle Classes.* Oxford University Press, 1951.

[12] Maddi, Salvatore R., and Costa, Paul T. *Humanism in Personology: Allport, Maslow, and Murray.* Chicago: Aldine-Atherton, Inc., 1972. pp. 1-200.

[13] Lowry, Richard J. *Dominance, Self-Esteem, Self-Actualization: Germinal Papers of A. H. Maslow.* Monterey, Calif.: Brooks/Cole Publishing Co., 1973. p. 162.

[14] Oakley, Donald. "Ripoffs From Both Collars." *The Radford News Journal* (Radford, Virginia). October 1975.

[15] *Ibid.*

[16] McDaniels, Carol O. "The Role of Leisure in Career Developments for Girls and Women." *Conference Proceedings: New Dimensions in the Career Development of Women.* Blacksburg, Va.: Third Annual Conference, Career Counseling and Vocational Education, March 1974. pp. 50-60.

[17] Hoyt, Kenneth. "What the Future Holds for the Meaning of Work." *American Vocational Journal* 48: 35-37; (No. 1) 1973.

[18] U.S. Department of Health, Education and Welfare. *Trends in Vocational Education Fiscal Year 1973.* Washington, D.C.: Office of Education, Bureau of Occupational and Adult Education, Division of Vocational and Technical Education, June 1974. pp. 1-25.

[19] Carnegie, Dale. *How To Win Friends and Influence People.* New York: Pocket Books, Inc., 1965.

[20] Lancelot, W. H. *Permanent Learning.* New York: John Wiley and Sons, Inc., 1929. pp. 10-47.

[21] Hunsicker, N. H. "Understanding Cooperative Education." *The Agricultural Education Magazine* 48: 99-100; (No. 5) 1975.

A Framework and Strategy for Examining Environmental Values, pp. 235-242.

[1] Boulding, Kenneth. Question and answer session with the Select Subcommittee on Education, Washington, D. C. *The Environmental Problem: Selections from Hearings on the Environmental Education Act of 1970.* (Edited by Irving Morrissett and Karen B. Wiley.) Boulder, Colo: The Social Science Education Consortium, Inc., Publication No. 140, 1971. p. 153.

[2] Ibid., p. 155.

[3] Martin, Paul S. "Pleistocene Overkill," *Natural History*, 76 (December 1967), pp. 32-35. This thesis was advanced by Sir Charles Lyell, *Geological Evidence of the Antiquity of Man* (London 1866), p. 143 cited in George M. Marsh, *The Earth as Modified by Human Action* (NY: Chas. Scribner's Sons, 1907), p. 80.

[4] Wagner, Richard W. *Environment and Man* (NY: W. W. Norton and Co., Inc., 1971), p. 25.

[5] George M. Marsh, *op. cit.*, Study of Critical Environmental Problems. (SCEP), *Man's Impact on the Global Environment* (Cambridge, Mass.: MIT Press, 1970).

[6] Kluckholn, Florence, and Strodtbeck, Fred, *Variations in Value Orientations* (Evanston, Illinois, Row, Peterson, 1961).

[7] For an annotated bibliography of tradebooks, write to Dr. Elmer U. Clawson, Center for the Development of Economics Education, School of Education, University of the Pacific, Stockton, CA 95211.

Future Values for Today's Curriculum, pp. 257-267.

[1] Lippitt, Ronald. "The Dimensions of Change: In Our Society, Our Students, and Our Social Studies Curriculum." Publication 134. Boulder, Colo.: Social Science Education Consortium, 1971. pp. 2-3.

[2] The notations in parentheses indicate what a survey of approximately 100 prominent futurists judged would happen with each value. The key is as follows: (+ + +) very probable positive change; (– – –) very probable negative change; (+ +) probable positive change; (– –) probable negative change; (+) possible positive change; (–) possible negative change; (0) little or no change.

[3] From "Forecasts of Some Technological and Scientific Developments and Their Societal Consequences," a research report for The Institute for the Future, Inc., 2725 Sand Hill Rd., Menlo Park, Calif. 94025.

The Challenge of Value Commitment, pp. 277-287.

[1] Bronowski, J. *The Commonsense of Science.* Cambridge: Harvard University Press, 1953.

[2] Fromm, Eric. *Escape From Freedom.* New York: Rinehart & Co., 1941.

[3] Maslow, Abraham. *Religion, Values, and Peak Experiences.* New York: Viking Press, 1970. p. 58.

[4] Dewey, John. *Democracy and Education.* New York: Macmillan Publishing Co., 1916.

Acknowledgments

310 ♦ VALUES CONCEPTS AND TECHNIQUES

The following acknowledgments are continued from page 2:

"The Cognitive-Developmental Approach to Moral Education" by Lawrence Kohlberg. *Phi Delta Kappan,* June 1975. Copyright © 1975 by Phi Delta Kappa. Reprinted with permission.

"The Claim to Moral Adequacy of a Highest State of Moral Judgment" by Lawrence Kohlberg. Table 1, excerpt, pp. 631-32. Copyright © 1973 by *The Journal of Philosophy.* Used with permission.

"Values Clarification: It Can Start Gently and Grow Deep" by Sidney B. Simon and Polly deSherbinin. *Phi Delta Kappan,* June 1975. Copyright © 1975 by Sidney B. Simon and Polly deSherbinin. Reprinted with permission.

Figure II, "Relations between Piaget logical stages and Kohlberg moral stages" from "The Adolescent as Philosopher" by Lawrence Kohlberg and Carol Gilligan. *Daedalus,* The Journal of the American Academy of the Arts and Sciences, Vol. 100, No. 4; Fall 1971, p. 1072. Copyright © 1971 by *Daedalus.* Republished with permission.

"Moral Education in a Canadian Setting" by Clive Beck and Edmund V. Sullivan. *Phi Delta Kappan,* June 1975. Copyright © by Phi Delta Kappa. Excerpted with permission.

"Schooling and Future Society" by Johan Galtung. *School Review,* August 1975. Copyright © 1975 by The University of Chicago Press. Excerpted with permission.

Culture Against Man by Jules Henry. Copyright © 1963 by Random House, Inc. Excerpted with permission.

Moral Education: Five Lectures by James M. Gustafson and others. "Introduction" by Nancy F. and Theodore R. Sizer. Copyright © 1970 by Harvard University Press. Excerpted with permission.

"Confrontation, Insight, and Commitment: Moral Education and the Teacher" by David Purpel and Kevin Ryan. *Phi Delta Kappan,* June 1975. Copyright © 1975 by Phi Delta Kappa. Adapted with permission.

Part Two

"Analyzing Value Conflict" is from a forthcoming 1977 publication by Jack R. Fraenkel, *How To Teach About Values.* Adapted by permission of Prentice-Hall, Inc., Englewood Cliffs, New Jersey.

Acknowledgments (continued) ♦ 311

"Conducting Moral Discussions in the Classroom" by Barry L. Beyer. *Social Education,* April 1976. Copyright © 1976 by Barry L. Beyer. Reprinted with permission.

"Humanizing Through Value Clarification" by Mary M. Yanker. Reprint permission granted by Thresholds in Education Foundation, Dekalb, Illinois. Originally published in *Thresholds in Secondary Education,* Vol. 1, No. 3; August 1975.

"Values Education vs. Indoctrination" by Sidney B. Simon. *Social Education,* December 1971. Copyright © 1971 by the National Council for the Social Studies. Reprinted with permission of the National Council for the Social Studies and Sidney B. Simon.

Directory of Educational Simulations, Learning Games and Didactic Units by Ronald G. Klietsch and Fred B. Wiegman. Copyright © 1969 by Instructional Simulations, Inc. Excerpted with permission.

Teaching as a Subversive Activity by Neil Postman and Charles Weingartner. Copyright © 1969 by Neil Postman and Charles Weingartner. Excerpted with the permission of Delacorte Press.

Simulation and Society: An Exploration of Scientific Gaming by John R. Raser. Copyright © 1969 by Allyn and Bacon, Inc. Excerpted with permission.

The Sane Society by Erich Fromm. Copyright © 1955 by Erich Fromm. Reprinted by permission of Holt, Rinehart and Winston, Publishers.

"Developing Values Awareness in Young Children" by Alan J. Hoffman and Thomas F. Ryan was originally published by the American Association of Elementary-Kindergarten-Nursery Educators under the title "Psycho-Social Development of the Young Child: An Instructional Paradigm." *Educating Children: Early and Middle Years,* Vol. 17, No. 4; 1972. Copyright © 1972 by EKNE. Used with permission.

"The School Assembly as Creative Pace-Setter for Moral Development" by Lisa Kuhmerker. *Character Education Journal,* Winter 1973. Copyright © 1972 by the American Institute for Character Education, P.O. Box 12617, San Antonio, TX 78212. Used with permission.

"Teaching About Women in the Social Studies" by Jean Grambs. NCSS monograph. Copyright © 1975 by the National Council for the Social Studies. Excerpted with permission of the National Council for the Social Studies.

Touch the Earth: A Self-Portrait of Indian Existance compiled by T.C. McLuhan. Copyright © 1971 by T.C. McLuhan. Reprinted by permission of the publishers, Dutton-Sunrise, Inc., a subsidiary of E.P. Dutton & Co., Inc.

"Equality: Caught Smoking" developed by Douglas Risberg. St. Cloud College, St. Cloud, Minn. Unpublished paper. Used with permission.

Black and White Statue. Sound filmstrip. Copyright © by Prentice-Hall Media, Inc. Excerpted with permission.

"Anthropology and Environmental Education" by Buckley R. Barnes and James R. Richburg. *The Journal of Environmental Education,* Vol. 5, No. 2; Winter 1973, pages 1-3. Copyright © 1973 by Heldref Publications. Reprinted with permission.

"Understanding Our Environment: The Ethnological-Ecological Tradition of Anthropology." *Social Studies Review,* Vol. 14, No. 2; Winter 1974, pages 40-43. Copyright © 1974 by the California Council for the Social Studies. Reprinted with permission.

"Pop Music and Values Clarification" by Richard Simms. *The OCSS Review.* Copyright © by the Ohio Council for the Social Studies. Reprinted with permission.

"Black and White," words by David Arkin, music by Earl Robinson. Copyright © 1956, 1972, Templeton Publishing Co., Inc. Sole selling agent: Shawnee Press, Inc., Delaware Water Gap, PA 18327. Used with permission. Recorded in 1972 by "Three Dog Night" on their album *Seven Separate Fools.*

"The World Is A Ghetto" recorded by "War" on their album *The World Is A Ghetto.* Copyright © 1972 by Far Out Productions, Inc. Used with permission.

"Lean On Me" by Bill Withers. Copyright © 1972 by Interior Music Corp. (BMI) Administered by Irving Music, Inc. (BMI) All Rights Reserved. Used by Permission.

"Values and Health Education" by Robert D. Russell. Adapted from "Some March to Different Drums" in *Health Education* by Robert D. Russell. Copyright © 1975 by the National Education Association of the United States. Adapted with permission.

"Future Values for Today's Curriculum" by Richard Van Scotter and Jon Cauley. *Scholastic Teacher,* February 1974. Reprinted by permission from *Scholastic Teacher.* Copyright © 1974 by Scholastic Magazines, Inc.

"Interview: Alvin Toffler on the Role of the Future and Values in Education" by June and Harold Shane. *Today's Education,* January-February 1974. Copyright © 1974 by the National Education Association of the United States. Reprinted with permission.